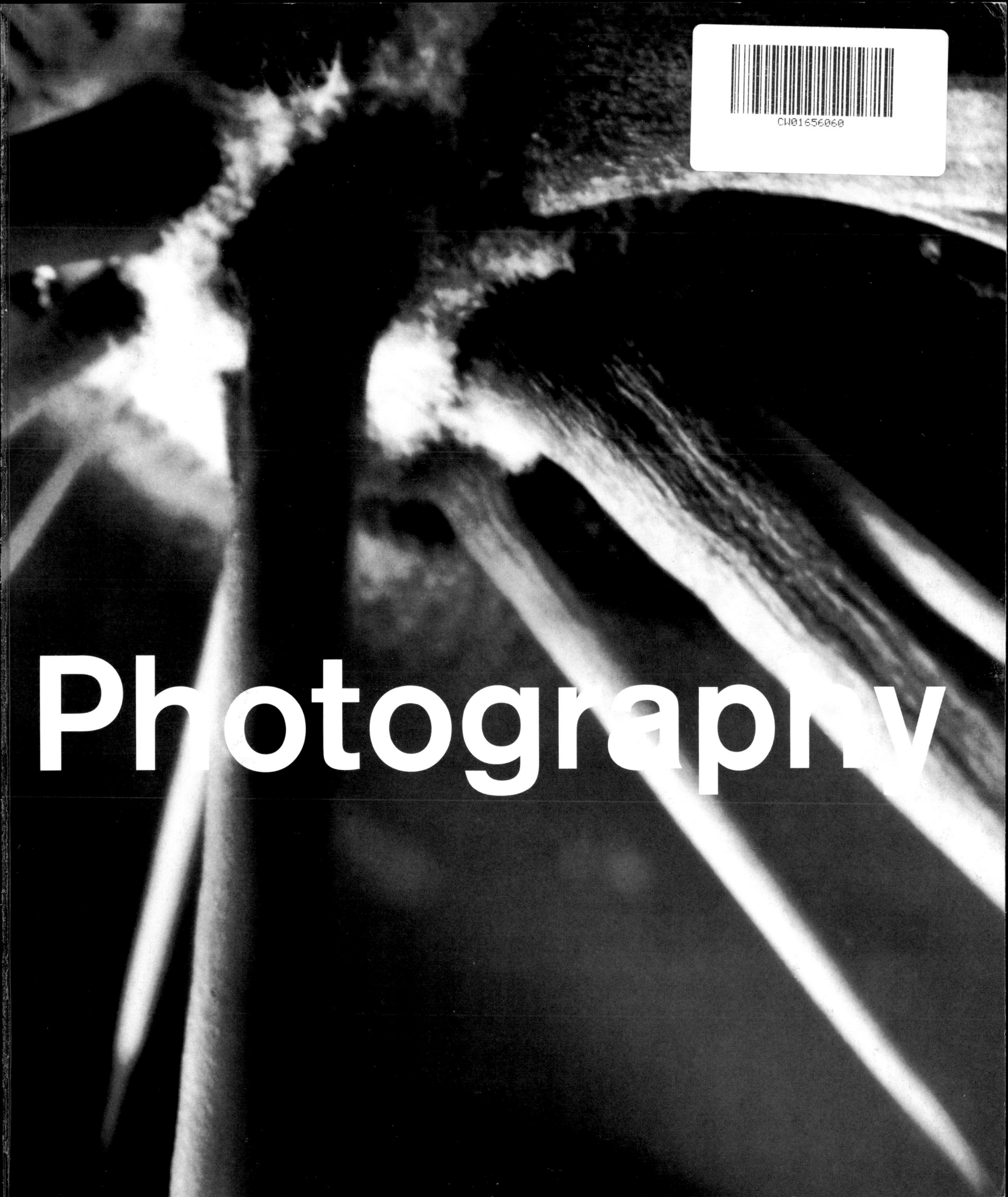

Photography

A RotoVision Book
Published and distributed by RotoVision SA
Rue du Bugnon 7
CH–1299 Crans-Près-Céligny
Switzerland

RotoVision SA, Sales & Production Office
Sheridan House, 112/116 A Western Road
Hove, East Sussex BN3 1DD, UK

Tel: +44 (0) 1273 72 72 68
Fax: +44 (0) 1273 72 72 69
E-mail: sales@rotovision.com
Website: www.rotovision.com

RotoVision

ISBN 2–88046–549–4

Book design by Dan Moscrop at Navy Blue Design Consultants

Production and separations in Singapore by ProVision Pte. Ltd.
Tel: + 65 334 7720
Fax: + 65 334 7721

Introduction

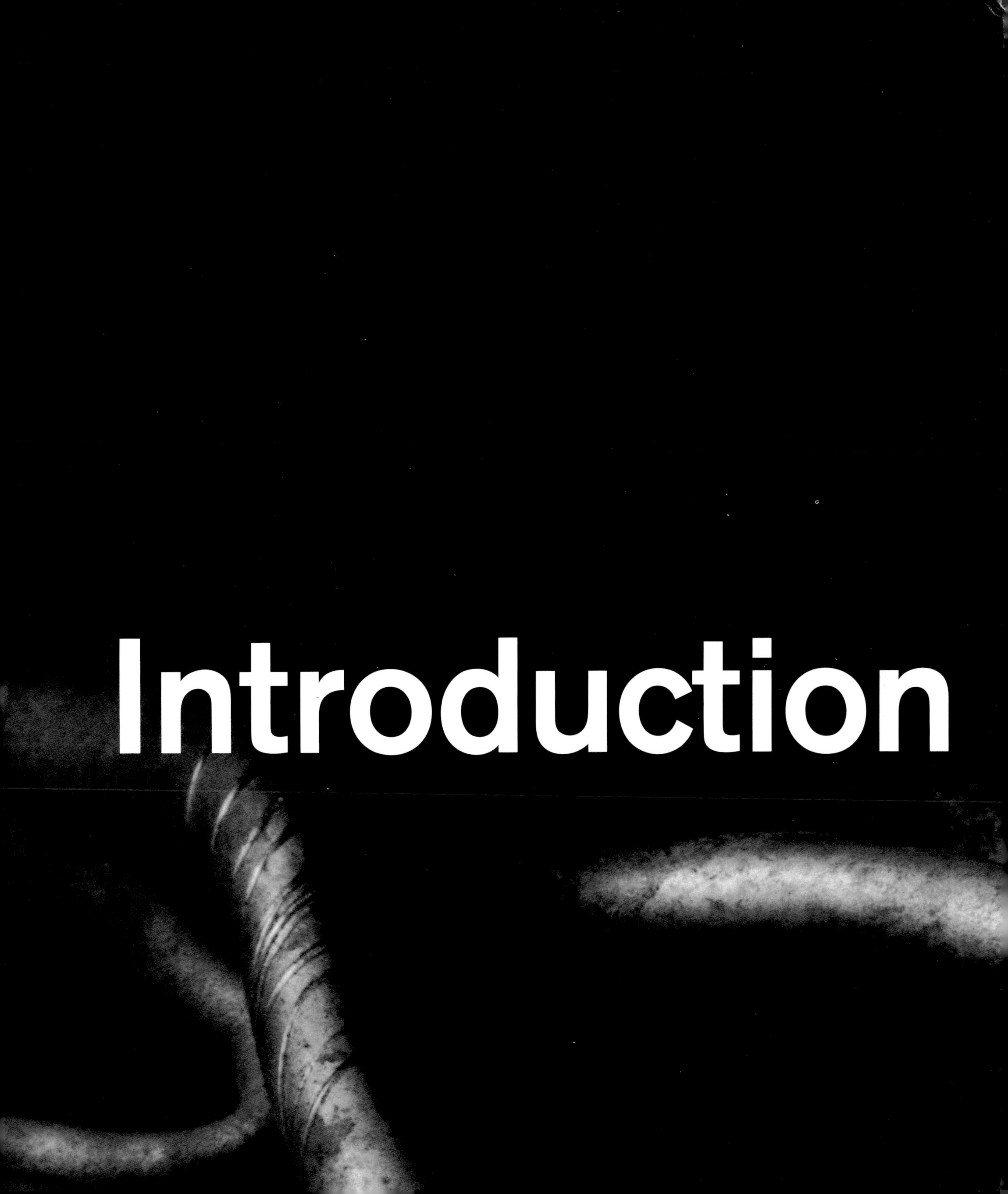

This is a book that's as much about images as it is about technique. It's as much about having an eye for a picture as it is about having a mastery of the technicalities of black and white. And hopefully, for all the things that are passed on through the words of the photographers who created this collection of incredible images, one of the main benefits of the book will be its ability simply to inspire. If, having seen the quality and the sheer breadth of imagery that makes up these pages you feel the irresistible urge to pick up a camera and to go off and try some of the ideas for yourself, then the book will have achieved its purpose in style.

Still life has so many aspects to it that in many ways it's difficult to produce just one book that will do the complete job. Certainly it would be almost impossible for a single photographer using his or her own pictures as examples to try and explain the variety of ways that this subject can be tackled. A still life can be many things, as you'll see throughout this book. It could be a classic collection of objects, painstakingly arranged and immaculately photographed, a style of picture that was popular at the very dawn of photography with practitioners such as Roger Fenton and which is now being recreated by young and creative photographers like Allan Jenkins. The new generation is attracted by the discipline that's required, while also enjoying the challenge of working with early printing processes.

A still life can also be the texture seen in a twisted piece of scrapyard metal sheeting or the decaying form of a piece of fruit. It can be an extreme close-up that reveals something hitherto unsuspected and beautiful about an everyday object or, through the lens of one of the world's great masters such as Ralph Gibson, it could be a seemingly trivial moment that has, through skilful observation, been turned into a classic study of form and light.

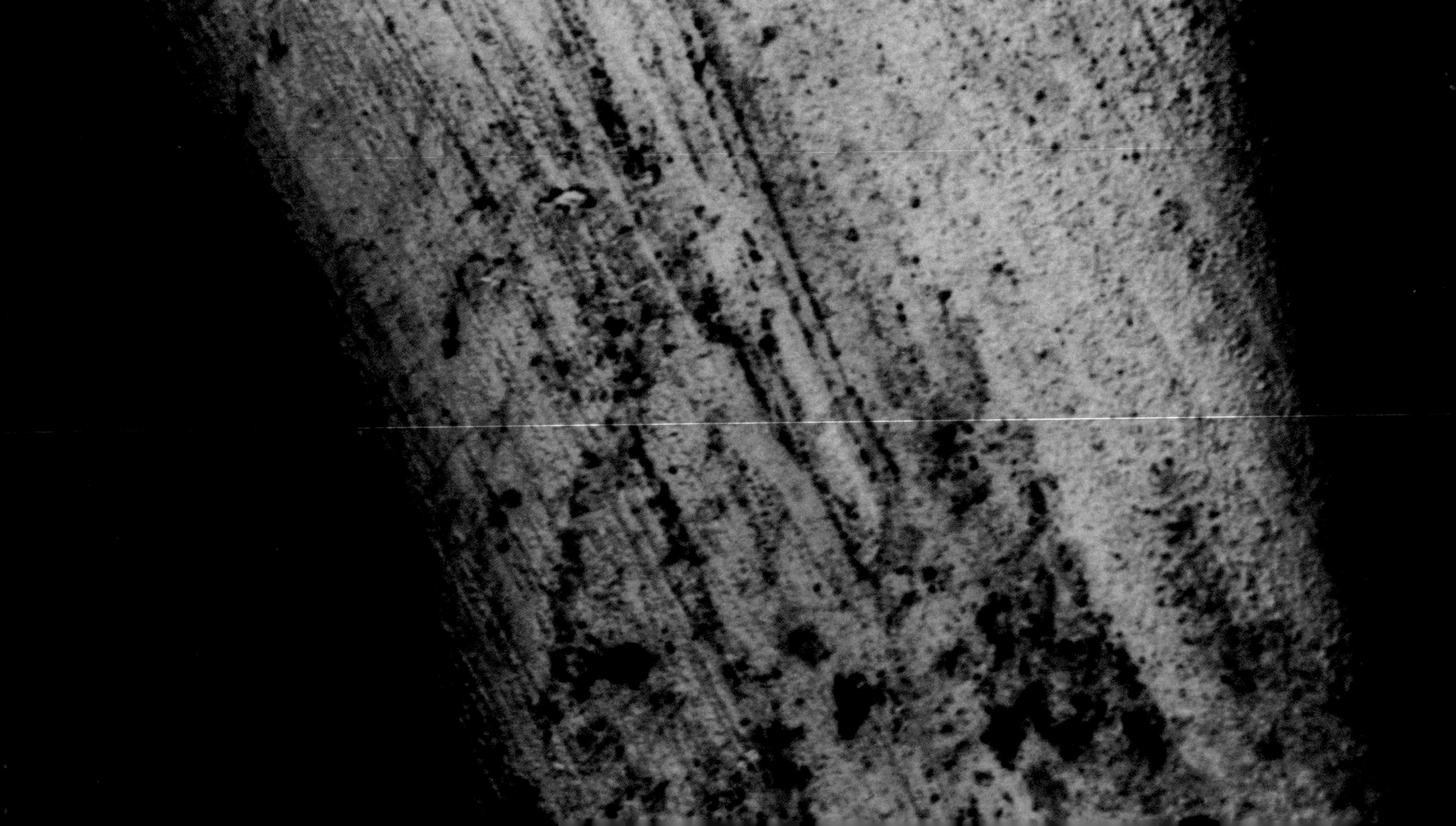

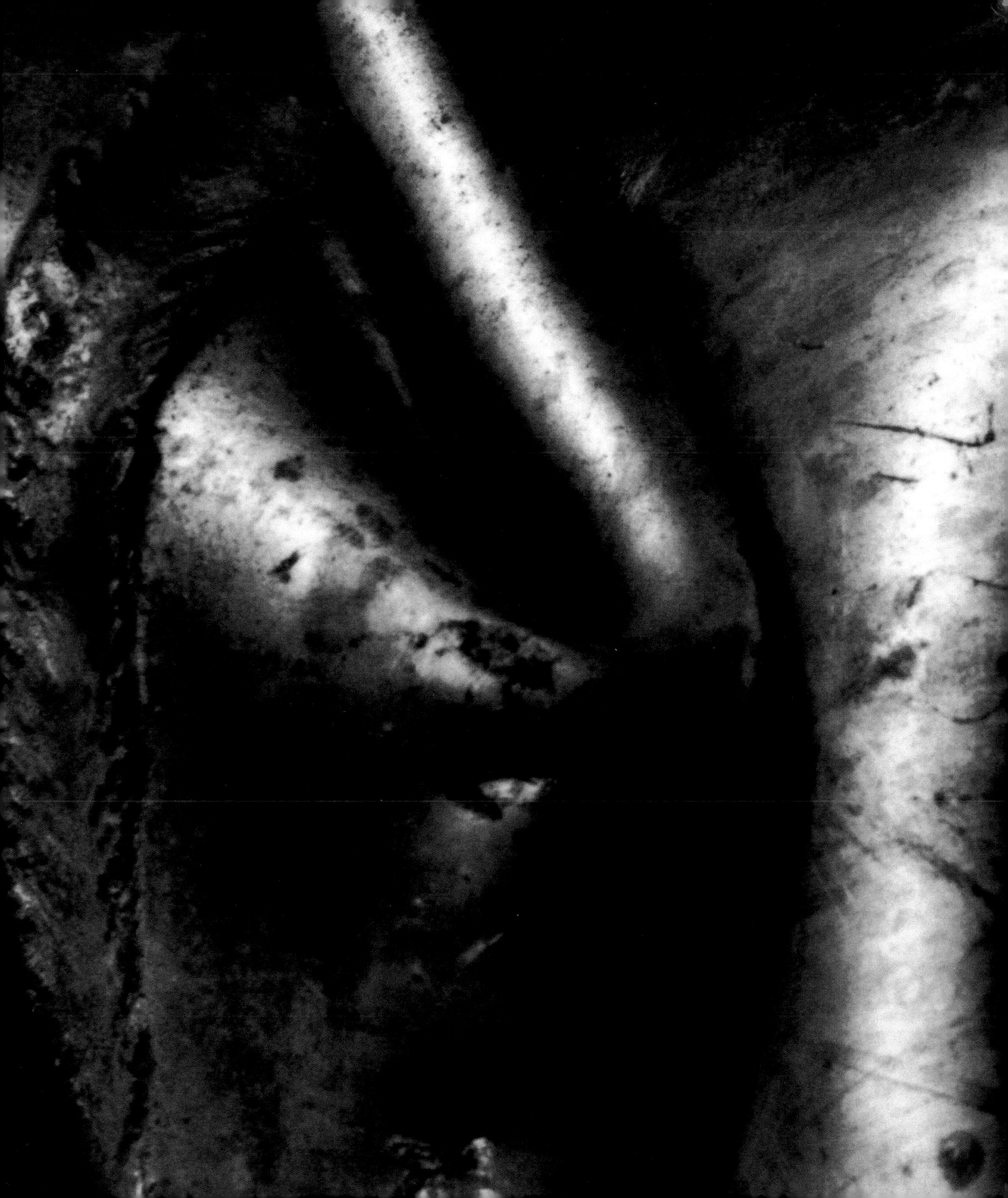

A still life could be produced without a camera even being present, as Manuela Höfer has shown through her thought-provoking photograms, or it might have its origins on a huge camera such as the giant 20x14in Deardorff employed by the Japanese fine art photographer Kenro Izu.

Still life pictures can be set up, they can be 'found', they might be an instant that is over in 1/125sec and is never repeated or they could be planned for weeks beforehand. They could even be part of a series that will keep a photographer occupied for years, and which will continue to stimulate and inspire for all that time, as in the case of John Blakemore and his adored tulips. That's the beauty of this and so many other photographic subjects: the individual can make of it what they will, there's no set agenda that has to be followed. Even the golden rules that others have established over the years for photographers to follow are there to be broken and turned on their heads, as so many of the photographers featured here take the greatest delight in proving over and over again.

So much for the subject: what about the medium? What is it about black and white that makes it so enduring? Sheer logic should dictate that, with colour film so accessible and of such high quality now, black and white should have been relegated to the history books long ago. But instead the opposite has happened. It's taken on a new life of its own, and is gaining a steady and growing following across the world.

Black and white is now seen as the natural medium for fine art prints and, as the digital side of photography becomes ever more important, those who choose to indulge in silver halide and the skills of the darkroom will increasingly be seen as artists in their own right.

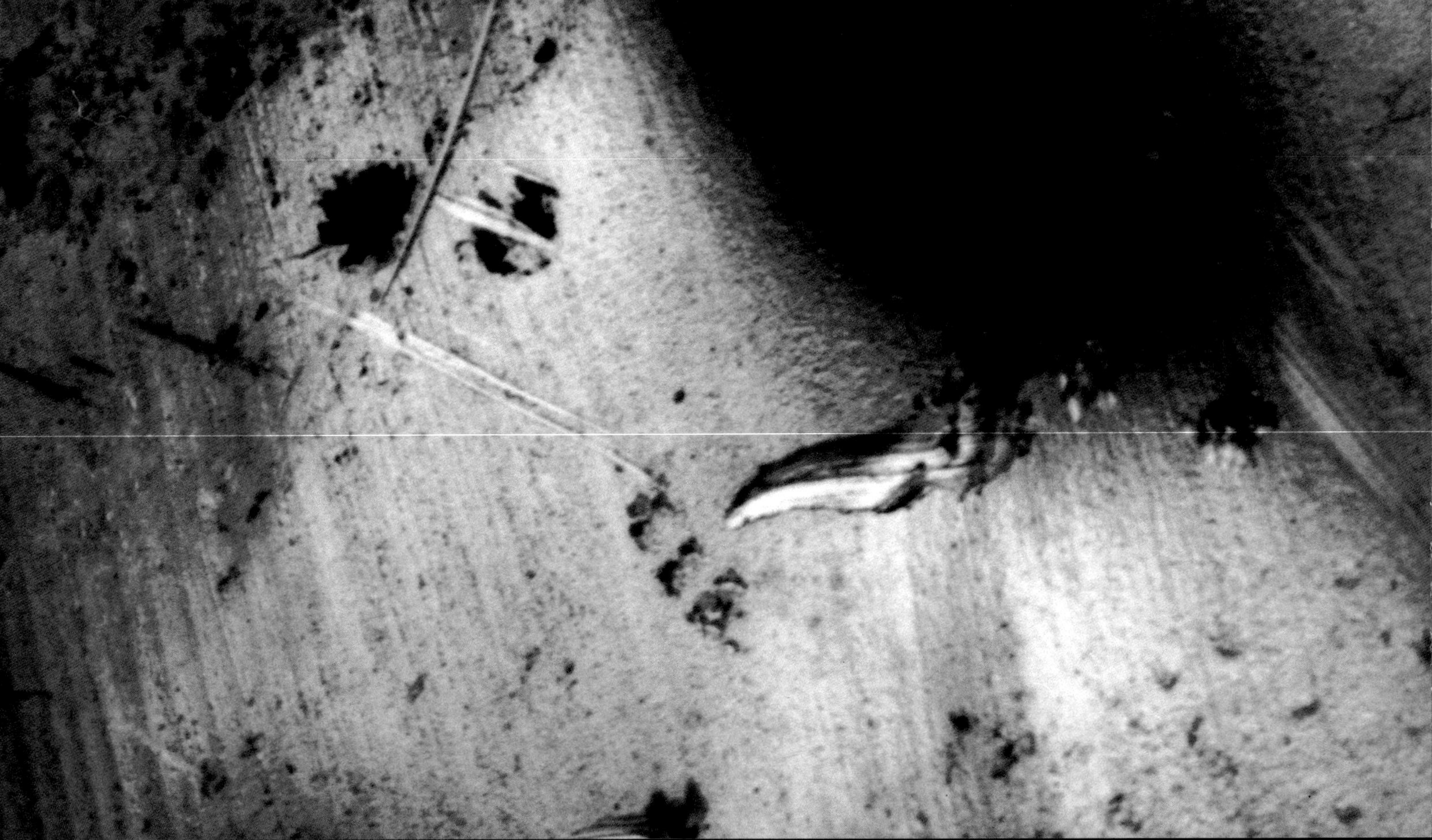

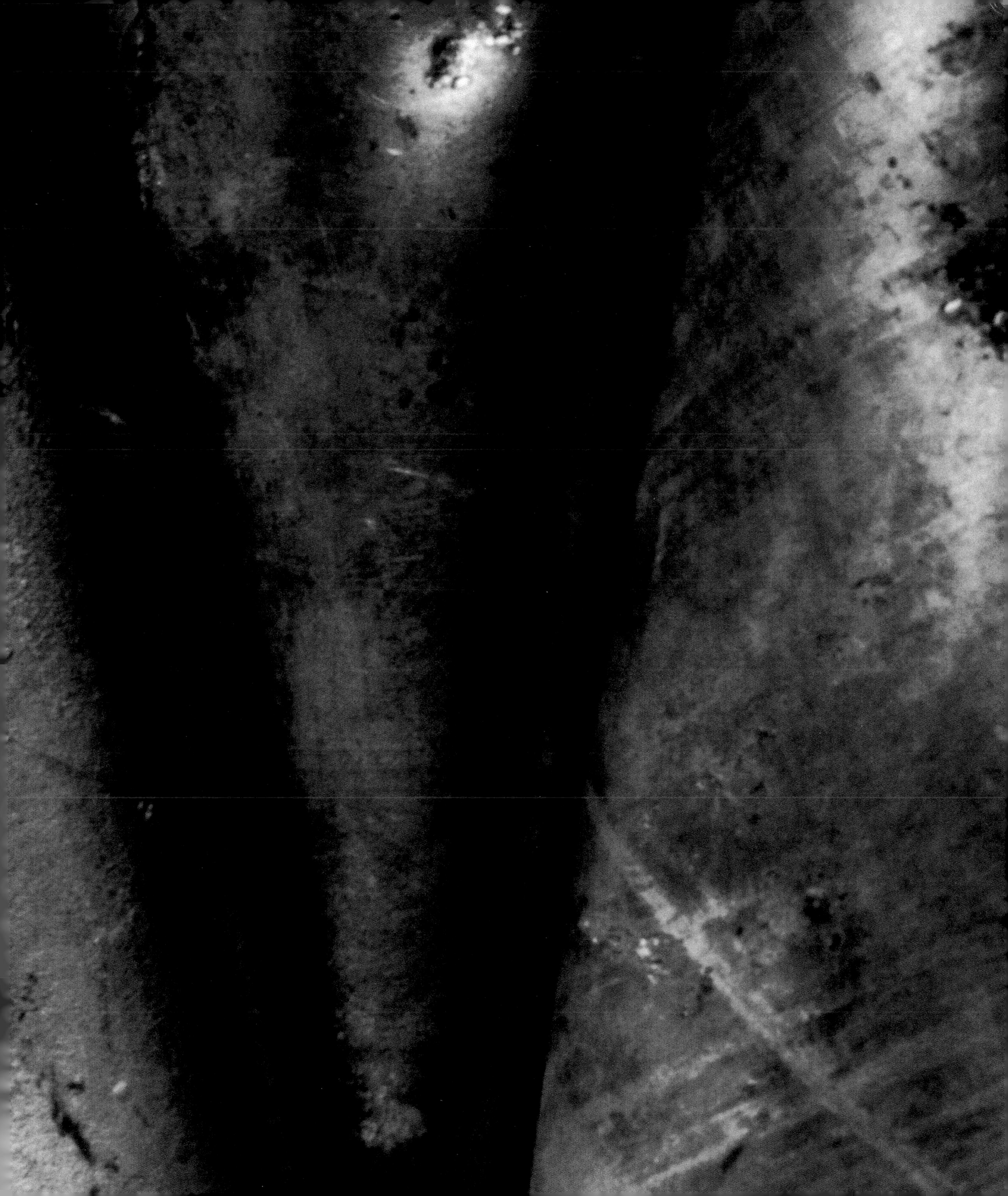

A whole new generation of photographers is discovering that black and white can offer them a different way of looking at the world, one in which the simplicity and subtlety of tone and shadow triumphs over the distractions of colour. Time and again black and white somehow captures a mood and a feeling that colour, for all its accuracy, simply can't. Perhaps that's exactly the point: photography is about so much more than a simple rendering of what's in front of the camera. We want to achieve an interpretation of life, and colour somehow sometimes gets in the way.

There's also a lot more flexibility built into black and white in the way that it can be manipulated and made to become what we want it to be. Instead of the computer screen, the traditional photographer has the darkroom, where all kinds of miracles can be performed. The rediscovery of ancient toning methods and half forgotten early printing processes has provided an extra dimension, and allowed photographers to produce pictures that wouldn't look out of place in an art gallery. As a bonus, many toners will also give a print a life expectancy of well over a hundred years as well, provided that the ground rules for display are followed.

A glance through the images in this book will show that black and white, thanks to these toning methods, can be surprisingly colourful at times, and equally impressive is quite how effective the final results can be. This is photography proudly proclaiming its history and heritage, and establishing a niche for itself that technological progress in the world of imaging won't erode.

The future of black and white looks secure, and its following will continue to grow as more and more photographers discover its advantages. So, listen to what the photographers in this book have got to say, pick up your camera and get out there and find out what black and white can offer for yourself. You won't be disappointed.

Terry Hope

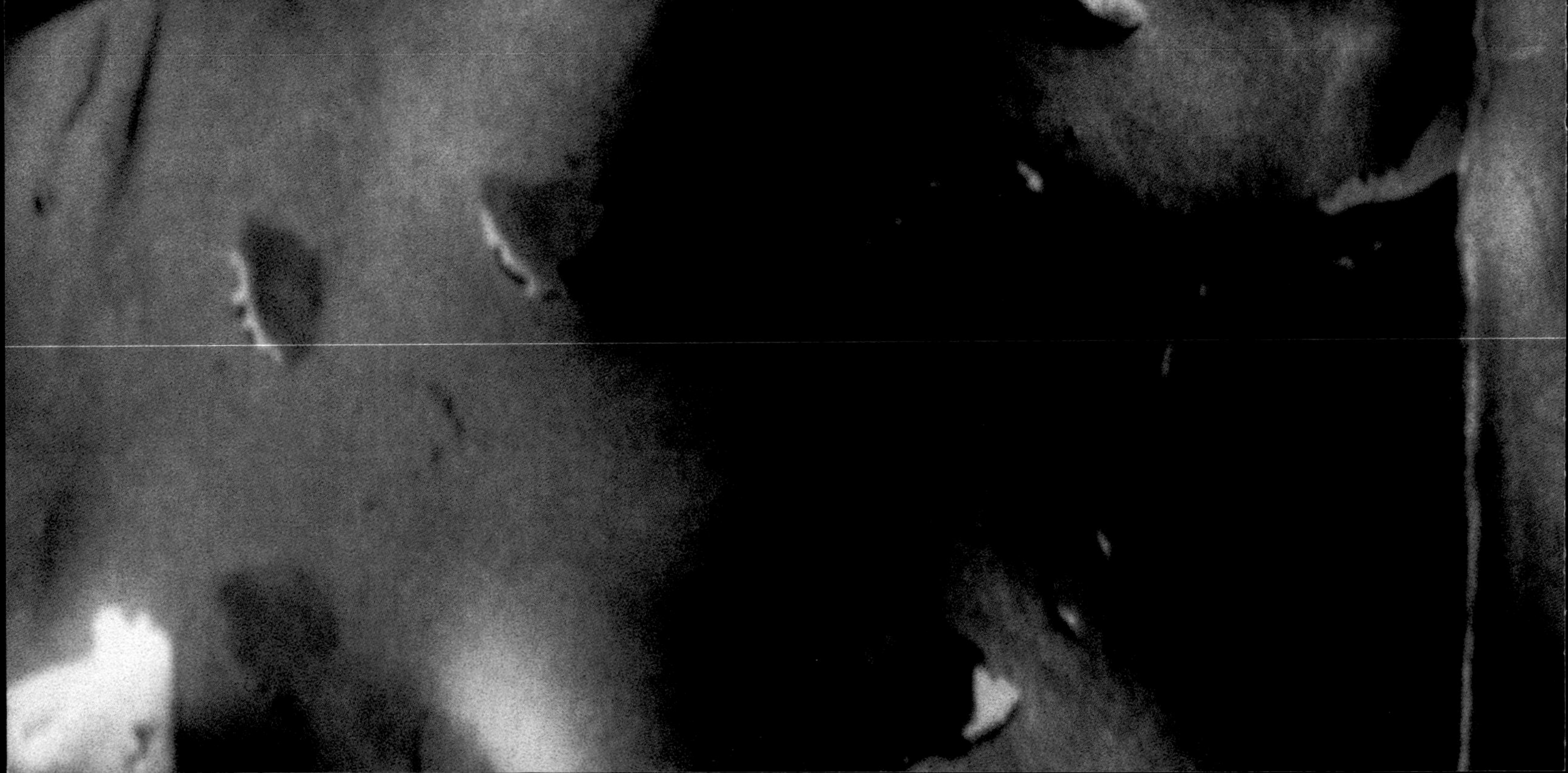

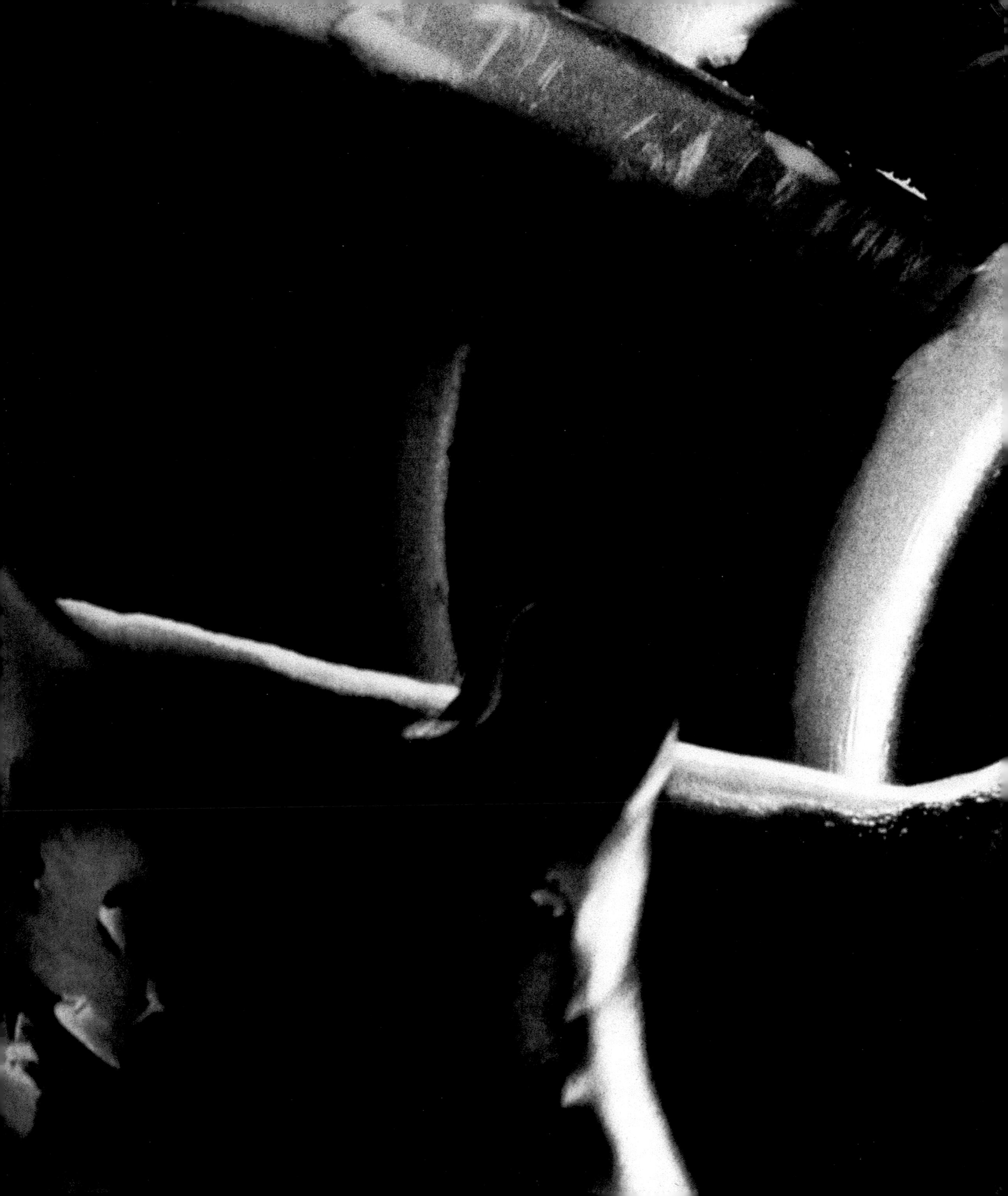

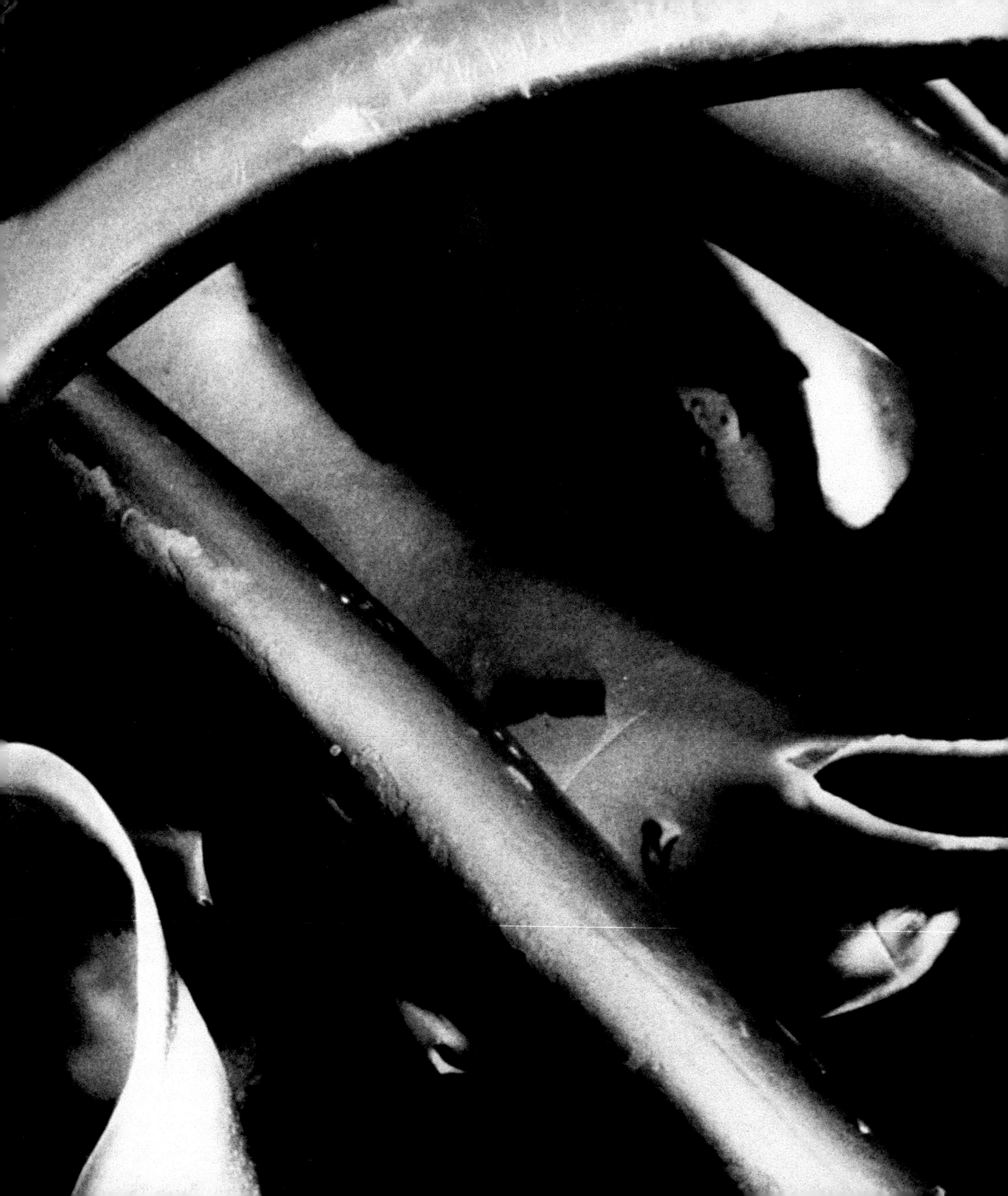

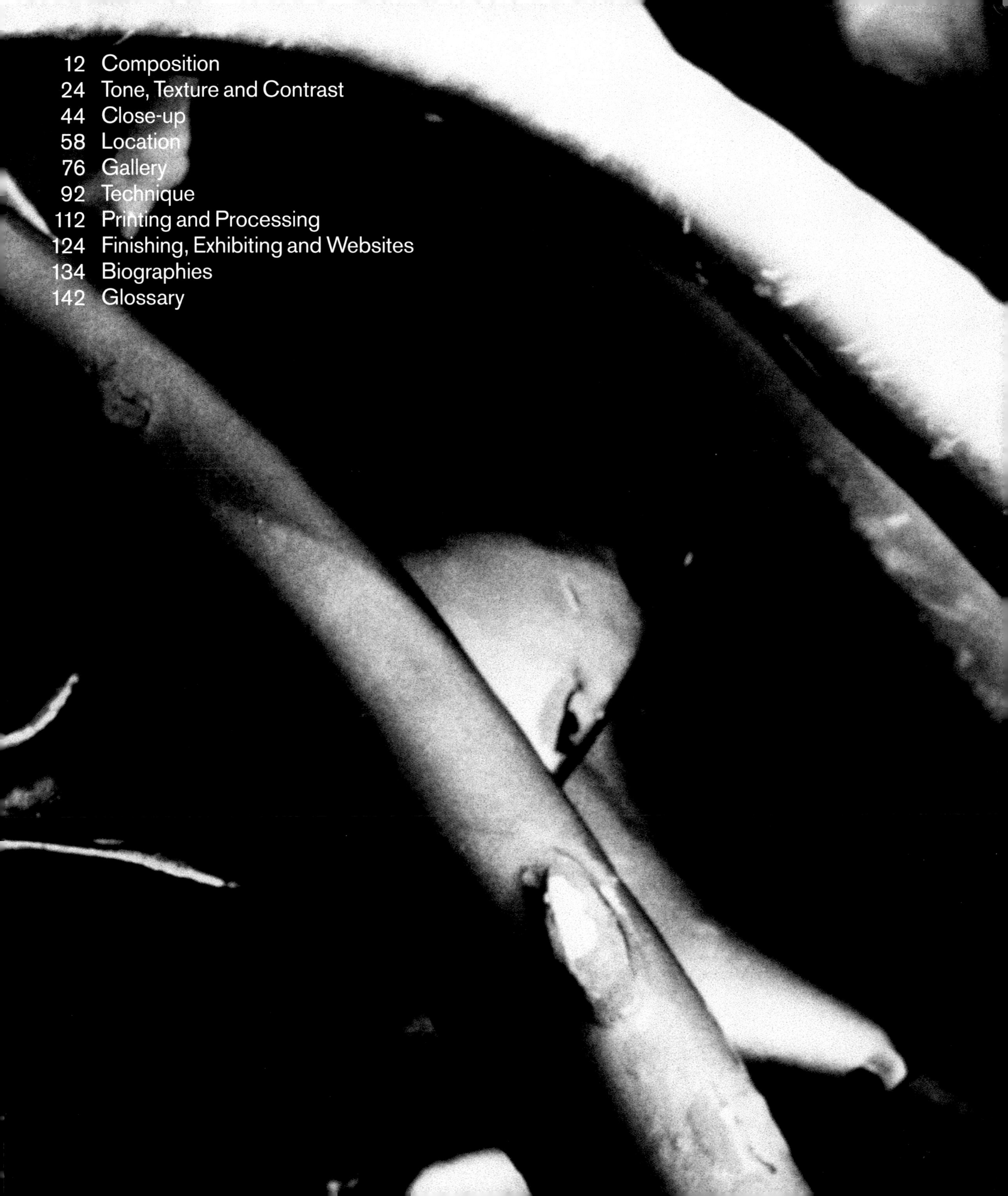

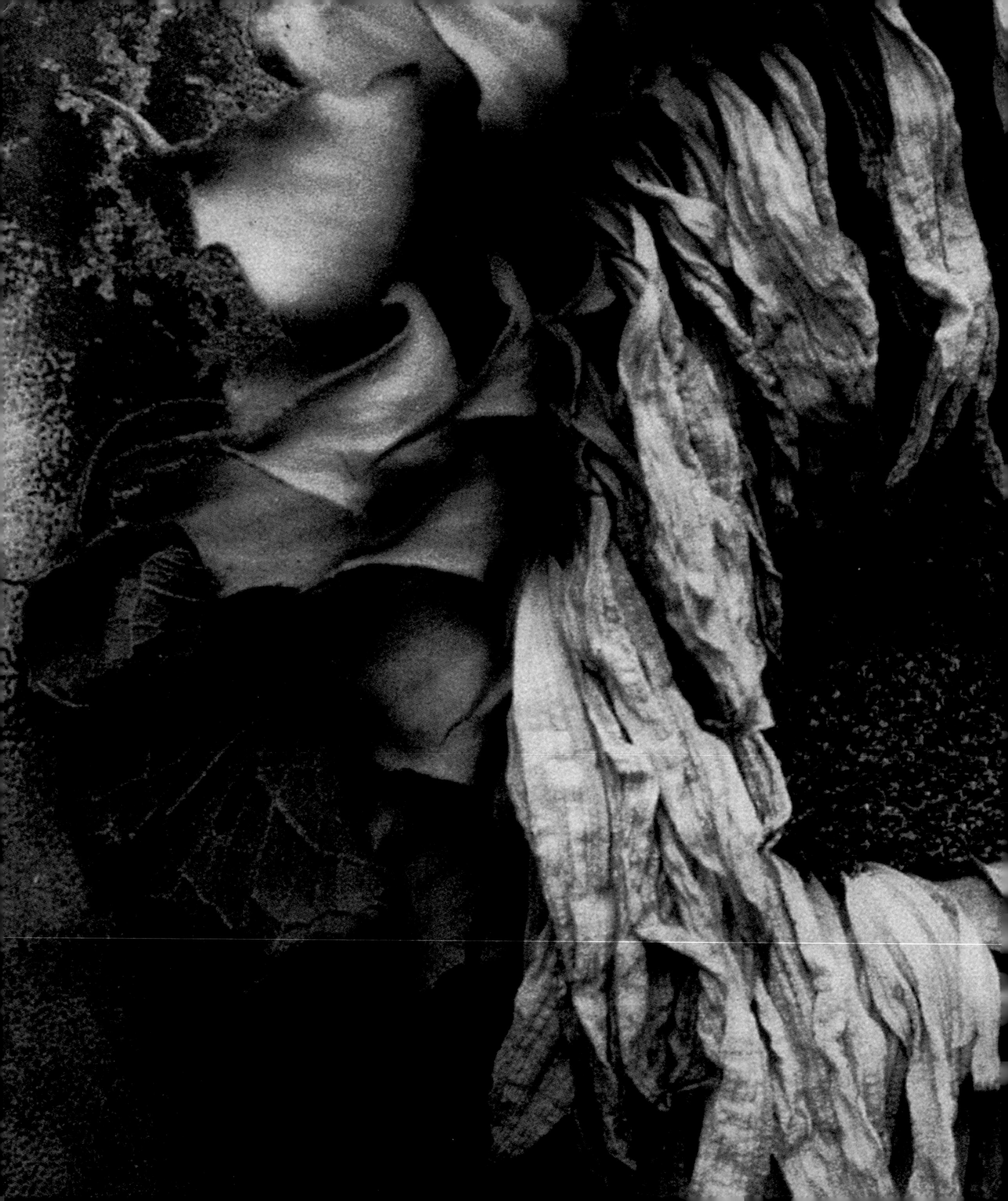

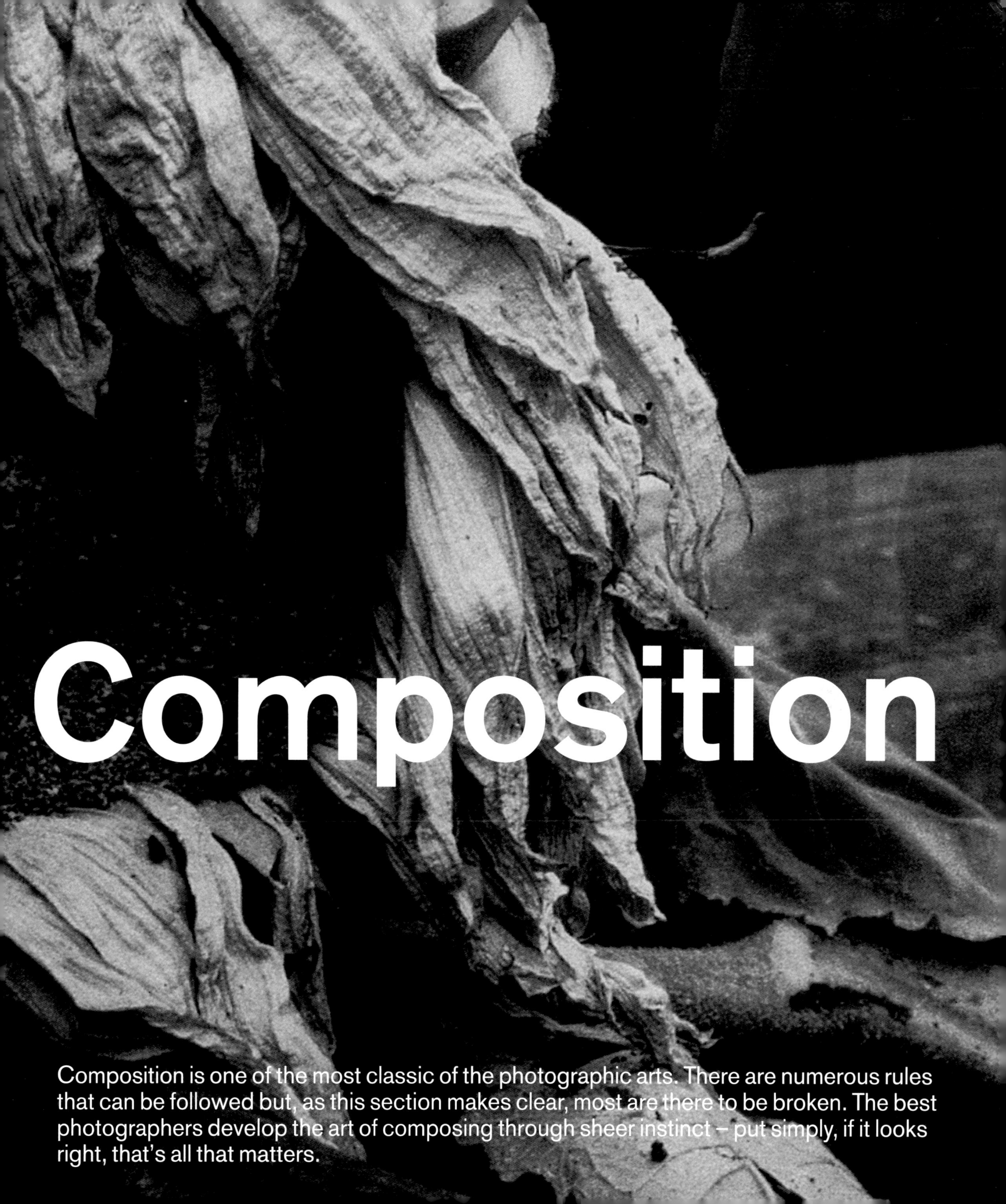

Composition

Composition is one of the most classic of the photographic arts. There are numerous rules that can be followed but, as this section makes clear, most are there to be broken. The best photographers develop the art of composing through sheer instinct – put simply, if it looks right, that's all that matters.

Still Life by Ralph Gibson
Leica M2 camera, 50mm lens, Kodak Tri-X film, processed in Rodinol. Exposure unknown

I had just stepped off the ferry after arriving in Corsica, and this scene was virtually the first thing that I saw. In order to compose the picture in the way that I wanted, I moved in towards my subject, gradually subtracting all of the things in the scene that weren't necessary until I achieved the picture that I wanted. It's the way I always work when I see still life in a location, and it's the opposite of the additive way you would work if you were to produce a drawing. With my photography I like to be highly selective, and eventually all that I'm left with is the essential element that attracted me in the first place. What you see in the picture is what attracted me to the scene, and nothing more. The way that I work is one of the reasons why I choose to use the Leica rangefinder camera. While I'm looking through the viewfinder my other eye is able to take in the wider picture, and it helps me to decide on the composition that I want. If I worked with a single lens reflex camera this wouldn't be possible.

Ralph Gibson

Pointer Ralph Gibson produces extraordinary still life images from the most ordinary of subjects, and has developed a remarkable eye for natural detail, shape and form. He finds material everywhere he travels: "I would never go anywhere without a camera", he says. "There would be no worse feeling for me than to see a picture and not to have a camera with me to record it." Meanwhile, the absence of colour allows his work to be one step removed from so-called reality. "Black and white is the essential photographic truth", he says, by way of explaining how the subtle tones of monochrome allow the natural geometry he's exploited within his pictures to be given greater prominence.

Location It's a fallacy to imagine that you have to start with a dramatic subject in order to make a memorable still life. As great photographers like Ralph Gibson have proved endlessly, there is potential in the most everyday of subjects, but it takes a trained eye to see how this can be realised. Learn to read the way that light affects a scene, make a feature of shadows and textures and don't be afraid to move in close or to introduce an extreme in-camera crop to extract only the most telling elements of your subject.

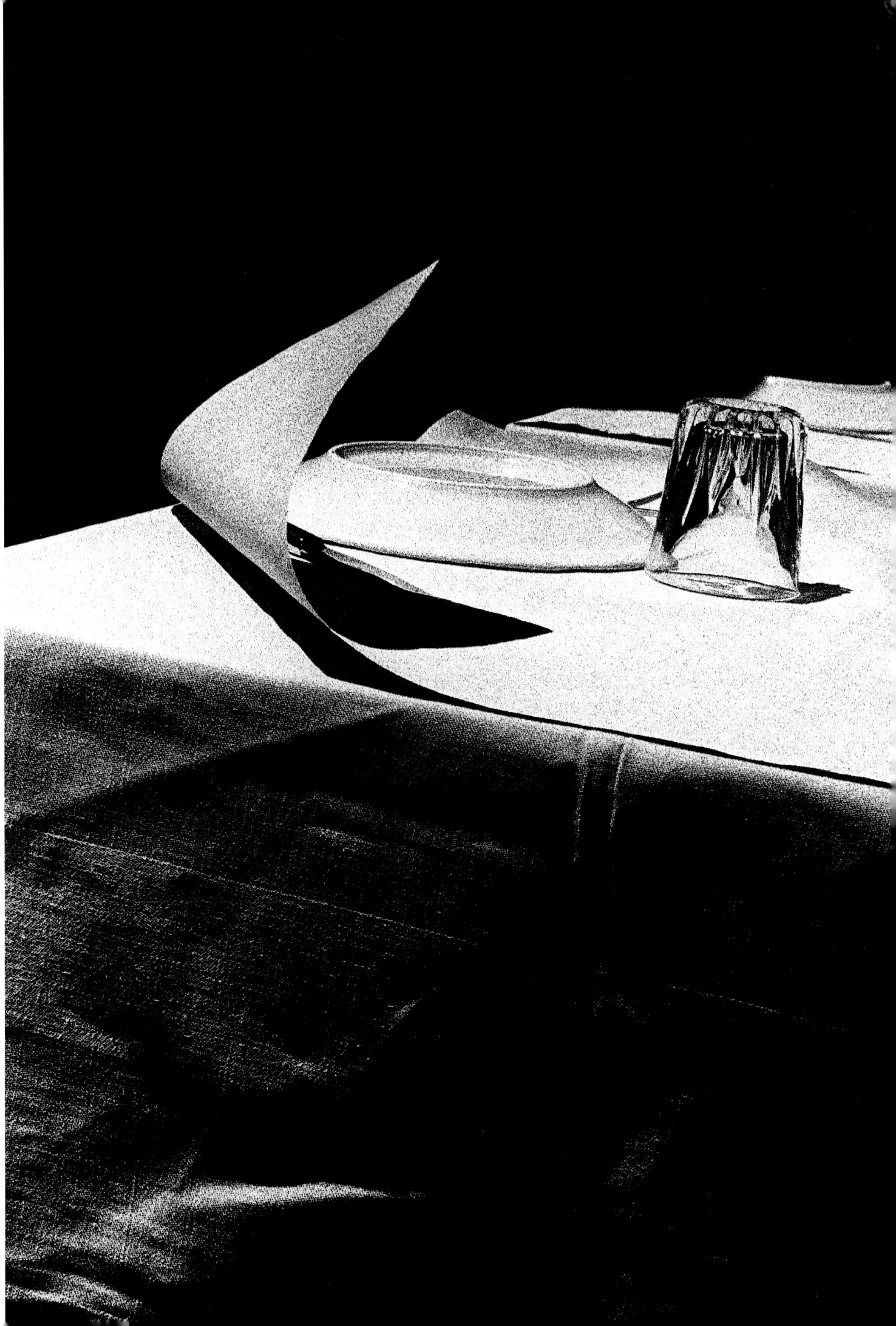

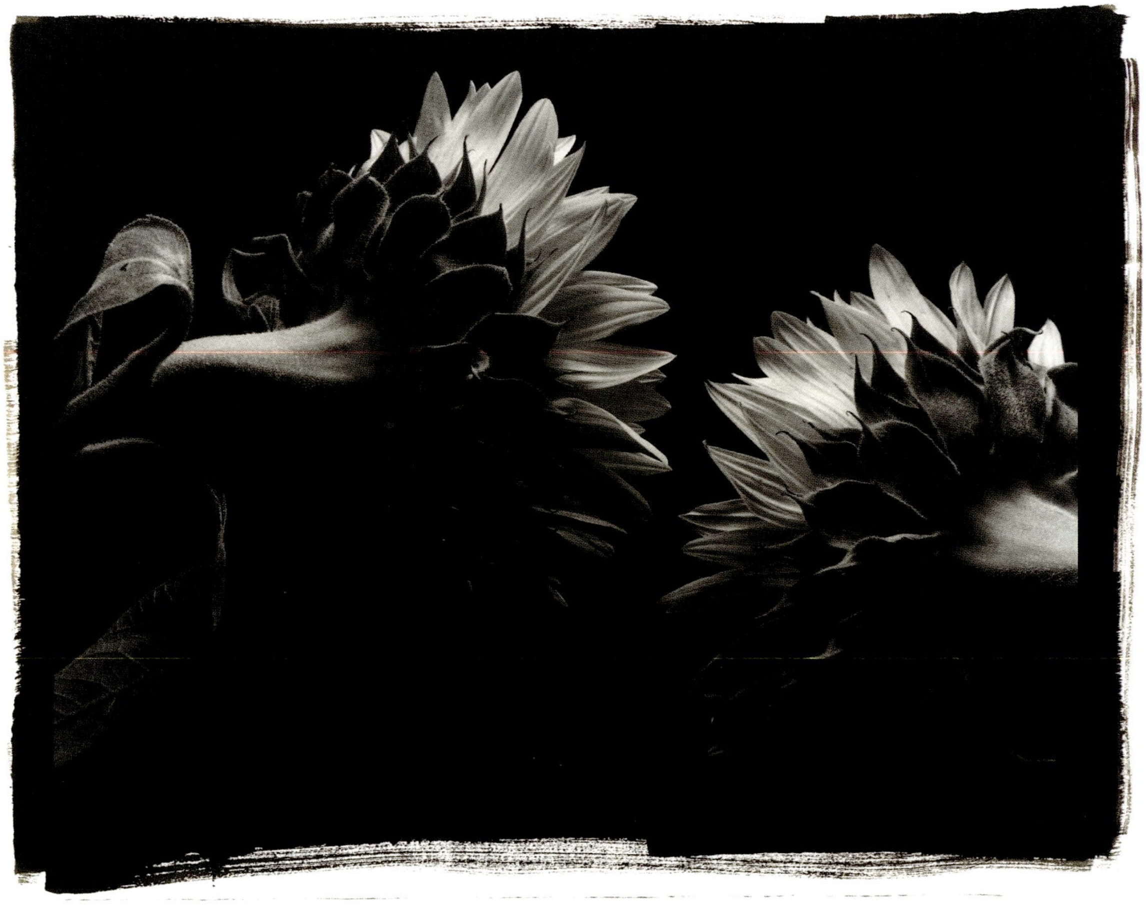

Composition

Sunflowers by Kenro Izu
Deardorff 20x14in camera, vintage lens, Kodak Plus X film ISO 125. Exposure not revealed

Sometimes a picture can be composed spontaneously, while at other times you can struggle for hours to produce an image that you're happy with. When you're dealing with two subjects that have to relate to each other, such as here, the problem can be compounded. There's no great secret, you have to persevere until you achieve a set-up where everything works together, and that's down to time and patience.

I usually don't use the camera when I'm setting up a still life. Rather I'll compose my subject with my eyes, and then decide what kind of lighting will best suit the arrangement that I have. Only when the subject and arrangement resonate to my heart will I bring the camera into my viewing position and prepare to take a photograph. I've found that there's nothing better than the naked eye for judging an arrangement, and this approach works for me in the studio and on location too.

Due to the extremely large format, the depth of field that I'm working with is very narrow, usually just an inch or so in front and behind the subject, and this gives me complete control over the image I produce. It's my choice which elements are in focus, and which aren't, and just the smallest adjustment will change the feel of the image that I produce. Here the focusing is on the petals of these sunflowers, while the nearest leaves and furthest petals are slightly softened as the focus drops away.

I like simplicity in my pictures. I used to use props occasionally, but lately I've discarded them and have moved in closer and closer to my subject and have worked to eliminate as much of the background as possible. All you can see here is an area of black behind the subject: this represents infinity and contains nothing to distract the viewer, while a grey background introduces tone and gradation, and takes the impact away from the subject.

Kenro Izu

Pointer This picture was taken with a Deardorff 20x14in camera that was made especially for me. I've had it for over 17 years now, and it's a unique format. The prints I produce are made by contacting, so I was looking for the largest negative size I could find, and a 20x14in camera and accessories turned out to be the largest that I could carry on location by myself. The film that I use, Plus X, is not made in 20x14in size, but if I order a large enough batch Kodak will make an order just for me and then I'll keep this in the fridge and use it over a lengthy period. Using a film as large as this concentrates my mind, and ensures that I always observe a subject very carefully, even the most subtle of details, before taking a picture.

Printing and Processing I produce all my own prints using the platinum /palladium method (see Printing and Processing section), and make up the emulsion and coat my own paper. Usually I produce around 20 sheets of paper in a batch, which I will need to use up within a day or so: it is very time consuming and laborious, but it means that I have complete control over the results.

Composition

Arum Lilies by Ray Spence
Mamiya RB67 camera, 90mm lens, Ilford FP4 film ISO 125.
Exposure 1/2 sec at f/11

I'm an ex-botanist, and have always been fascinated with flowers. These arum lilies, or lords and ladies as they're more commonly known, particularly appealed to me on several fronts: although very common in the hedgerows where I live they are beautiful plants, with the most exquisitely long and graceful stems. The botanist side of me is also intrigued by their amazing reproductive cycle, which involves tempting in flies to carry out pollination and then trapping them inside the flower heads through downward facing hairs for 24 hours before releasing them once their work is done.

I've often photographed them and, on this occasion, the composition just came naturally, the two plants that were more developed being positioned on either side of one that was at an earlier stage. I arranged them so that these two bigger plants leaned in towards one another, and there was just a slight overlap between them at the top of the frame to pull the whole set-up together. I think the shapes are extraordinary, and quite sexual in many ways in their appearance, which is what I was alluding to when I set this up.

The camera was set up on a copying stand, so that I could look directly down on my subject, and could guarantee to keep everything dead level, which was vital if the perspective was to appear undistorted. I kept everything very clean and uncluttered, and this allowed the shapes of these flowers to become the focus of the picture.

Ray Spence

Technique The illumination for this still life was provided from a light box – normally used for viewing transparencies – that the lilies were placed on. Although this is a very simple approach, it can be highly effective when used with subjects such as these, which are translucent enough to allow a little light to penetrate their form, so that they don't turn into pure silhouette. No frontal lighting was required, and the brightness of the light source ensured that the background to the flowers – the surface of the light box – recorded as a pure white. Exposure was determined by taking a straight meter reading directly from the light box itself.

Pointer In my work I've been very heavily influenced by the work of the artist Georgia O'Keeffe (1887–1986), who produced wonderful paintings of plants, in which she really explored their shape and form. A photographer should be open to influences from all sources, and be prepared to learn from the way that others, even if they're using a different medium, have approached the same subject.

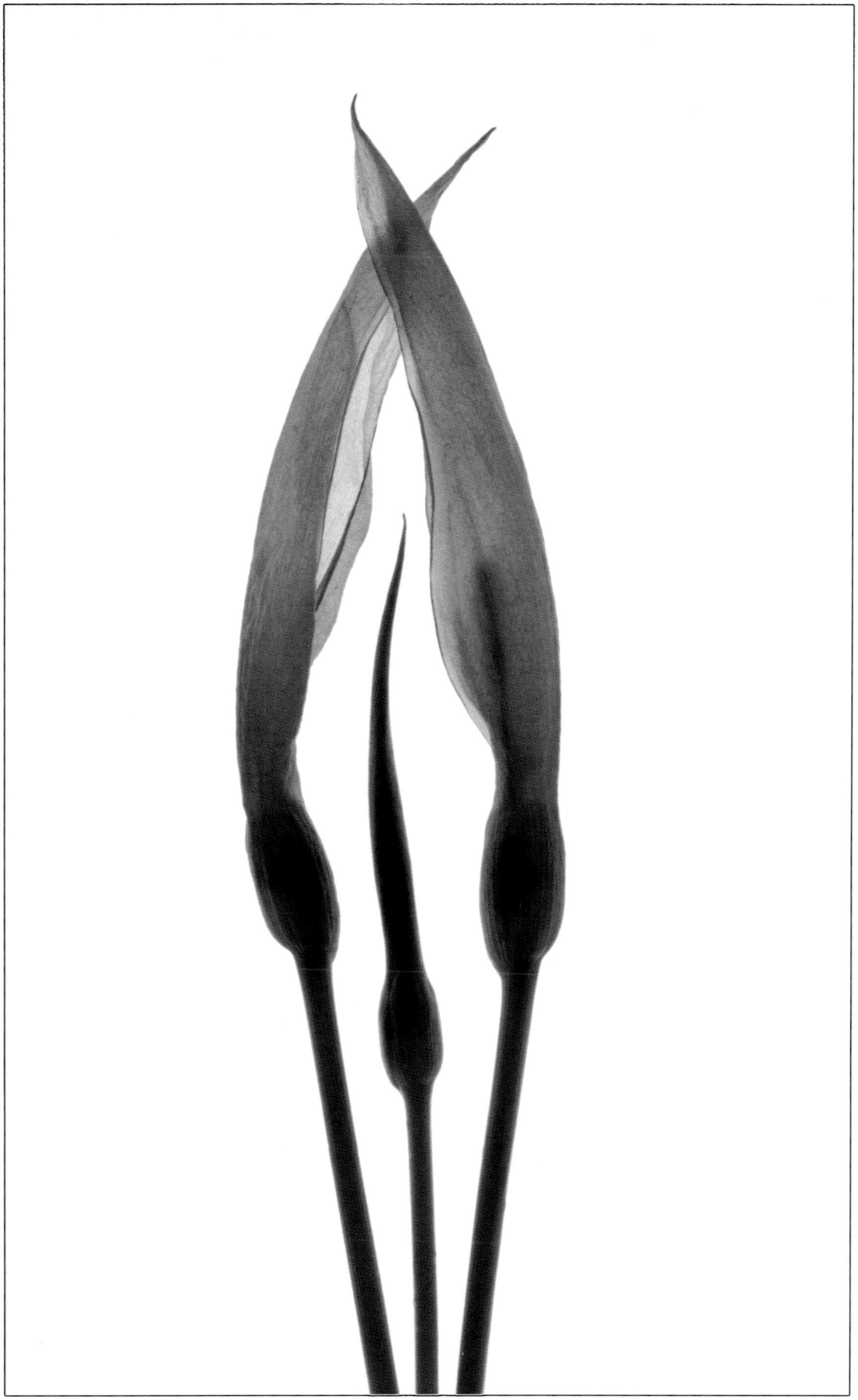

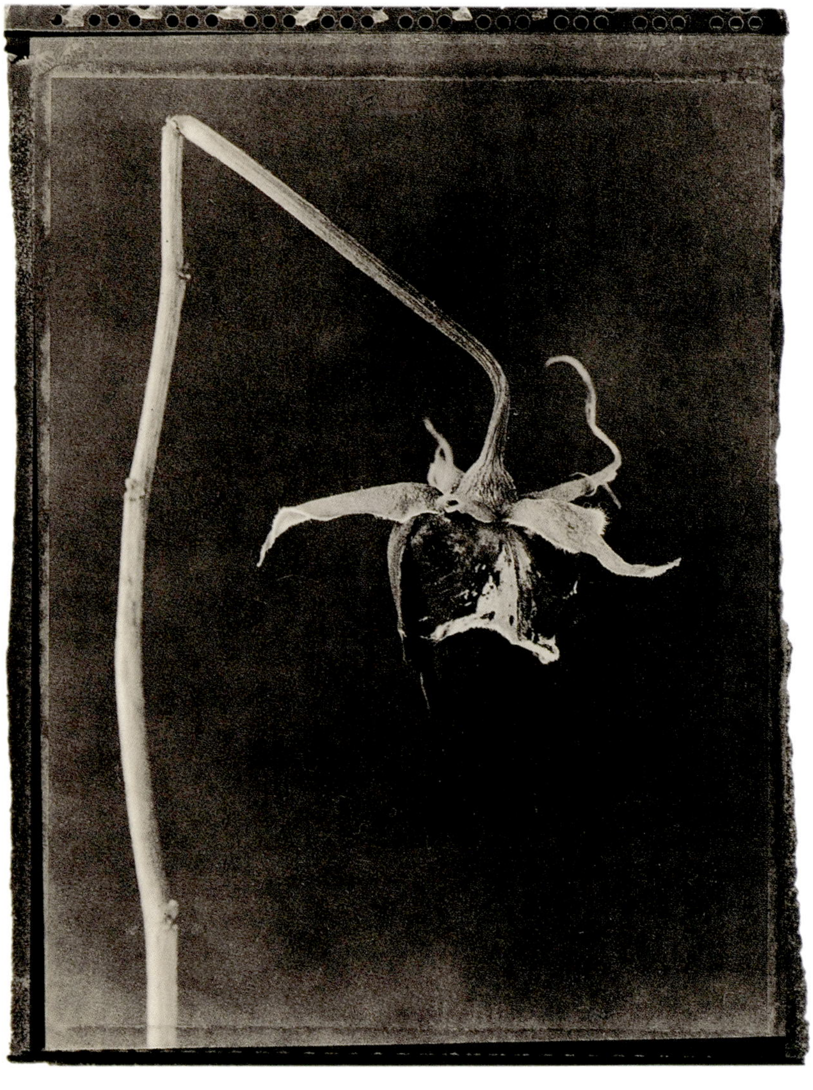

Bent Rose by Joseph Ortenzi
Crown Graphic 5x4in camera, 210mm lens, Polaroid Type 55 film.
Lit by tungsten light, exposure four seconds at f/16
Picture: The Michael Trevillion Picture Library

Still life composition can be remarkably simple, and yet still be highly effective, and often it's the really subtle designs that work the best.

I picked this single rose from my garden, and it sat for some time in a small jar on a desk in my studio. Eventually it began to die and then decay, and as it did so it took on this remarkable shape, and I realised that it would make a powerful photograph. The composition was largely dictated by the angle of the broken stem and the shape the dying rose had naturally worked itself into. I pulled the camera back to ensure a little space around the subject and set up a plain background to ensure there was no unnecessary detail anywhere else in the picture that could act as a distraction.

Most of my still life work utilises subject matter that has decayed to some degree. It allows the texture to become more interesting as the smoothness of surface areas starts to break up, and tones may change and perhaps become darker, while the subject will take on a new quality. The most exciting thing about work of this kind is that you never quite know what to expect and, for a photographer, that's a tantalising thought.

I used tungsten lighting for this picture, and set two lights, one high, one low, to the right of the camera to ensure quite a flat result, while a further light behind the subject helped to pick out some of the fine detail on the flower's surface.

Joseph Ortenzi

Technique Simple compositions require plain backgrounds to set them off, and I decided here to go for one that was black. All this required me to do was to put something behind the rose that was dark and non-reflective: often I'll just use a sheet of black card or even the back of my jacket, because when using a large format camera you have great control over depth of field. This means that the background doesn't need to be far behind the subject to be thrown out of focus and to be turned into something that is unrecognisable. To make the background more interesting here I developed the print in lith developer, which caused the overall dark tone to break up and become mottled, and then selenium toned the print to cut back on the pink hue that the lith treatment had produced.

My Favourite Tip Although this particular rose had taken up this shape quite naturally, you can, as a photographer, lend a helping hand to exercise a little control over the way that plants will decay. You can hang flowers upside-down, for example, to influence the direction that the petals will face, while it's also possible to place your flower in a certain position, i.e. facing a bright light such as a window, to encourage it to bend in the way that you would like. But, as I say, you never know quite what to expect, and that's part of the attraction!

Composition

Sunflower by Edward Steichen
Toned gelatin silver print, c1920.
Picture: The Royal Photographic Society, Bath

This beautiful sunflower study is perfectly composed, yet deceptively casual in appearance. The weight of the picture is in the top half of the frame, while the decaying petals of this mighty flower flow downwards to lead the eye into the bottom half of the picture. Here a single leaf can be seen in the shadows, which carries a line down to the edge of the print: block this line out with your finger for an instant and just see how much power is lost should this line not exist. It was placed there for a purpose, and there is nothing accidental in this picture, because Edward Steichen took enormous care over every aspect of his composition, and his still life work was meticulously planned.

Note how the sunflower head is also placed slightly off centre of the picture, rather more towards the left. It's a subtle thing, but highly effective, because the composition otherwise would have appeared too formal and contrived.

Tone, Texture and Contrast The picture makes the valuable point that often it is the subjects which are not perfect that are the most interesting for the photographer. This sunflower head is well past its prime as its seeds have dried out, so its form has collapsed and the once-fresh appearance has become tattered and worn. It's all helped to add texture and shape to the study: an immaculate flower will often look too perfect and will have less to interest the still life photographer.

Pointer Edward Steichen didn't just photograph one sunflower and then move on to the next subject. Rather he stuck with his theme over a long period, to ensure that he really got to know his subject and through this was then able to explore its true form in his work. With sunflowers he produced a series that looked at every aspect of the plant – from the seed, through to sprouting, then growing, fully open and decaying and finally back to the seed again. Steichen also photographed the mundane in order to hone his still life skills to perfection. For example, he pictured a white cup and saucer over a thousand times against a graduated scale of tones from white to black, to see and to note for himself exactly what the results would be, and how his final picture would be affected. The discipline that this approach required produced a new sort of artistic freedom in his work.

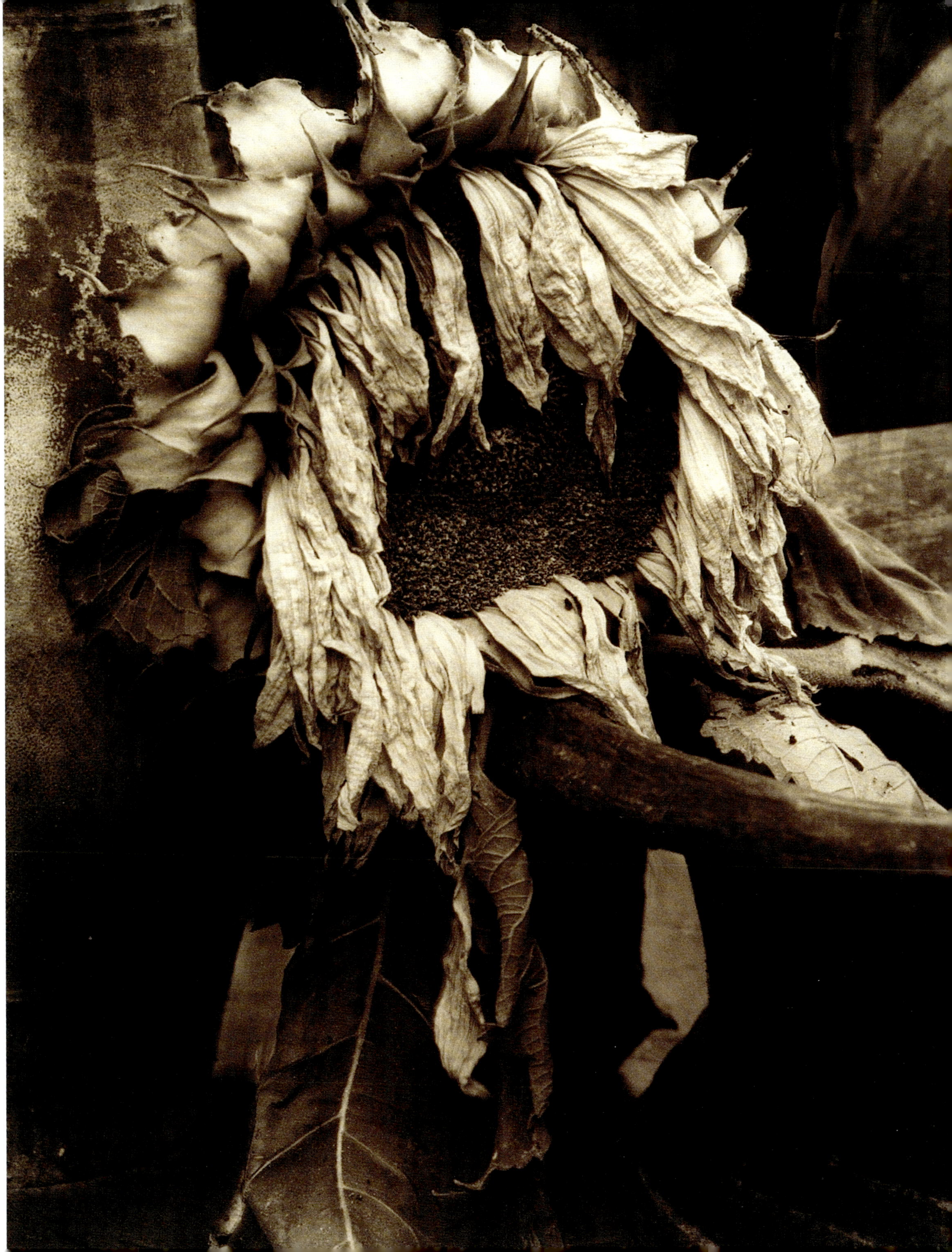

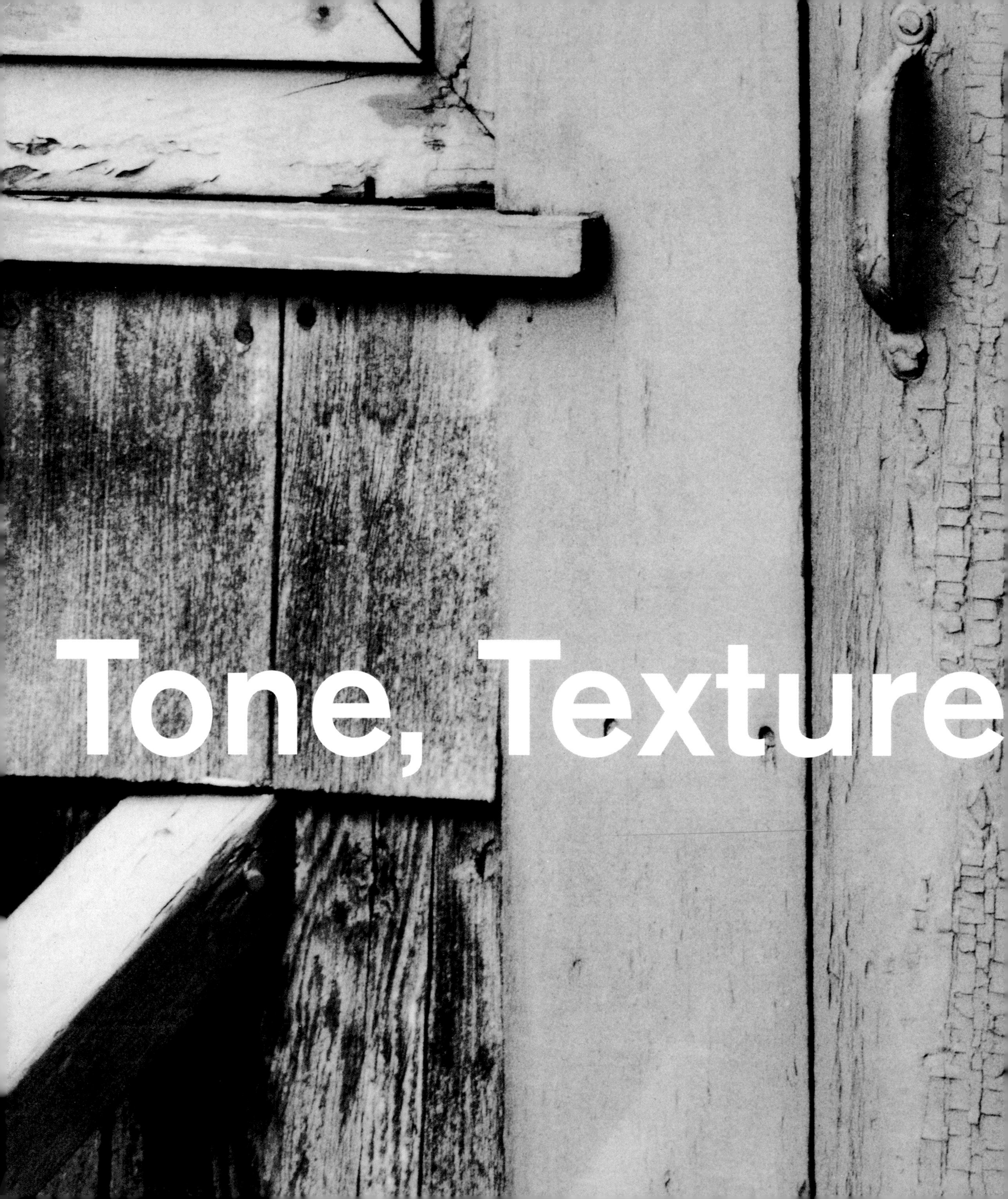
Tone, Texture

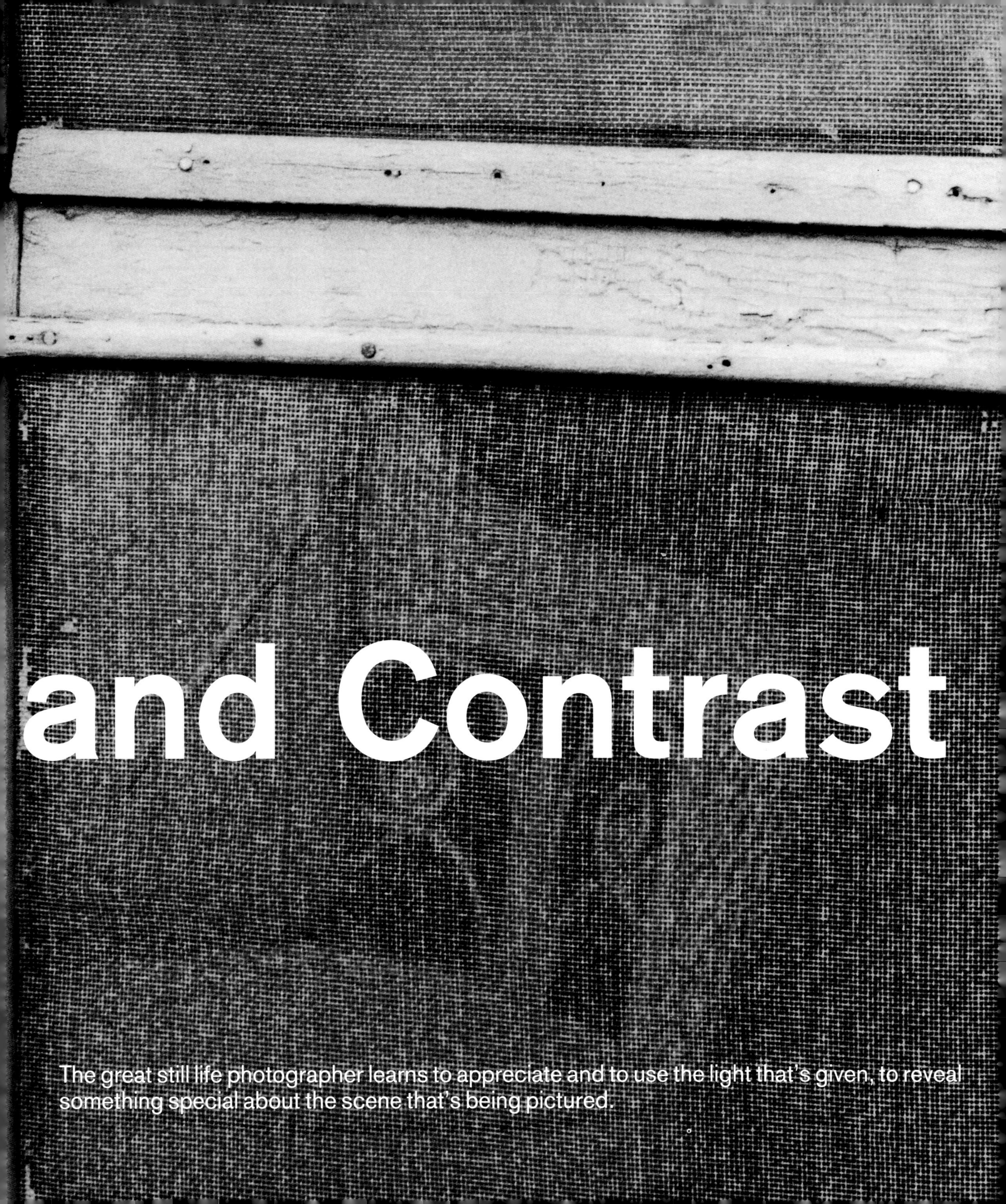

and Contrast

The great still life photographer learns to appreciate and to use the light that's given, to reveal something special about the scene that's being pictured.

I had noticed one day how a bunch of flowers that had been placed on a window sill glowed when backlit by strong sunlight, and I decided to try to set up the same high contrast effect for a picture. Initially my efforts to shoot from the room out through the window didn't meet with a great deal of success, because the glass was difficult to clean sufficiently and the detail of neighbouring houses registered too distinctly in the background. I overcame the problem by hanging a sheet of semi-opaque tracing paper over the window, which acted as a diffuser and spread the light evenly without allowing any detail to show through. This still left me with the problem of how to support the flowers that I wanted to photograph without these then moving too far away from the paper causing the loss of the glow that I was so keen to capture.

The answer that I eventually came up with was to cut a slit in the paper so that I could place the stem through it. The flower was consequently held firmly at the precise distance I wanted from the background. The result was even better than I had anticipated: because the stem was now seen through a thickness of tracing paper, it became softer and less of a distraction, while the flower itself still held the glow that I had been after.

Seamus Ryan

Printing and Processing In the straight print of this gerbera, the stem leads out of the bottom of the picture, and I decided the result would be far better if I dodged the lower half to two thirds of the image so that it simply faded away into the white background. Because there was no tone in the backlit background this was fairly easy to achieve, and the result appears very seamless and unforced. My biggest challenge in printing this image was to ensure that, once the Kodak Ektalure paper I was using had dried down, the glow of the flower still remained. There was no easy way to achieve this, and several prints were ultimately disappointing, but eventually I was able to retain the contrast that I wanted.

Pointer If something works for me then I tend to stick with it, and I've standardised my working methods as a result. I use just the one lens, stick to Ektalure for my printing and use Polaroid's Type 55 film for virtually all my work. This has served to give my pictures a strong and immediately identifiable look and, of course, a rigid format.

Type 55 is one of the oldest Polaroid film materials available, and it gives the photographer both a print and a negative. It's inserted into a Polaroid back that slips into the back of the camera in the normal way and, on exposure, it's pulled out to release the chemicals held inside. Then it's given the usual processing time of one minute whereupon it can be peeled apart and a black and white contact print examined.

This print needs to be coated quite quickly with a chemical film to prevent it oxidising, while the negative has to be cleared with a salt solution, but it's a brilliant way to work because you can see exactly what you're doing as you go along. You do have to take particular care, however, to frame the picture exactly as you want it, because if you intend to feature the edge of the picture there's no possibility of cropping. Again this is quite a useful discipline to learn.

Tone, Texture and Contrast

Gerbera by Seamus Ryan
Horseman LX 5x4in camera, 150mm lens, Polaroid Type 55 film.
Exposure unknown

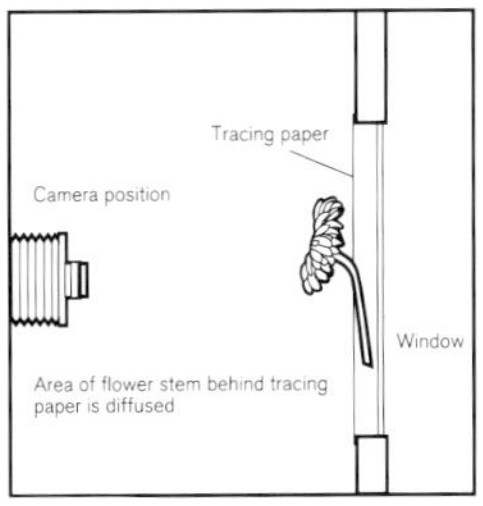

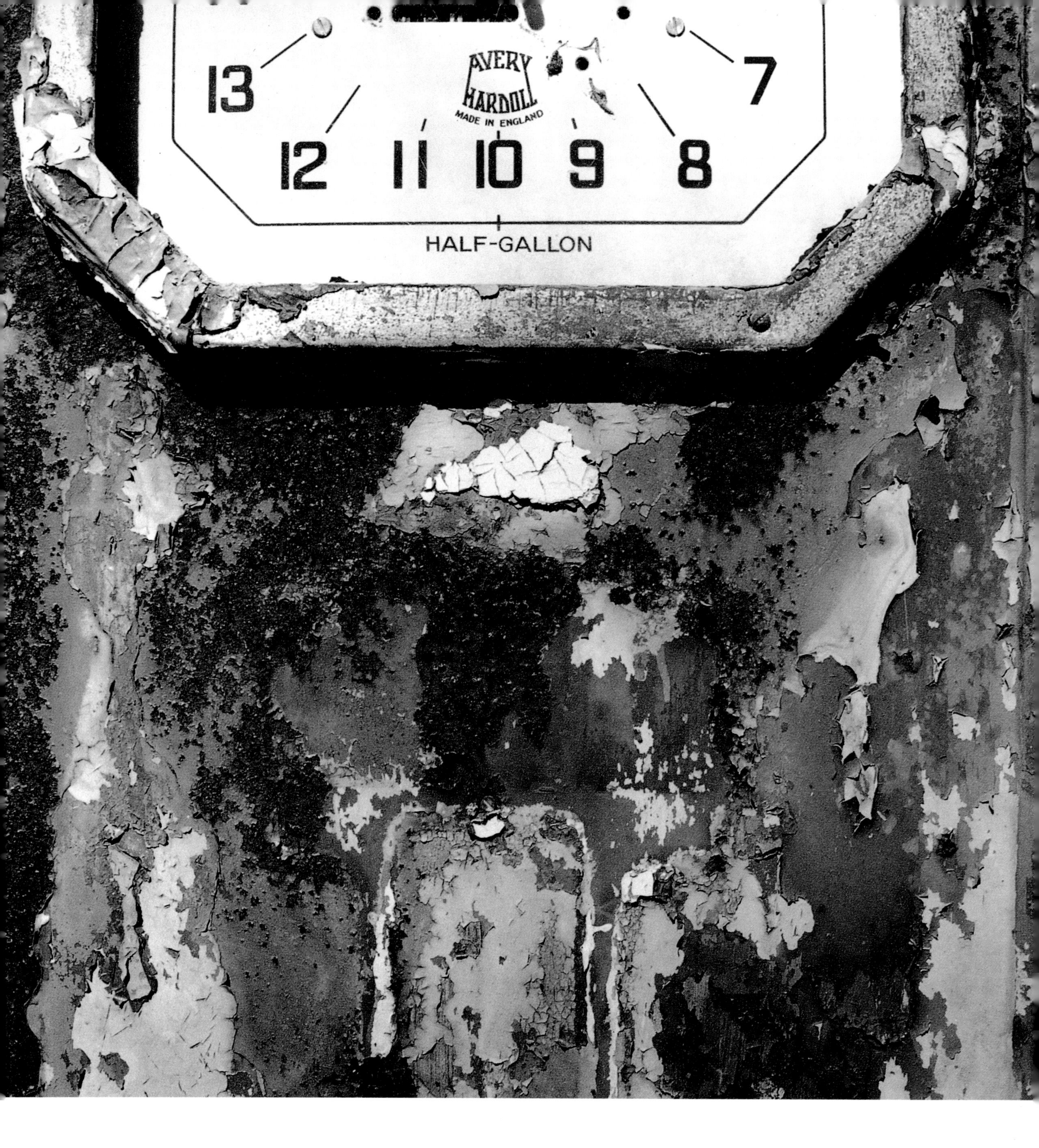
13
7
AVERY
HARDOLL
MADE IN ENGLAND
12 11 10 9 8
HALF-GALLON

Imperial Measure by Gerry Coe
Bronica 6x6cm camera, 80mm lens, Number Two close-up filter, Agfa APX 100 film. Exposure 1/125sec at f/11

I photograph people for a living, but my personal work is far more about objects and shapes and textures, and I'm always on the lookout for subjects that I can photograph. Out driving one day in County Down, Northern Ireland, near the town of Newtownards, I saw an abandoned petrol station, and realised that it might have potential. I was particularly intrigued by the petrol pump that was still standing: it had obviously not received any attention for some years, and the 'Half-Gallon' inscription that it still carried proved its age, and gave me a focus for this picture. I looked at it from a number of different angles, and took several pictures that featured the whole pump. Eventually, however, I realised that its decaying surface, which contained a whole mixture of textures and tones created by the rust and peeling paint alongside each other, was the major point of interest for me. I'm fascinated by the random way that decay takes hold, and I start to see all kinds of details, such as imaginary faces and shapes, the longer I look at something like this. A pristine surface would hold little interest for me, because it would simply be too bland: the weather-beaten surface I photographed here was unique and will continue to change with time, and that was the appeal for me.

Gerry Coe

Close-up I started by photographing the pump in long shot, and then moved in closer and closer as I started to strip away the details in the scene that were not relevant to its strength. Eventually I fitted a Number Two close-up filter, which screwed into the front of the lens in the way that any normal filter would do. This enabled me to take my theme to its logical conclusion and to exclude everything but the elements that tell the viewer what this object is. You don't need to see the entire pump to get a feel for the decay that's taking place here – you don't even need to see the whole face of the pump. By cropping in this tightly I reduced the picture to its bare bones, and increased the graphic feel of the scene at the same time.

Printing and Processing I decided to tone the final result, because I felt that this helped to bring out the textures in the picture more. I used sulphide toner, a form of sepia toner: the print is immersed initially in a bleach solution and then, when the tones have faded to the degree that's required, it's transferred to a second bath where re-development takes place, with tones now rendered a soft brown. To complete the print I washed it and then toned it further with selenium to achieve a colder final result that I felt was appropriate for the subject.

Tone, Texture and Contrast

Thai Village Detail by Stephen Widdows
Nikon FM2 camera, 28mm lens, Kodak Tri-X film. Exposure 1/30sec at f/8

I was visiting a hill tribe village in the Chang Mai region of Northern Thailand, and the details of the life that the people lived there fascinated me. Because I was working with a 35mm camera, I was able to move around and cover a variety of things, but some of my most successful pictures came about as the light turned more contrasty towards the evening, and streamed into the huts in the village, highlighting the textures that could be found there. It was one of those occasions when even the most ordinary of objects suddenly became photogenic, and I looked for scenes that had a pleasing symmetry and which said something about the location I was in. This cooking pot and its surroundings had it all: the picture that resulted was full of the most amazing shapes and graphic details, from the rough wall that made up the background through to the uneven surface of the earthen floor.

What I liked most about it was that the scene wasn't manipulated by me in any way, it's completely natural and as found. I think that this is extremely important when looking for still life in its natural environment. You can work on an image in the studio to make it perfect, but on location it's the imperfections that add to the charm and make the picture real.

Stephen Widdows

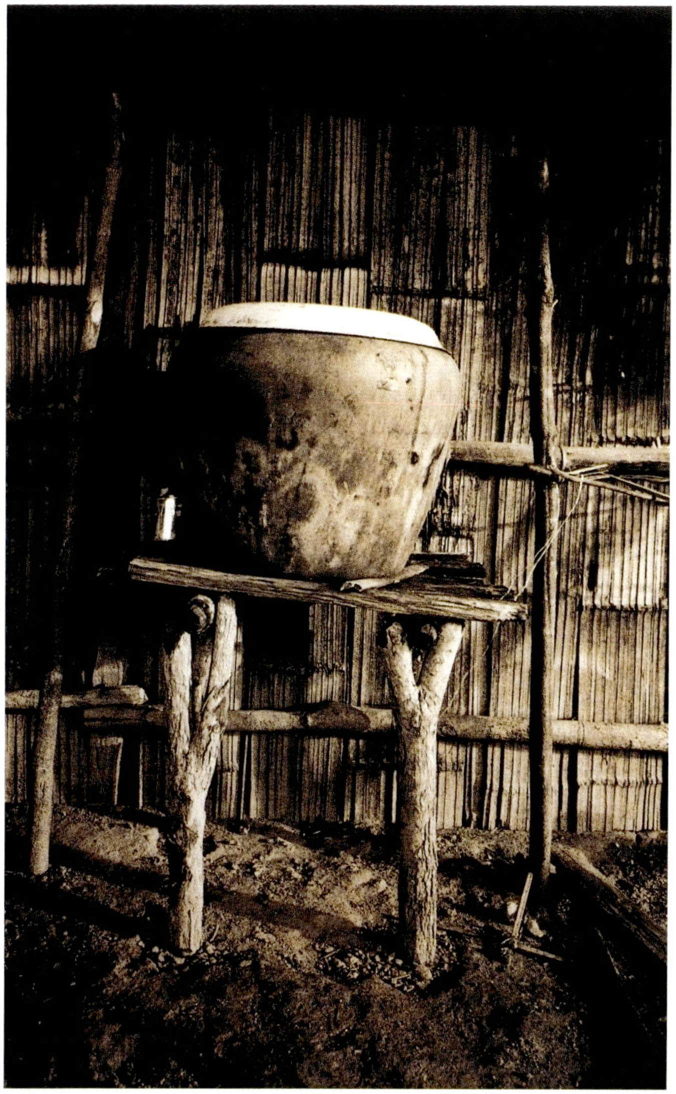

Pointer Still life is all about the skill that a photographer has in being able to extract an extraordinary picture from an ordinary scene. The great master Irving Penn produced one of the most memorable series of studio still life pictures ever seen, simply by collecting discarded cigarette stubs in the street and then photographing them against plain backgrounds before blowing the results up to a giant size so that they appeared out of context and a little unreal. The subject you choose to feature doesn't have to be conventional, nor does it have to be studio based. Develop an eye for detail in the most mundane of scenes and try to anticipate how lighting at different times of day might affect your subject for better or worse.

Printing and Processing I toned the final print in sepia toner, which I made up myself to ensure that I got exactly the colour that I wanted. The two chemicals that make up the toner are thiocarbamide and sodium hydroxide, and I usually mix them in equal measures as a starting point, and then add more of the sodium hydroxide if I want the result to appear cooler.

"Because I was working with a 35mm camera, I was able to move around and cover a variety of things."

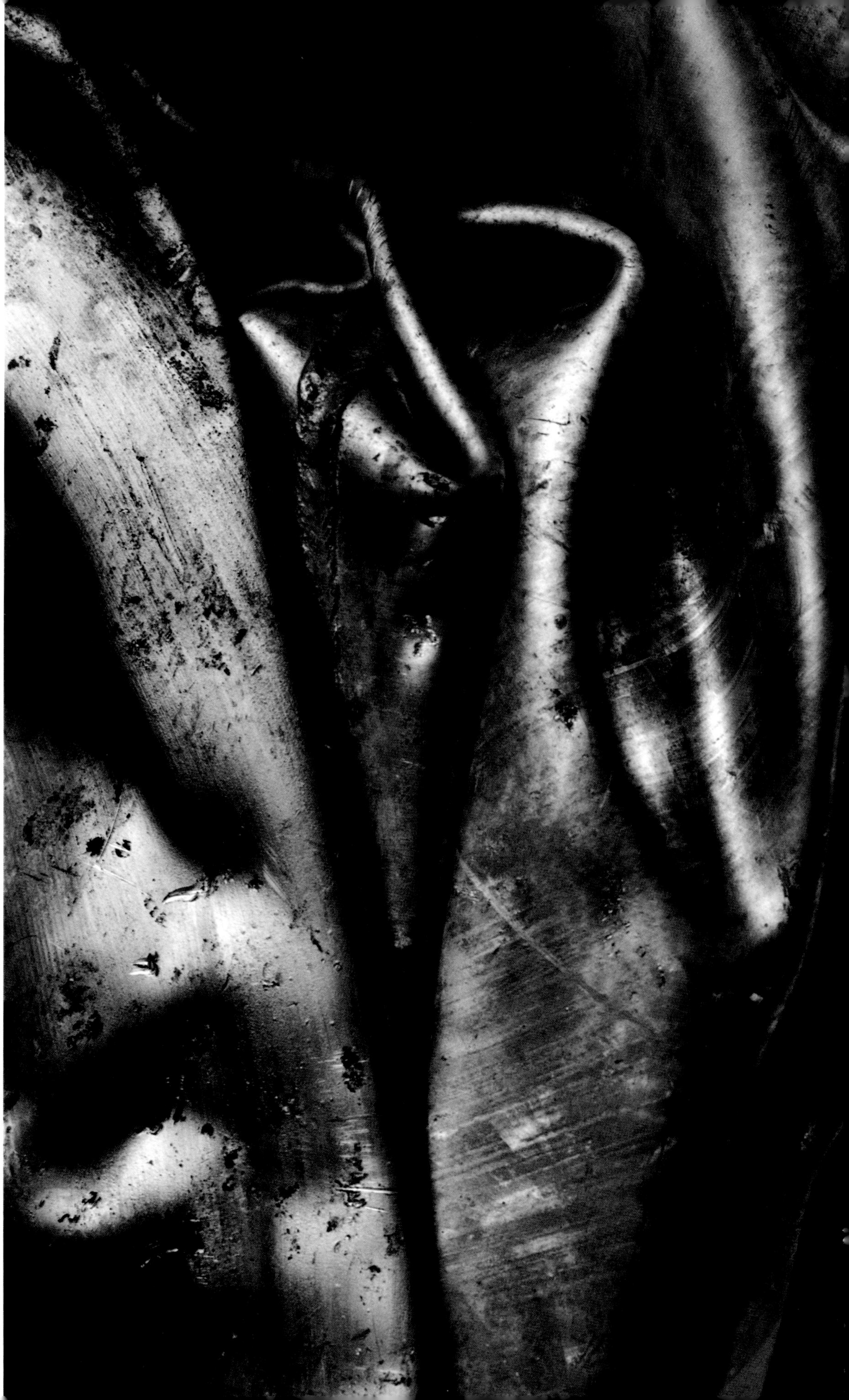

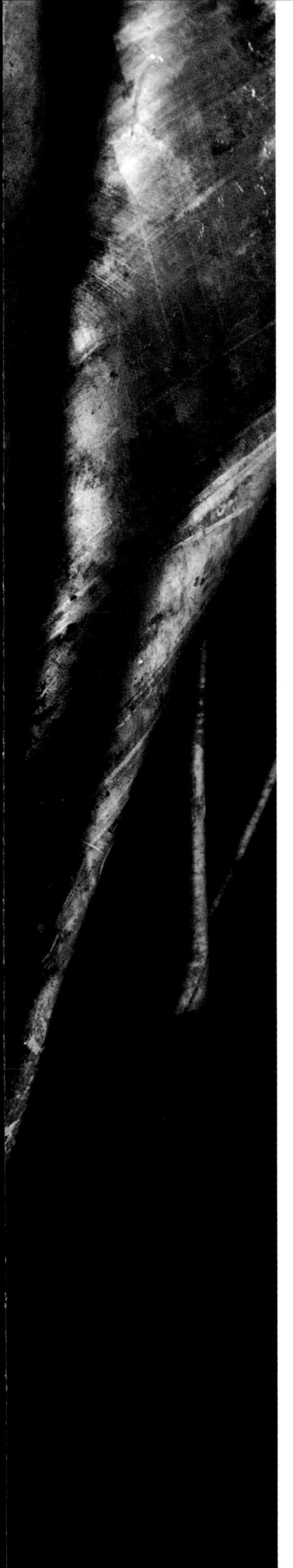

Metal Detail by Robin Broadbent
Sinar 5x4in camera, 150mm lens, Agfa 100 film.
Exposure two seconds at f/32

I love exploring the texture and form of metal through the camera, so when I came across some old water heaters that had been crushed and bent into the most amazing sinewy shapes, I knew I had to take them into the studio and produce some pictures of them.

Each water heater was around two and a half feet across, but quite deliberately this picture of one of them gives no idea of scale, and by moving in close the result I've achieved is pure abstract. I used just one tungsten light – chosen because this source is more controllable and easier to judge – to pick out the shine on the metal's surface and to highlight some of the imperfections in its surface that I found so beautiful. I find that the fewer lights I use the easier it is to keep the object I'm photographing in its purest form.

Behind the metal I arranged a sheet of black velvet, so that any background that was visible, as it is here in the bottom right hand corner, would register as pure black tone, and would cause the minimum of distraction.

The picture shows a section of the water heater exactly as I found it, because if you start to work on an object to 'improve' it for the camera, then you're doing something that's beyond a photograph. My philosophy is to enjoy something and to see it for what it is. This is a found object, and the joy of such things is seeing something in it that everyone else may have missed.

Robin Broadbent

My Favourite Tip My first stage of photographing this heater was to produce a 10x8in Polaroid print of the whole object, and then I set about playing with crops within this, and finding areas that would work as pictures in their own right. Only after this process did I start to photograph my subject in detail, knowing by this point of course exactly how I intended to tackle each study.

Exhibitions This picture is one of a set I produced all based around the theme of metal and the shapes and textures that it can produce. Eventually I gathered enough together to make up a show, MetalFlesh, which was exhibited in London, and the experience was a wholly positive one. An exhibition is a useful outlet for pictures and a great opportunity to show a wider audience the kind of work that you're capable of producing.

Porch Door by James Flanagan
Zone Six 4x5in field camera, 150mm Schneider lens, 6in bellows extension, Kodak Tri-X film ISO 400. Exposure 1/2 sec at f/45

I was staying with friends in Chatham, Massachusetts, and came in and out of this doorway every morning and evening, and I never noticed anything special about it. Then one morning, when the light was soft and misty, I happened to see this delicate shaft of sunlight falling across the porch, and suddenly the picture just came together. As I looked, I was struck by all the textures that this most simple of scenes contained. There was the roughened appearance of the peeling paintwork, the fine mesh of the screen that made up part of the door, and which was allowing the outline of a chair to show through, and the dried and ageing panels of wood that hung on the outside of the building. So much was here, and yet it was so easy to overlook. I decided to move in close and to extract just a small section of the scene, because that was all that was needed to tell the whole story. A wider viewpoint that included more of the scene would have lessened the impact by giving the viewer far too much information.

James Flanagan

Technique As with most of his still life work, James utilised the Zone System to achieve an accurate exposure that would allow him to produce exactly the print that he wanted. This system relies on a scene being broken up into areas of differing exposure values, each one of which is allocated a zone within a range that normally runs from one through to nine. Zone One is almost black and Zone Nine almost paperbase white, and the difference between each is one stop. Most meters build in a Zone Five mid-tone assumption, which is roughly equivalent to the 'average' tone featured on a grey card, and in this scene that falls on the part of the door frame which is in the shade. The part of the door frame which is in the sun, however, falls into Zone Five and a half, and represents the lightest area of the picture, while the dark part of the screen, the densest area of tone in the picture, is in Zone Three. By taking into account how a scene breaks down like this, the photographer is able to calculate an exposure reading that will provide a perfect negative.

Pointer Taken with a 5x4in camera, the image that was presented on film was slightly too elongated, and so James decided to make the composition a little tighter by cropping just a fraction off the top of the picture. There is a philosophy that refuses to contemplate cropping of any kind, but often the best result is achieved by taking a pragmatic approach.

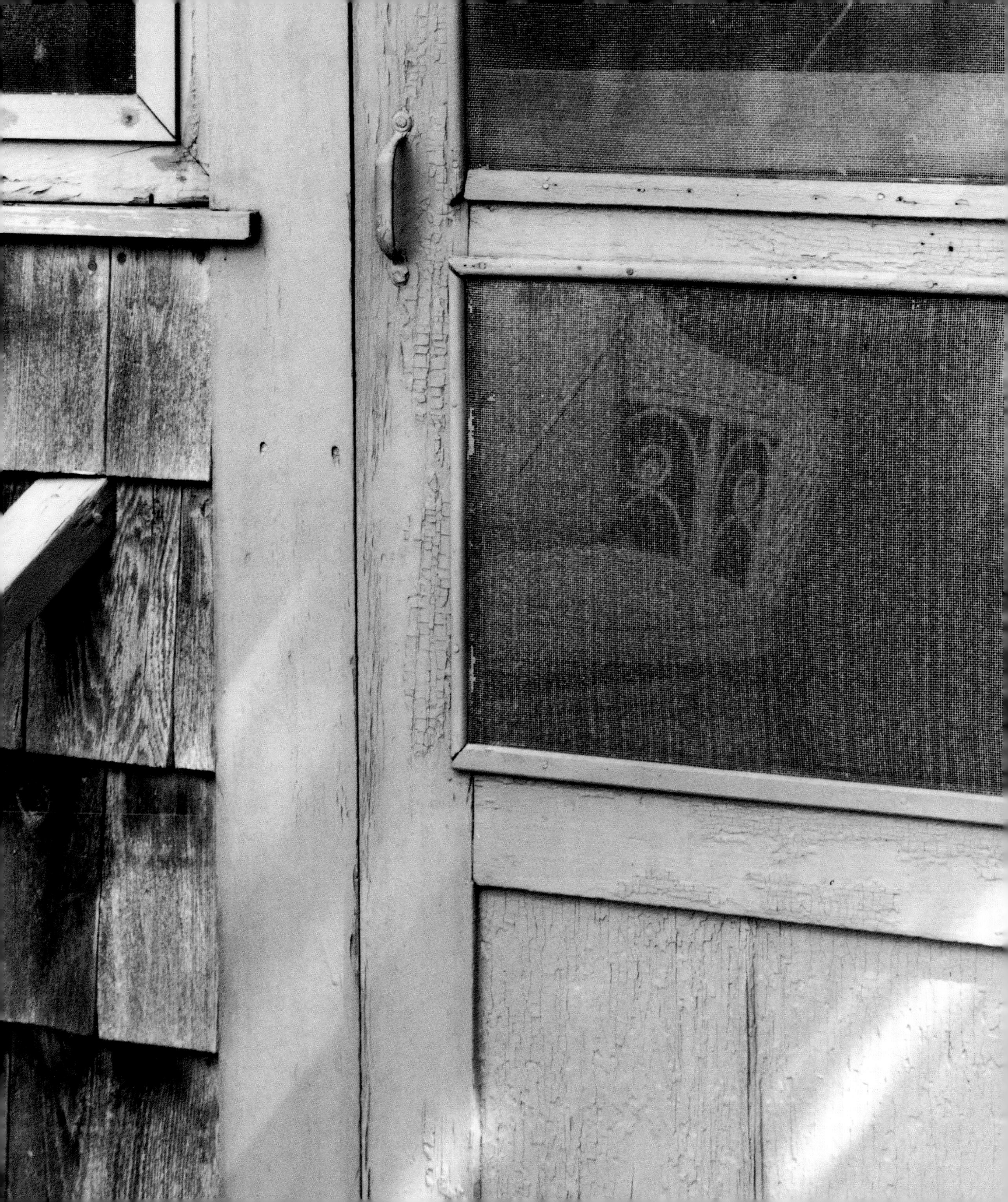

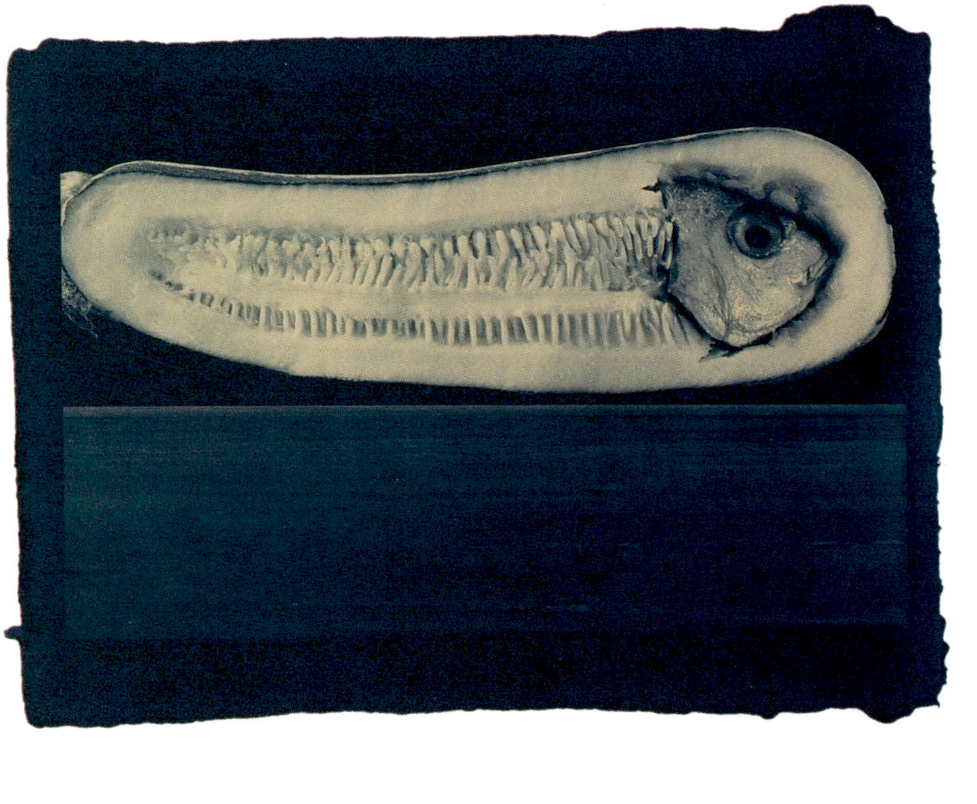

Marrow and Fish by Jason Bate
Studio 5x7in camera, 180mm lens, Ilford FP4 film. Exposure two minutes at f/64. Printed as a Cyanotype on cotton paper

Tone, Texture and Contrast

As a fine art photographer who has come to the medium via painting, my work has less to do with hard and fast photographic technique, and instead is more image led. I specialise in still life studies of organic objects such as fish, animals and vegetables, and what has always fascinated me is the natural texture these contain, and it's inevitably what I try to capture.

I'm also interested in the relationships that different subjects may have with each other, and often my aim will be to try to produce something that blends elements together in an interesting way. This was the case with this study of a fish and a marrow. I was intrigued by the texture created by the marrow's pips, and realised that they resembled, in some ways, the bones of a fish, and from then on I had the image in my mind and it was simply a case of setting it up.

I use an unusual format, 5x7in, because I found that 5x4in was slightly too small for the contact printing which my use of the Cyanotype process demanded, while the use of 10x8in was too expensive. I was studying at the time, and was able to obtain the 5x7in camera from my university, and it's ideal for my requirements, although the film size is not available in the UK, and I have to buy imported stocks of FP4.

Because I want things to be uncontrived and to feature as much of the natural ambience as possible, I always try to use available light for my pictures. I simply set my still life up next to a window so that it receives the bulk of the light from the left-hand side, and the shadow this creates helps me to highlight the textures that I want to capture. This, coupled with a very small f-stop, does lead to very lengthy exposures – up to six minutes at times – but I've got a very sensitive light meter which will give me exposure times up to one minute, and I've become adept at working out how much extra time to allow if the light is so low the meter has gone off the scale!

Jason Bate

Printing and Processing Since I was so determined to accentuate the texture in my still life studies, it seemed logical to me to find a print process that would emphasise this element of the picture still further. This led me to look at hand-coated emulsions and, in particular, the Cyanotype process, which allowed me to produce prints on heavily textured cotton paper. Along with the final look of the picture, which I found very pleasing, I also loved the idea that this was a Victorian printing process, and it seemed to me to give the whole project a reference to photography's history. I mix up the emulsion and coat it myself, and print out using either daylight or an ultraviolet facial tanning unit. Interestingly, different light sources create different kinds of tones in the final print, and it's an area I'm planning to explore more in the future. (An explanation of the Cyanotype process appears on page 117.)

My Favourite Tip The straight Cyanotype print can be a very garish blue, which isn't always what I'm after, and so, as I've done here, I will often tone the final print in a bath of cold tea. It's very cheap but effective, and you simply take it out and wash it once it's reached the point you want.

The Studio Table No 14 by John Blakemore
MPP 5x4in camera, 180mm Symmar lens, Ilford FP4 film developed in ID-11. Available light, exposure five minutes at f/45

The exploration of a theme, be it a particular location or a motif, allows both the development of knowledge about the subject and the discovery of different ways of picture making. One comes to a new subject with preconceptions of which pictures are possible, and these images are what one first makes. An extended period of photographing the same subject matter leads to new ideas and to unexpected responses and possibilities. The intensive exploration of a subject has always been part of my working method; in documentary, in the landscape and in still life. I have photographed tulips for nine years, making hundreds of negatives, and the images I made towards the end of my project I could not have imagined when I began.

The photograph of my studio table is one of 13 made to show the processes of collecting, drying, storing and arranging tulips, all of which support the activity of photographing them. The photograph relates to the tradition of photographs made in artists' studios, showing tools and work spaces: this reference to other traditions is for me an important element of working with still life, a genre which has a history predating the invention of photography and affords a wide reference to different systems of representation. Whilst making the tulip photographs I have investigated botanical illustrations, flower paintings by many artists, the Dutch tradition, the history of the tulip, all areas which suggest different ways of working.

The elements shown in this image were partly incidental and partly arranged – they include illustrations from botanical works, dried and arranged tulips, the decaying blooms I have already photographed and, in the foreground, newly arrived blooms ready for my next images. I have also included other tools important to my work such as the tape, film holder and spirit level.

The acquisition of suitable subjects was a constant problem. I grew some tulips in pots so that they could be removed, photographed as complete plants and then replanted. Most however I bought as cut flowers, both from local florists and from florists in London. I would telephone each Wednesday to give the florist an idea of what I wanted, and she would explore the flower markets. On Thursday morning the box would arrive at Derby station, but I would not know exactly what it contained until I opened it. There was always an element of surprise, it added a little of the unknown to the project, and I enjoyed the challenge that this presented.

John Blakemore

"When you decide to follow a theme, make sure that you stick with it and explore everything that it can offer you, because it's the only way to really see it."

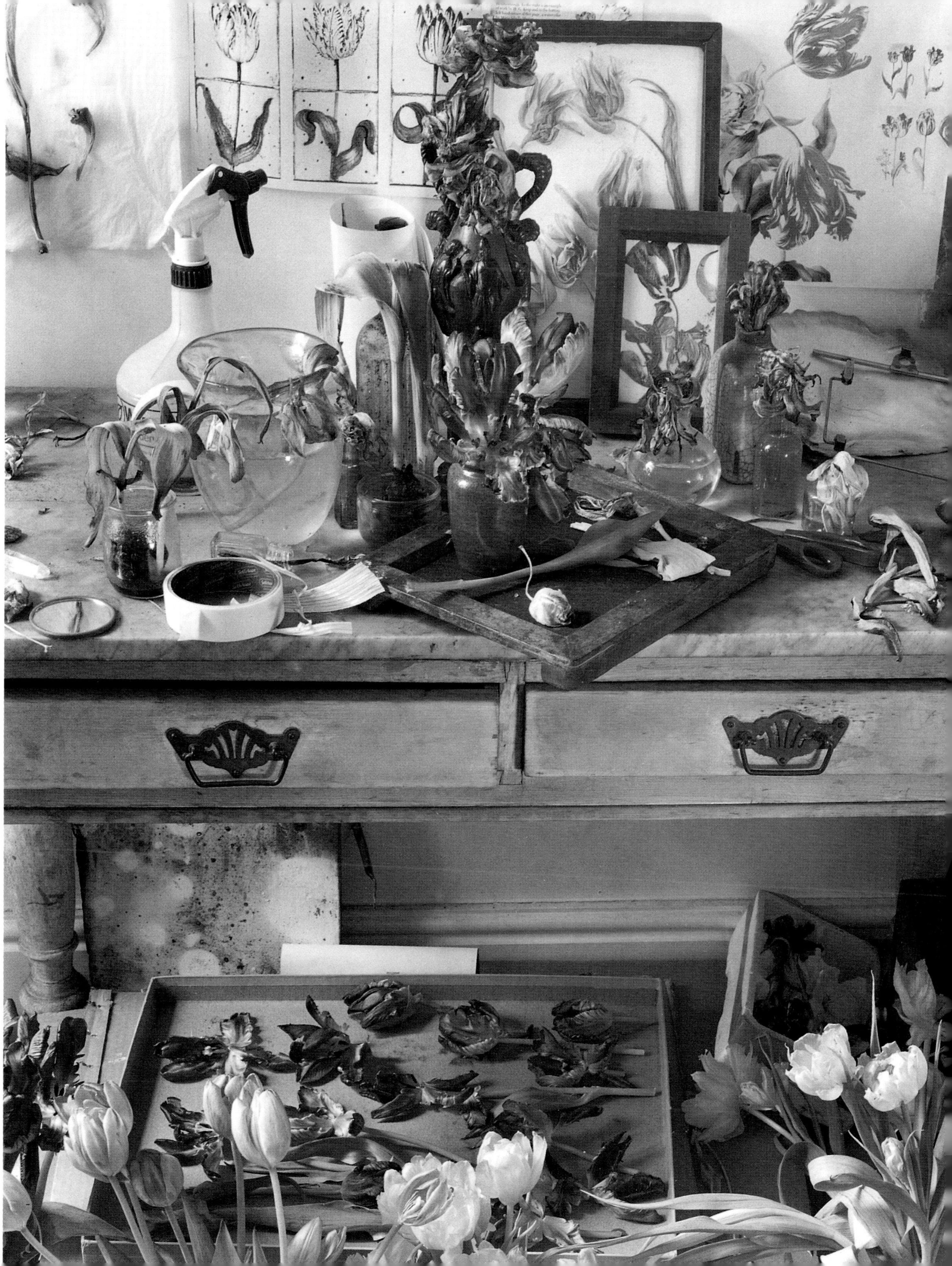

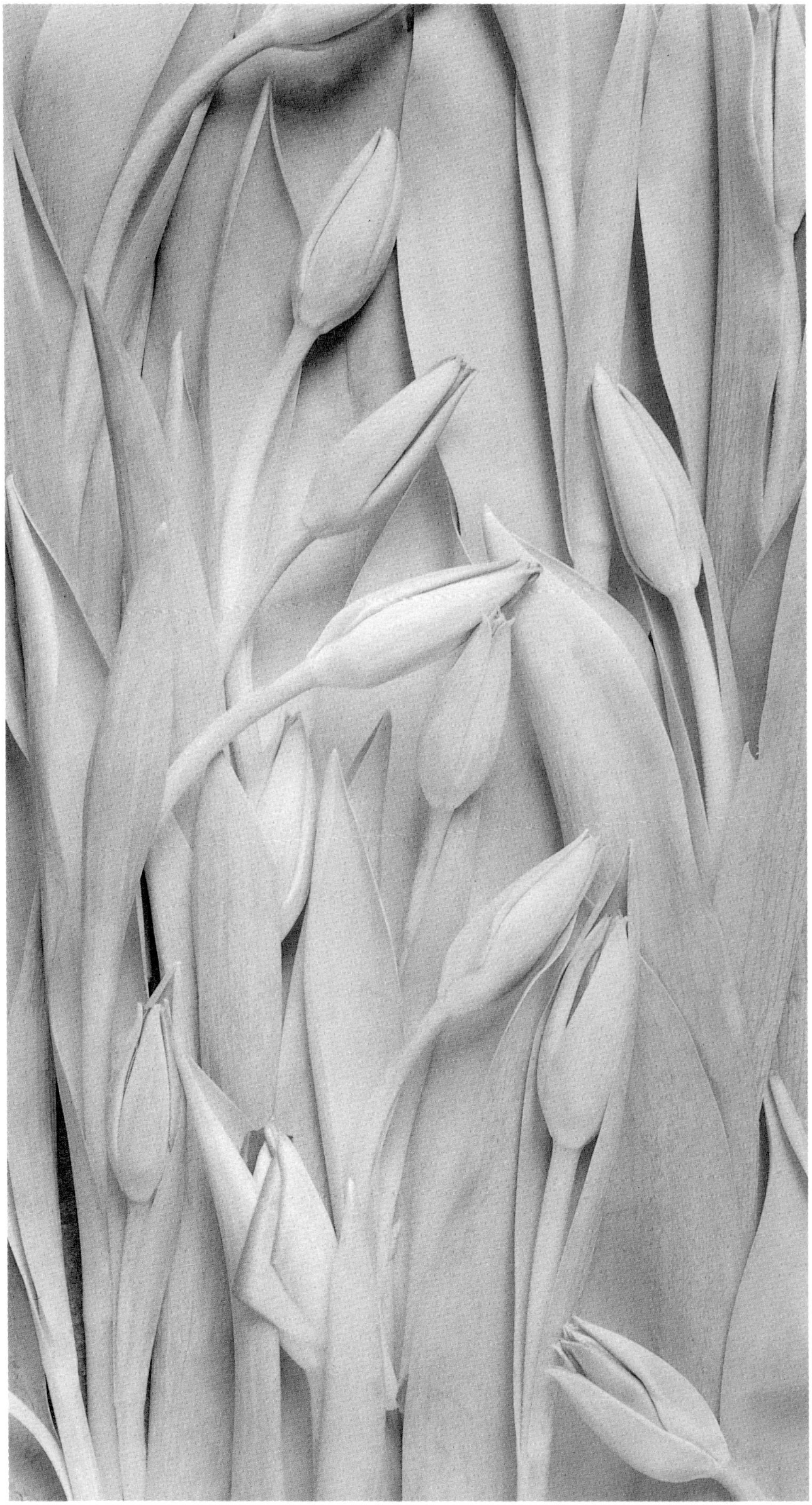

Tulipa, 1990 by John Blakemore
MPP 5x4in camera, 180mm Symmar lens, Ilford FP4 film developed in ID-11. Exposure around five minutes at f/45

I've established great continuity in my work, because I believe that this is the only way to learn and to progress in your photography. The camera and the lens that I use, for example, has been the same since 1974, which means that I know its workings intimately and understand how the way in which I use it affects the picture that I achieve. I've also used what is known as the Zone System of calculating exposure since that time, because it's a perfect accompaniment for still life photography. Devised by Ansel Adams, it's a way of controlling precisely the kind of negative that is produced and ultimately, of course, the tones that you achieve. This picture, as with most of my work, was exposed using this method, and I decided that I wanted a look that was full of light tones, while still allowing full detail to be recorded. I could just as easily have decided that I wanted a picture that was full of dark tones (see next page), and I could have achieved a completely different look simply through exposure and development control. The beauty of the Zone System is that, once you've mastered the thinking behind it, you know exactly what you're going to get, and you'll find it easy to control the tone you achieve in virtually any situation. It sounds complicated initially, but in fact is perfectly straightforward and logical in practice: this picture was achieved by opting for high shadow placement coupled with reduced development, and the subject was photographed in my house using daylight as the illumination.

John Blakemore

Technique The Zone System can't be fully explained in a few words, but this is the essence, and further reading and practice will start to make things clearer. The main point to understand is that any light meter, however accurate, will only be able to give a guide to correct exposure in an ideal situation, i.e. one where light is consistent and the scene being photographed is made up of average mid-tones. By using this reading simply as a starting point, and then reducing or increasing exposure as necessary, you can change the kind of negative you produce, particularly if you combine this with precisely controlled development.

The Zone System divides up a scene into areas of differing tones, usually nine, with Zone One being black and Zone Nine paperbase white, and the difference between each is one stop. This means, for example, that Zone Three represents twice as much exposure as Zone Two, but only half as much as Zone Four. The Zone System is based on this x2 relationship between Zones, and upon the Zone Five mid-tone assumption built into light meters. More information about how to use the Zone System in practice can be found overleaf.

Composition I wanted the tulips in this picture to appear to be leading out of the frame, and so I made sure that the frame of the print cut through some of the buds and leaves. I also wanted the print to have a shape that was long and thin so that the tulips appeared to be stretched out. Although the 5x4in format made this composition impossible to produce in-camera, I arranged the flowers in a way that fitted the crop which I knew I would introduce at the printing stage.

Tulipa, 1994 by John Blakemore
MPP 5x4in camera, 180mm Symmar lens, Ilford FP4 film developed in ID-11. Exposure five minutes at f/32

In many ways this picture is similar to the one on the previous page, but its tone is much darker, and consequently the feel that I've achieved is quite different, even though the subject and the set-up is virtually identical. I introduced darker tones into the picture through use of the Zone System, which allows me precisely to anticipate the kind of negative that I'm going to produce through a combination of exposure and development control.

Where the picture on the previous page was controlled so that the shadows were made lighter, the reverse was true with this image, but the negative that I produced still had a complete range of tones within it, so that detail was still apparent even in shadow areas.

As with all of my tulip still life pictures, I used natural light to illuminate my subject. I work in different rooms around my house, effectively following the light as it moves around throughout the day. I control this light through a hierarchy of reflectors, a task made simpler by the very long exposures I'm generally working with, which can be up to 20 minutes in duration. If I want to particularly emphasise different areas, for example, I'll work with a small mirror to direct a more intense light into the places where I want it. Other reflectors are made of card and have a much softer quality, and these help me to level up the rather uneven light that I might find myself working with.

I cropped this picture so that I cut across some of the tulips at the top of the frame, in order to give the idea that they continue beyond the confines of the picture. Cropping can be too symmetrical at times, and I've found that it can benefit a picture to introduce compositional devices such as this.

John Blakemore

Technique To prepare to use the Zone System, the photographer needs to adopt consistent methods, and to carry out tests to establish personal film speed and development times for use with particular cameras, light meters, enlargers and materials. Once in use, the Zone System allows the tones of a picture to be changed as the photographer sees fit, simply through selection of the appropriate subject brightness value. When using negative materials, this is usually taken from a shadow area in Zone Three, two stops less than the exposure indicated by the meter for Zone Five. This then allows the photographer to ascertain which Zone the highlights will fall into. If a scene has a brightness range of four stops for example – which can be calculated by taking spot meter readings from highlight and shadow areas – a shadow placed in Zone Three will result in a highlight falling in Zone Seven. With this in mind, it's then possible to adjust where the highlight will fall by adjusting which Zone the shadow is placed within.

The second part of the Zone System involves precise control of the negative development. Normal development should render a normal brightness range subject with a full tonal range in the print, when printed on Grade Two paper. Increasing development expands the tonal range of the negative and allows compensation to be made for low contrast subjects, while reducing development compresses the tonal scale of the negative and compensates when subjects have higher than normal contrast.

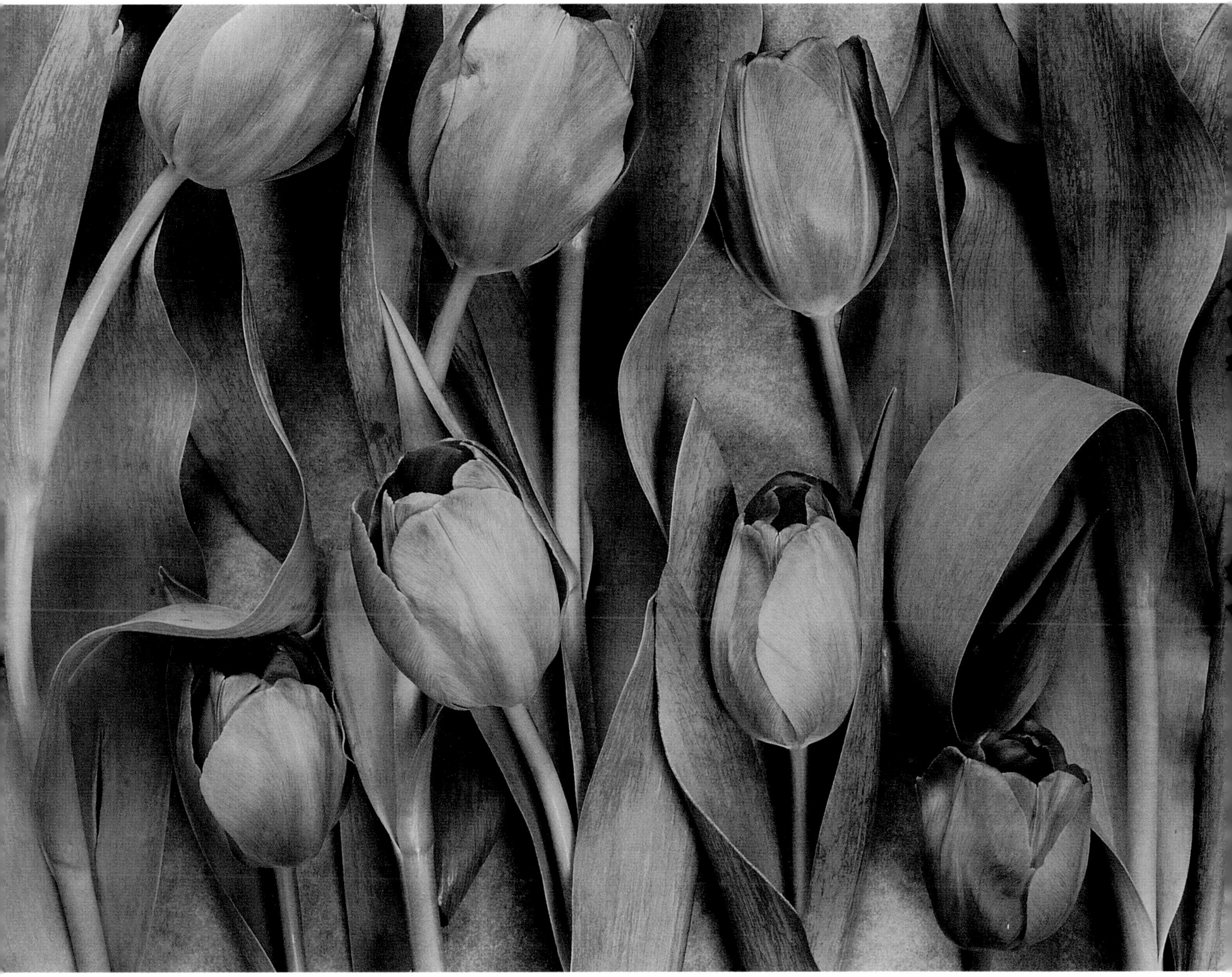

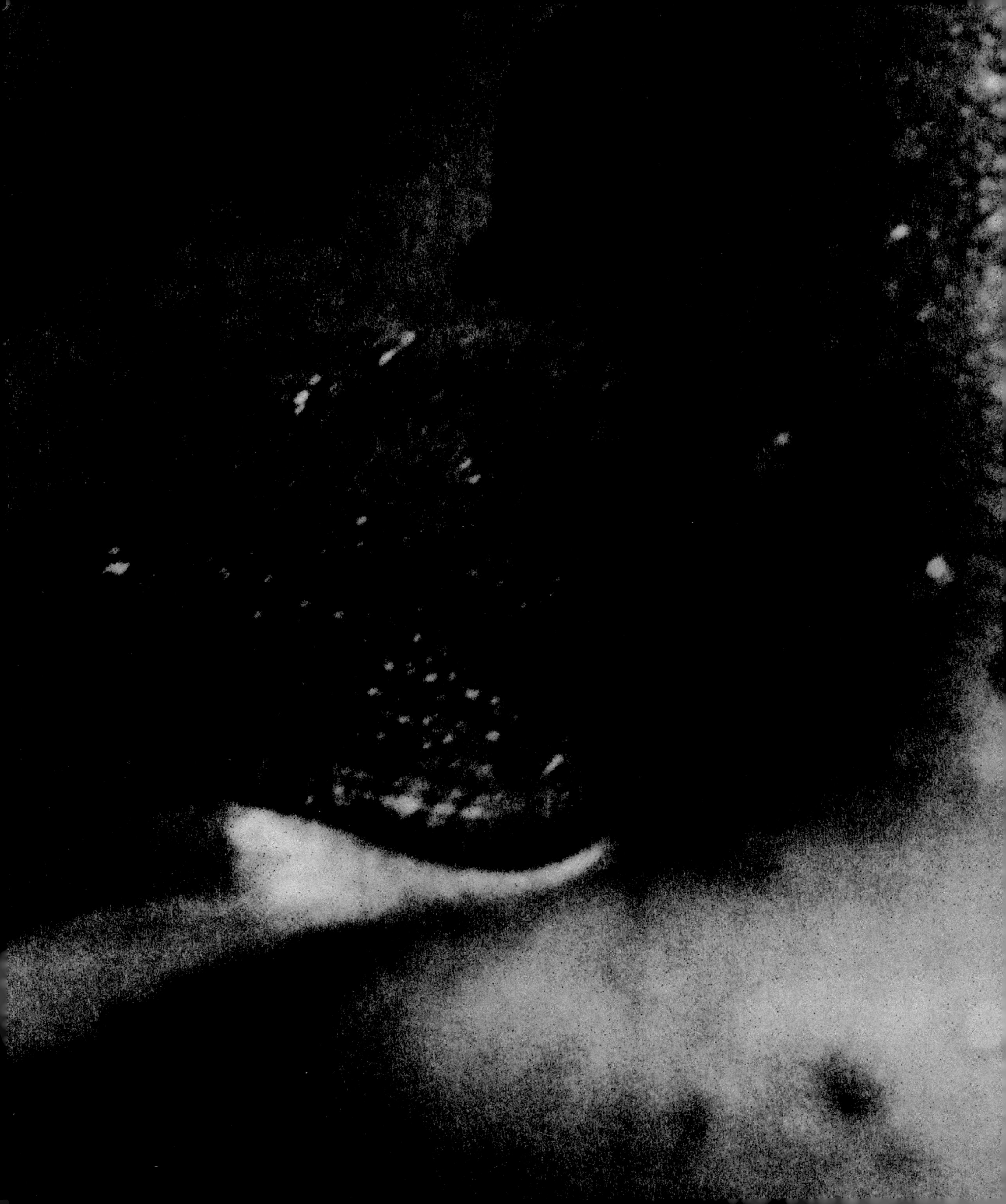

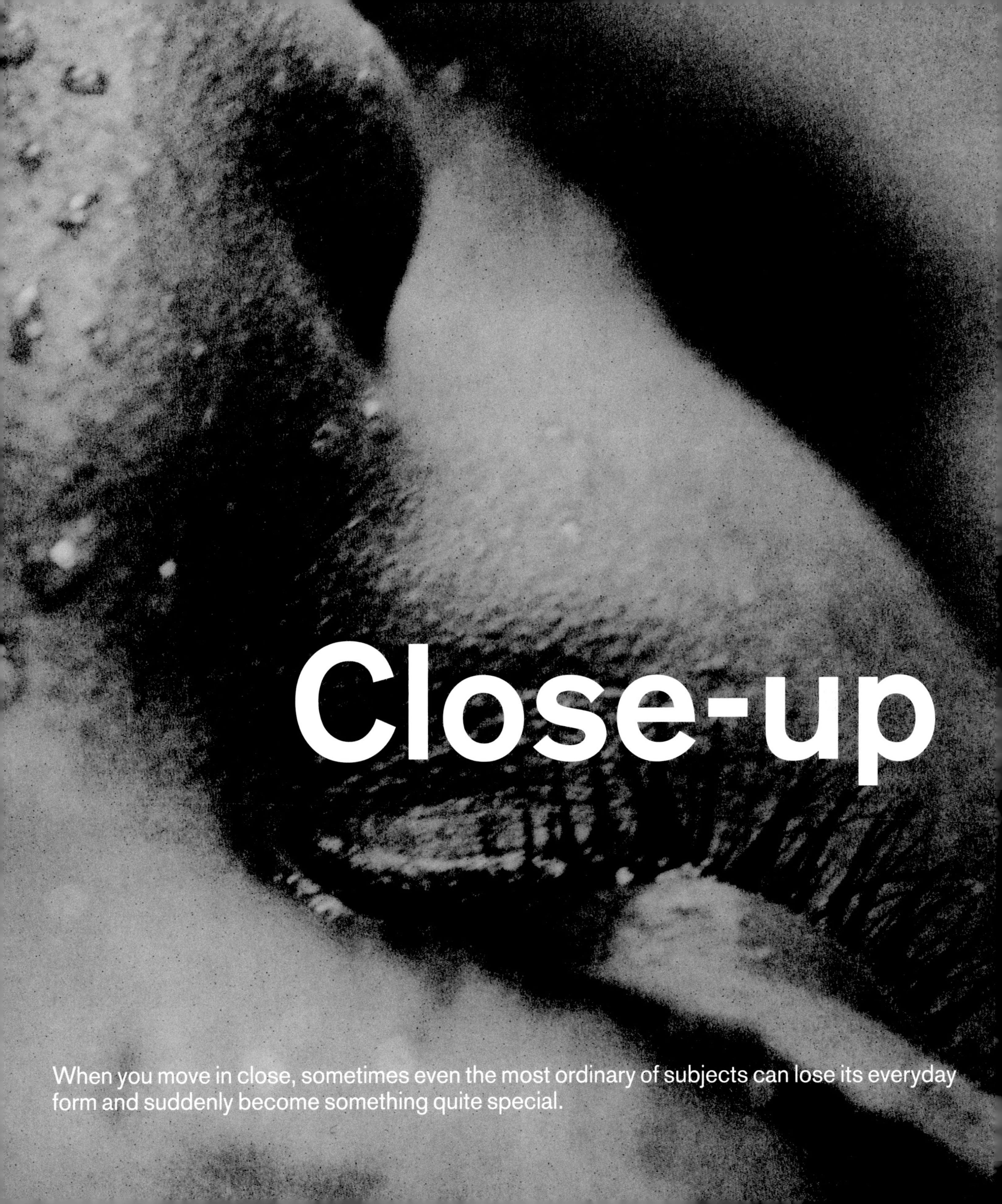

Close-up

When you move in close, sometimes even the most ordinary of subjects can lose its everyday form and suddenly become something quite special.

A friend of mine cultivates cacti, and I've had this specimen, known officially as Optunia Invicta, for something like 15 years now. Invicta translates as 'to puncture,' and refers to the formidable thorns that this cactus carries, and it was this feature that attracted me as a photographer to undertake a still life close-up.

Because studio cameras are equipped with a flexible bellows between lens and film plane, it's possible to rack out the lens by an appreciable amount beyond the position for focusing on distant objects. This is known as bellows extension, and it allows the cameras to focus on very close objects, and to produce extreme close-ups.

By extending the length of the bellows by a sometimes considerable degree, however, you're also increasing the distance that light will have to travel to reach the film, with the result that the effective f-stop of the lens is decreased quite considerably. This in turn means that meter readings will need to be increased substantially, and there is an involved mathematical calculation that will tell the photographer exactly how much extra exposure will be required.

Because I'd chosen to use a Polaroid material, however, and because the latitude of Type 55 is fairly wide, I felt that I could take a guess about how much extra exposure to give, and added two extra stops to my meter reading. Obviously, when the Polaroid film was processed just a minute later, I was able to check that my calculation was correct, and I could have added or subtracted from my exposure at that point.

Allan Baxter

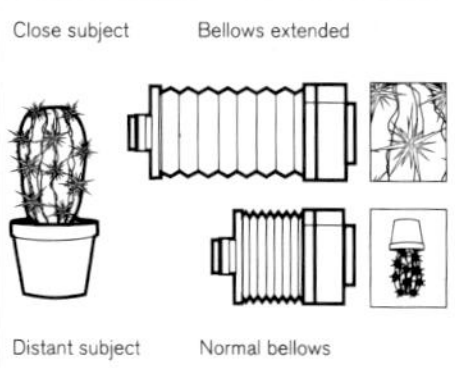

When working close to a subject the lens forms a larger and therefore dimmer image, at the same engraved f-number

Close-up

Cactus Spikes by Allan Baxter
Sinar 5x4in camera, 90mm Schneider lens, Polaroid Type 55 film.
Exposure two seconds at f/5.6
Picture: The Michael Trevillion Picture Library

Pointer Type 55 is one of the oldest Polaroid film materials available, and it gives the photographer both a print and a negative. After its one minute processing time, the print can be examined to ascertain exposure and composition, but needs to be coated quite quickly with a chemical film to prevent it oxidising. To preserve the negative for printing, it needs to be cleared with a salt solution, and subsequently needs to be handled with care since it's far more delicate than a conventional negative. I like to have the edges of the negative included in the print that I subsequently have made, because I think it adds to the picture and defines it, because no two edges will ever look exactly the same.

Technique The picture was lit with two tungsten Redhead lights. The main one was directed over my shoulder to throw a general light on to the scene, while a weaker one was positioned over to the right hand side to provide a fill light. The fact that the lights could be switched on while the picture was being set up was extremely helpful, because the length of the bellows extension restricted the light reaching the focusing screen at the back of the camera. Focusing in this case was particularly crucial because I had set the lens to its maximum aperture to keep the depth of field to a minimum so that I could isolate the thorns.

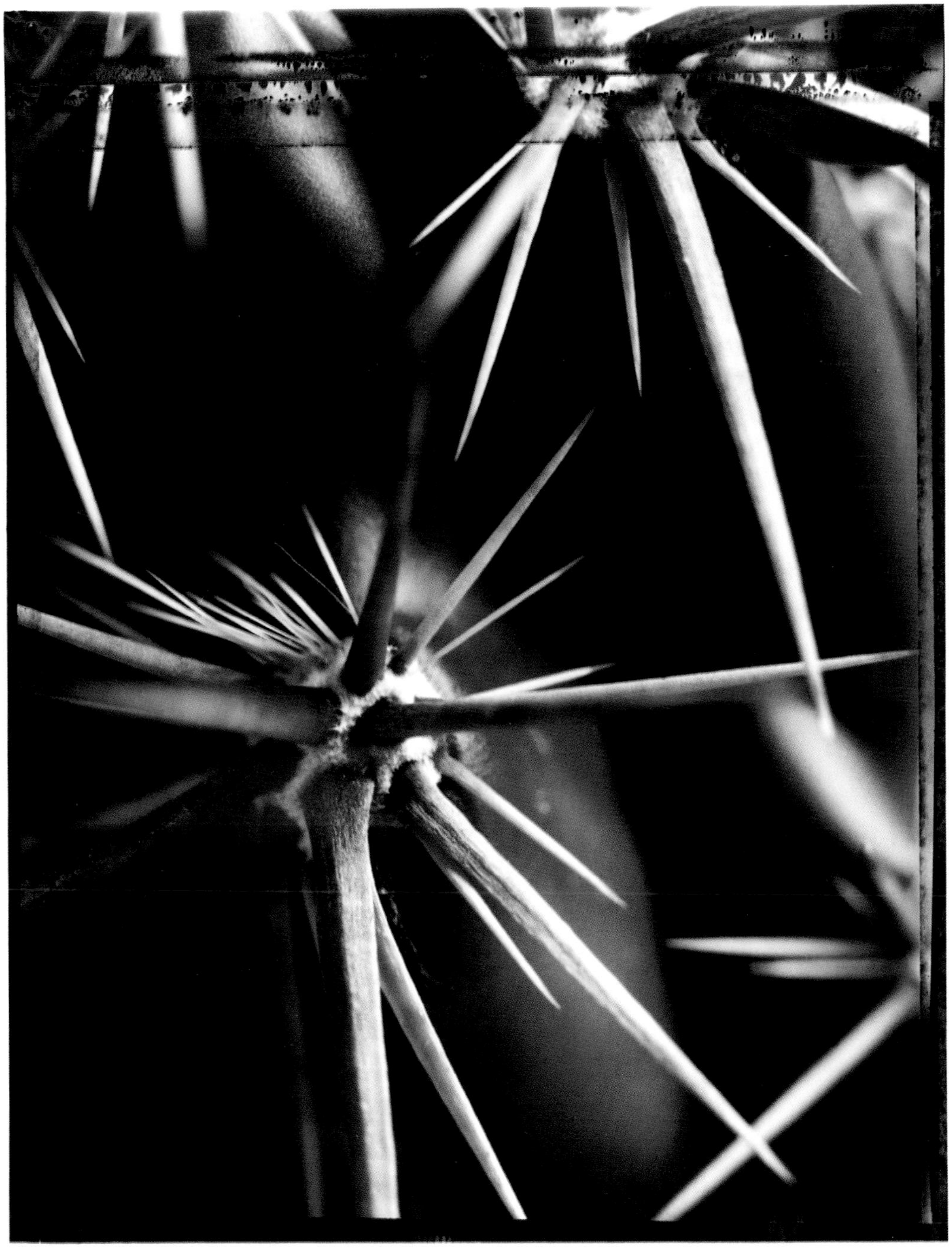

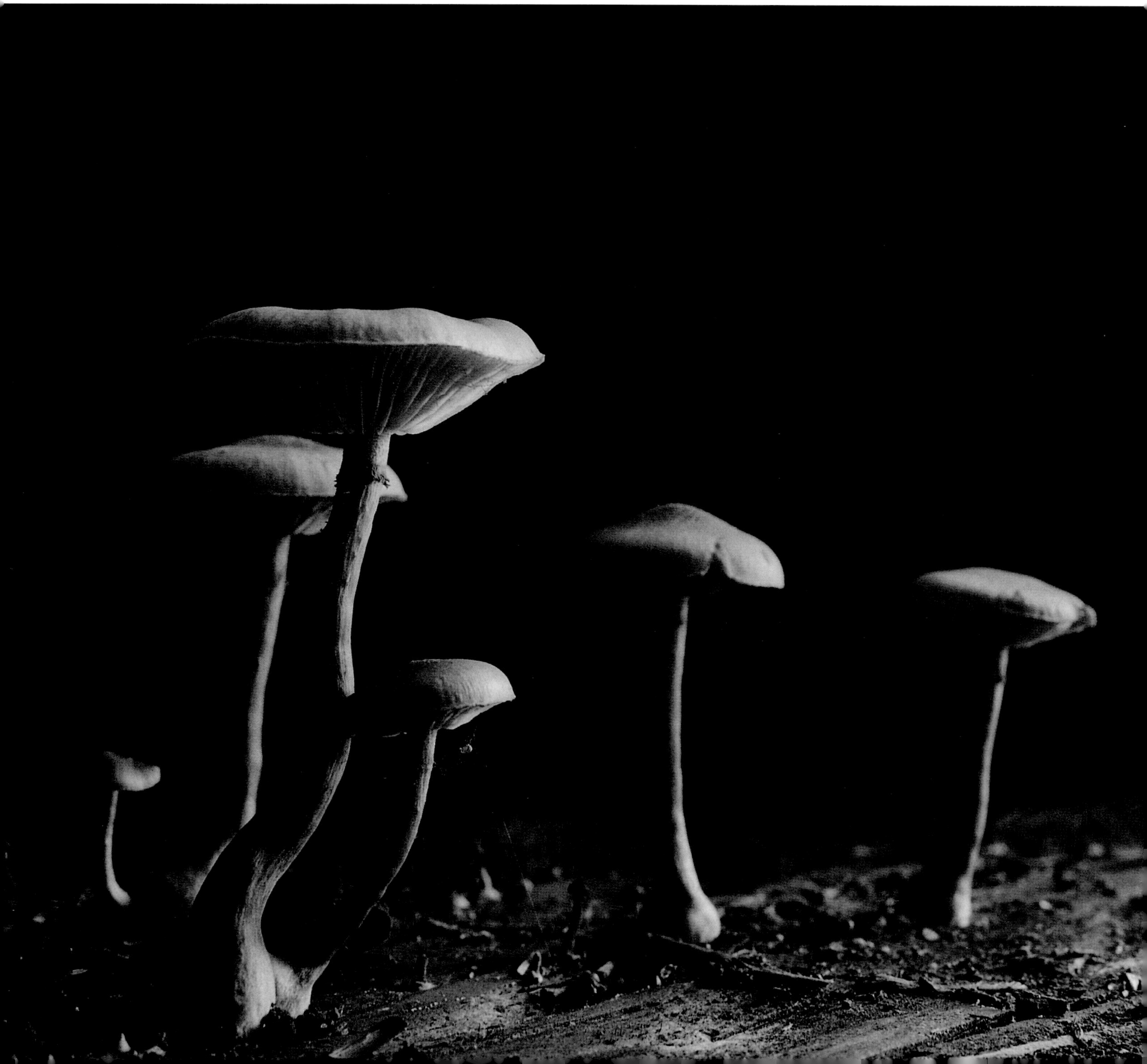

Close-up

I came across this group of mushrooms growing on the dirty wooden floor of an old barn in Ocean View, Delaware, and I was captivated by the fact that, despite being so tiny – perhaps just a few centimetres in height – they were perfectly formed. It was clear that any picture that I wanted to take which would feature the mushrooms as the central focus would involve the use of close-up techniques, and I decided to fit a 32mm extension tube to the Hasselblad camera that I was using. An extension tube sits between the lens and the camera body and has the simple function of moving the lens further away from the film plane, thus allowing closer focusing and an increased image size, albeit at the cost of extra exposure. Extension tubes generally come in sets of four, and it's possible to use one on its own, as here, or more than one in tandem to enable even closer focusing. Automatic tubes enable camera functions such as metering and aperture stop down to be maintained and because the camera I was using is a single lens reflex, I could see exactly the image that I was achieving, allowing me to frame from a very low level to give my subject greater emphasis in the frame.

I wanted a simple picture and so, to avoid any clutter behind my subject, I positioned a black plastic bin bag there, which kept things plain and soaked up any stray light. The picture was taken in late morning, and I directed the strong sunlight that was falling outside through the doorway of the barn with a Fill Flex reflector, creating dramatic sidelighting that picked out the subject against its dark background.

James Flanagan

Mushrooms by James Flanagan
Hasselblad 6x6cm camera, 80mm lens, 32mm extension tube, Kodak Tri-X film. Exposure 1/15sec at f/16

"Because I was using a single lens reflex, I could see exactly the image that I was achieving, allowing me to frame from a very low level to give my subject greater emphasis in the frame."

Printing and Processing James Flanagan decided to finish the picture in selenium toner, which has added a cold edge to the blacks. A brief immersion in selenium toner diluted at about one part concentrate to 15 parts water should not change image print colour too much but will improve the archival permanence of the print. Stronger concentrations of selenium toner, however, up to one to three, can produce a very strong change in colour and contrast, while a split-tone effect can be achieved with multi-contrast chlorobromide paper. One very important rider to remember when selenium toning, however, is to keep the area you're working in well ventilated, to avoid inhaling the fumes, which can be extremely dangerous.

Technique Like many photographers who want to control precisely negative and subsequent print quality, James Flanagan has adopted the Zone System as a basis for his work. This is a method, devised by Ansel Adams, that involves the placing of certain areas of the picture into separate zones that relate to their density. There are normally nine of them, with Zone Five representing the Kodak grey card, the average density that meters are calibrated for. Here the floor of the barn, being darker than average, was placed in Zone Four, while the highlights on the mushrooms were in Zone Six. Careful control of metering in combination with film processing allows the photographer using the Zone System to achieve remarkably consistent and predictable results.

Sand Shapes by James Flanagan
Zone Six 5x4in field camera, 210mm Schneider lens, Kodak Tri-X film ISO 200. Exposure 1/30sec at f/16

I came across these ripple marks quite early one morning while walking along the shoreline at Chatham in Massachusetts, and I just loved the intricate and delicate patterns that they made. I decided to move in close, and to exclude anything that would act as a scale, and by doing this I've created a picture that poses all kinds of questions. Is this a shot of a delta system taken from space perhaps? Are these patterns man-made, or have they been found in nature? I like the idea that it's not immediately obvious what the viewer is looking at here, and the eye is left to concentrate on the patterns, shapes and textures found here as a result.

A Zone Six field camera was used to take this picture and, by racking its bellows out to a distance of 11 inches, I was able to focus closely on my subject, and to increase its size on the negative. Bellows extension is one of the most straightforward ways to produce close-up pictures such as this, and you'll be able to see the result that you are going to achieve by checking on the ground glass screen of the camera before fitting the film holder. The further you extend the bellows, the greater the magnification of the image will be, but the price you will pay is an increase in exposure times as the lens becomes further away from the film plane.

James Flanagan

Technique The Tri-X film used here was rated at ISO 200, which I had calculated using the Zone System technique as the right speed to give the film when used with this particular meter and lenses. In this instance, however, I was faced with a low contrast subject that needed some help. Consequently I gave the film extra processing time, effectively uprating it, and I also fitted a No 8 yellow filter to the 210mm Schneider lens I was using to help lift the contrast level as well.

Printing and Processing This print was finally selenium toned. A brief immersion in selenium toner diluted at about one part concentrate to 15 parts water should not change print image colour too much but it will improve the archival permanence of the print. The toner must be used in well ventilated conditions.

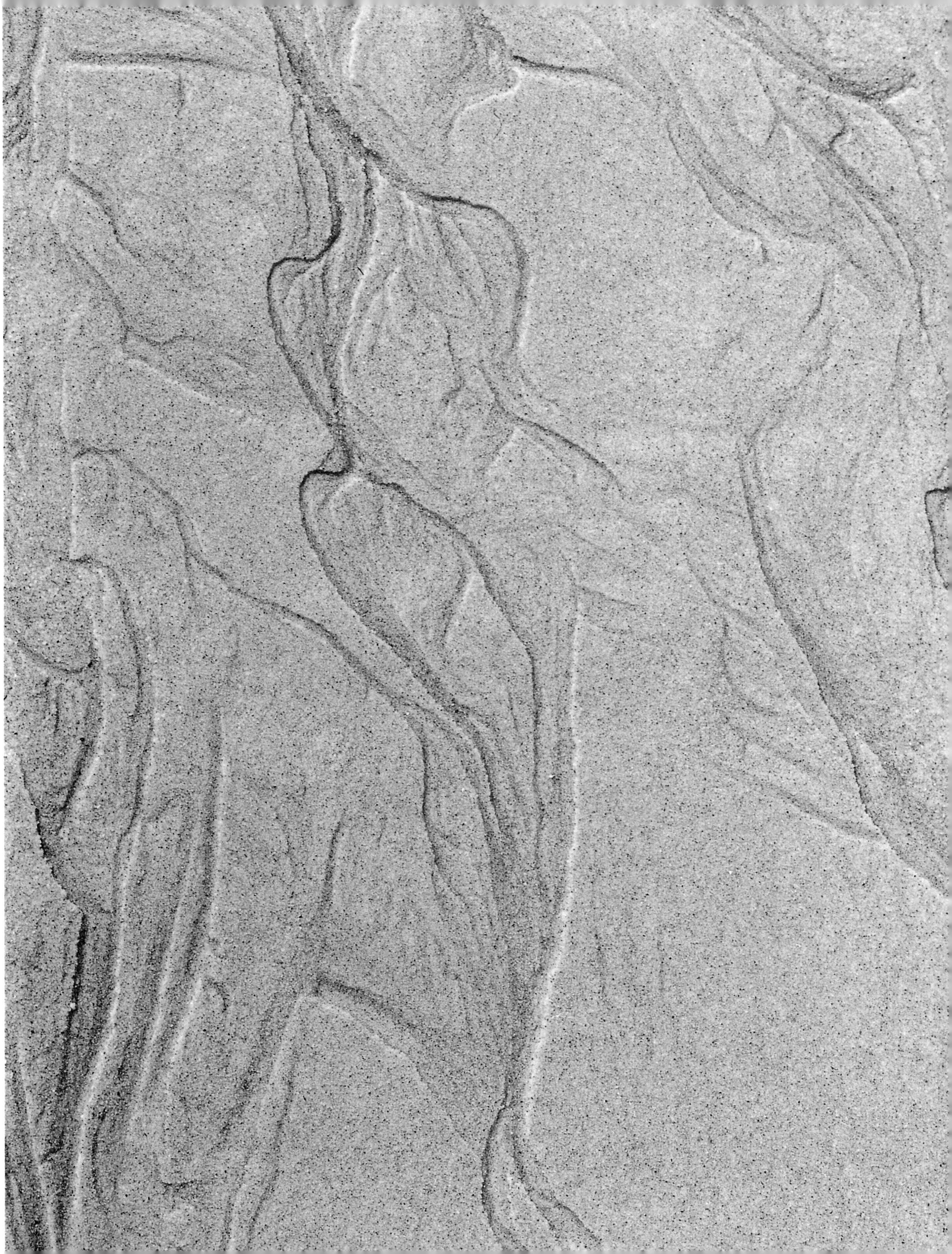

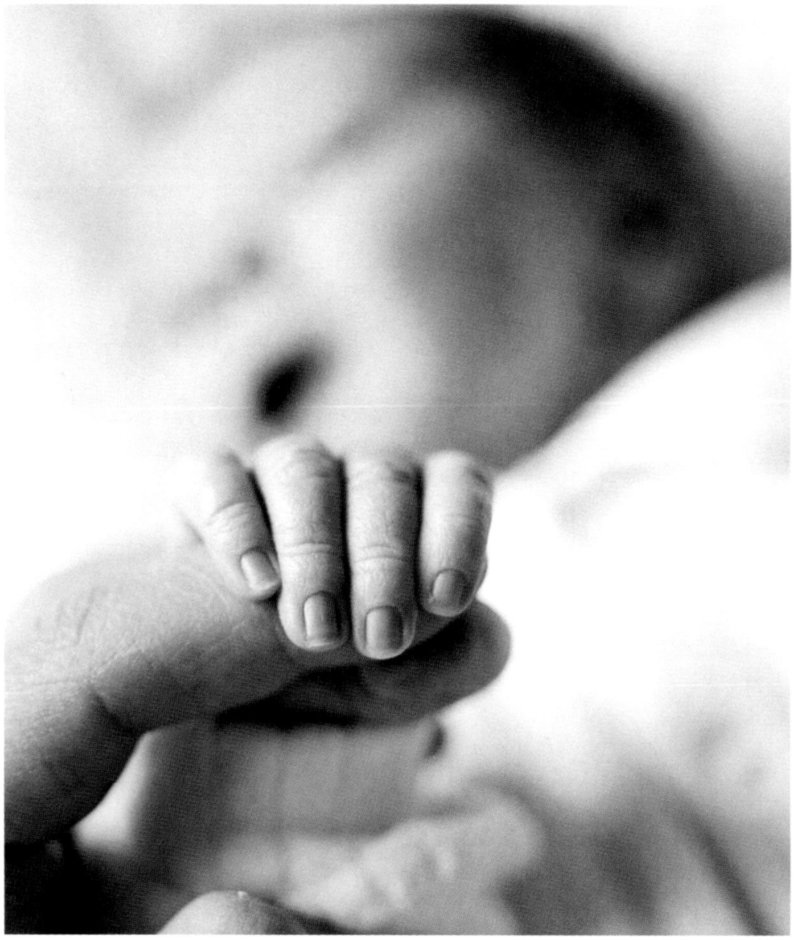

Close-up

My brother had just become the father of a new baby girl, Chloe, and he asked me if I would take some pictures for him to celebrate the fact. I didn't want to shoot something that was too traditional, however, and so I decided that I would tackle the portrait as though it were a still life, and concentrate on detail and the difference in scale between her tiny hand and the finger of her father.

Once I'd decided on my approach, it was a relatively easy picture to set up. I used my 90mm standard lens at its widest aperture of f/4.5, and then moved in to its closest focusing distance, around 12 inches. As Chloe instinctively grabbed my brother's finger I framed tightly and, making sure that Chloe's face, albeit just a softened series of tones, was visible in the background to make sense of the composition, I took several frames to try to give myself the best chance of getting one that was sharp enough to work. This wasn't particularly easy, because I was hand-holding quite an unwieldy camera at a very slow shutter speed, and Chloe was moving all the time. There was also a very narrow depth of field to play with, and I had to move the camera and myself slowly backward and forward to pull everything into focus.

Eventually I was sure that I had the image I wanted, and I was helped by the fact that the vital area of the picture that absolutely had to be in focus was in one plane of the picture, making it easier to judge. The result was an unusual portrait of a two-week old child that I feel has said something a little different about a father and daughter relationship.

Stephen Widdows

"There was a very narrow depth of field to play with, and I had to move the camera and myself slowly backward and forward to pull everything into focus."

Chloe's Hand by Stephen Widdows
Mamiya RB67 camera, 90mm lens, Kodak Tri-X film uprated one stop from ISO 400 to 800. Exposure 1/15sec at f/4.5

Technique In line with the simple nature of this picture, I decided to use available light as my illumination, and so I positioned my brother and his baby near to a set of patio doors, so that the light was hitting them from the side to provide a little modelling. I think it's a good discipline to stick with one light if possible, which is, after all, what nature will provide naturally. The light was fairly weak, which was good in one sense because it allowed me to set maximum aperture and to restrict depth of field, but it was leaving me with a shutter speed that was slower than I would have liked. I solved the problem by rating my ISO 400 film one stop faster at ISO 800, and I compensated by extending its development in line with the manufacturer's recommendation.

Pointer Control of depth of field is a useful weapon in the still life photographer's armoury, and allows dramatic effects as seen here. Use of an SLR camera or a large format camera will allow depth of field to be calculated precisely, because the photographer will see exactly what the lens is seeing. If using an aperture smaller than the maximum aperture, however, you'll need to be aware that depth of field will increase, something that you'll be able to check visually if your camera has a depth of field preview button. If you can't get as narrow a depth of field as you would like with a particular lens, try fitting one that is longer, and then adjusting your camera position back a little.

I have a personal fascination with seahorses, and have built up a collection of seahorse pictures as a result. Although they're very small – this example was just around one and a half inches in length – they are full of the most incredible detail and, when seen in close-up, they appear almost prehistoric.

With me, the idea of still life is to take a photograph of an object so that I can hold it up and show it to the world, and I liked the thought of blowing this seahorse up so that its scale was enormous. I set the picture up in my studio, and achieved what was effectively a life-size image on my 5x4in negative by racking out the bellows on my camera until I'd achieved the close-up that I wanted. I kept everything else simple: the lighting was tungsten, and was provided by one 2K blond, which was positioned to the left of the camera and was directed through a diffusion screen to take out some of the contrast. I also used a tiny bit of fill from a reflector to fill in shadows on the right of the picture.

This is the result, a picture of a seemingly ordinary subject that is suddenly remarkable, because you can see every detail. With the seahorse now an endangered species, I hope that images such as this might make people realise what a remarkable creature it really is.

Patrice De Villiers

Close-up

Seahorse by Patrice De Villiers
Sinar P 5x4in camera, 210mm lens, Agfapan 100 film.
Exposure eight seconds at f/45

My Favourite Tip With a subject as intricate as this, I didn't want a complicated background that would divert attention away, but I also wanted to use something that would enhance the subject and be sympathetic to it. Ultimately I decided to use a piece of slate, and this was perfect for the job. It gave the seahorse a surface to sit on that was complementary, while the lighting I used just picked out enough detail in it to show that it was a natural element and not a sheet of background paper.

Technique As a camera approaches a subject, the image is formed increasingly farther behind the lens and, on a studio camera or a smaller format camera fitted with a bellows extension kit, the bellows will need to be extended to retain focus. This means that the image will have further to travel from the lens to the film plane, and brightness will be reduced. This in turn means that a meter reading that would have been accurate for a picture at infinity, will suggest underexposure for a close-up. When the bellows extension has reached the point where the image being formed behind the lens is two focal lengths in distance, image illumination will have been quartered. A calculation will need to be carried out to estimate the extra exposure required, or you could carry out a Polaroid test giving at least two extra stops, and work the correct exposure out from there.

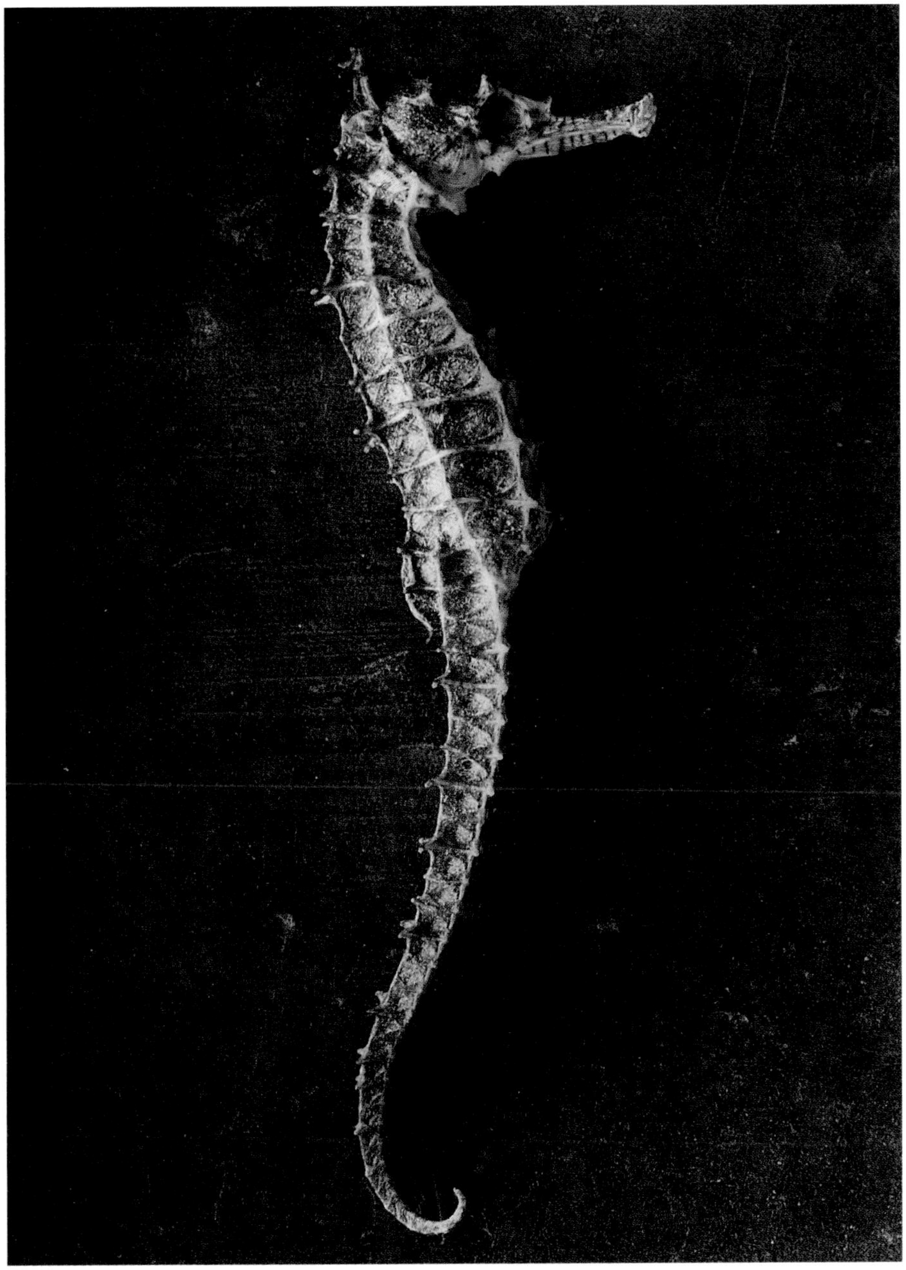

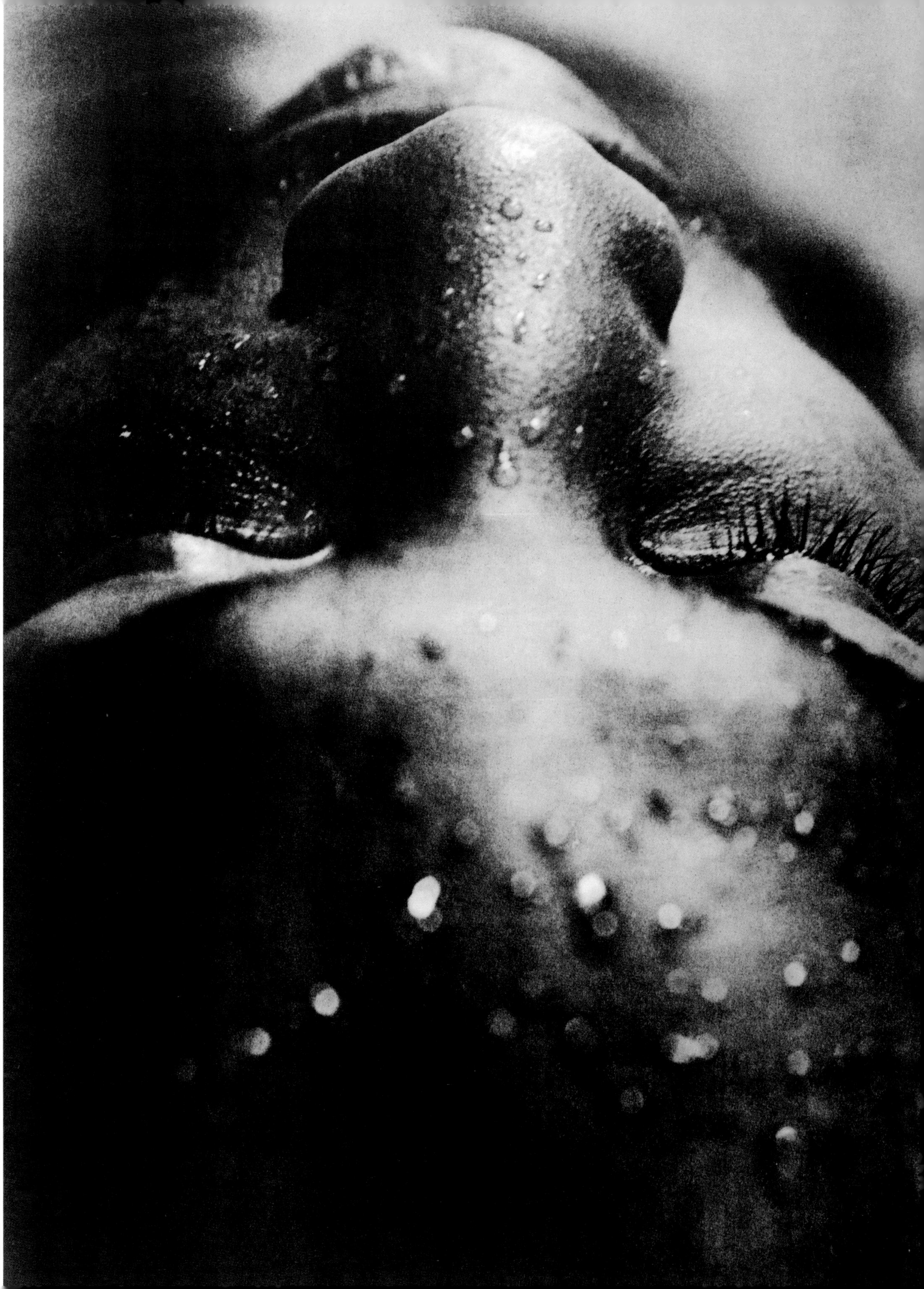

Close-up

Portrait of Julius Francis by Dean Rogers
Mamiya 645 camera, 100mm macro lens, Tri-X film.
Exposure 1/30sec at f/2.8
Picture: The Michael Trevillion Picture Library

I took this picture of boxer Julius Francis, resting in the Peacock Gym in London's East End during a break in his training, as part of a private commission from the British Board of Boxing. The macro lens I was using allowed me to move in ultra-close and to fill the entire frame with the head of the boxer, which created an intimate and powerful study. By moving in so tightly and setting a wide aperture I was able to keep the depth of field to an absolute minimum. I made the most of this by taking up a low angle of view so that just one narrow strip across his eyes and the bridge of his nose was rendered sharp. From a higher angle the view on to the face would have been flatter, the depth of field consequently greater and the overall effect much weaker.
The interesting thing is that the areas of the picture that are out of focus are just as important as those that are in focus here.

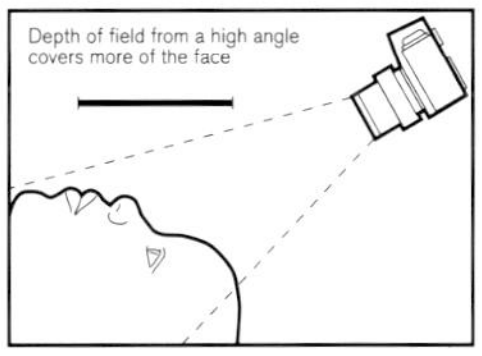

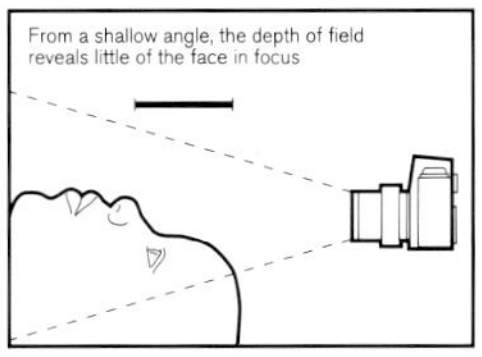

The beads of sweat, which have reflected tiny highlights of light towards the base of the picture, tell the story of the energy that's been exerted by this fighting man. It took me a while to gain the trust of those that I was photographing so that I was able to work as close in as this, but it came eventually, thanks mainly to the time that I devoted to the project. During a three-month period I visited the Peacock Gym and then subsequently a gym in New York, virtually every day, and I made sure that those I was photographing were given prints to thank them for their co-operation. I also worked throughout hand-holding the camera and using available light, since this was the least intrusive method I could cultivate.

Dean Rogers

Printing and Processing This is a print made on high contrast lith paper, and I decided that this was how I was going to present the picture before I ever pressed the shutter. It was important that I did, because to print on lith you need to adjust your exposure so that the results are effectively underexposed from what you would be trying to achieve if you were printing on to a paper that offered conventional tonal reproduction. In fact I would find it almost impossible to achieve a good print of this picture on regular printing paper, but on lith material the result is perfect, because the darker a picture is the more shadows you create and the more pleasing the brown of the highlights becomes.
Lith papers are exposed in the usual way, but have to be handled under deep red safelight conditions, and they also need to be processed in specialist lith developer.

Pointer Macro lenses are designed with focusing mounts with sufficient extension to permit continuous focusing down to one-to-one reproduction and, when their maximum close-up capabilities are being used, depth of field will be extremely limited. There has been a trend in recent years for some lenses to be marketed as having a 'macro' capability, when reproduction levels will fall far short of life size, and it's important to check carefully what a lens you may be interested in truly offers.

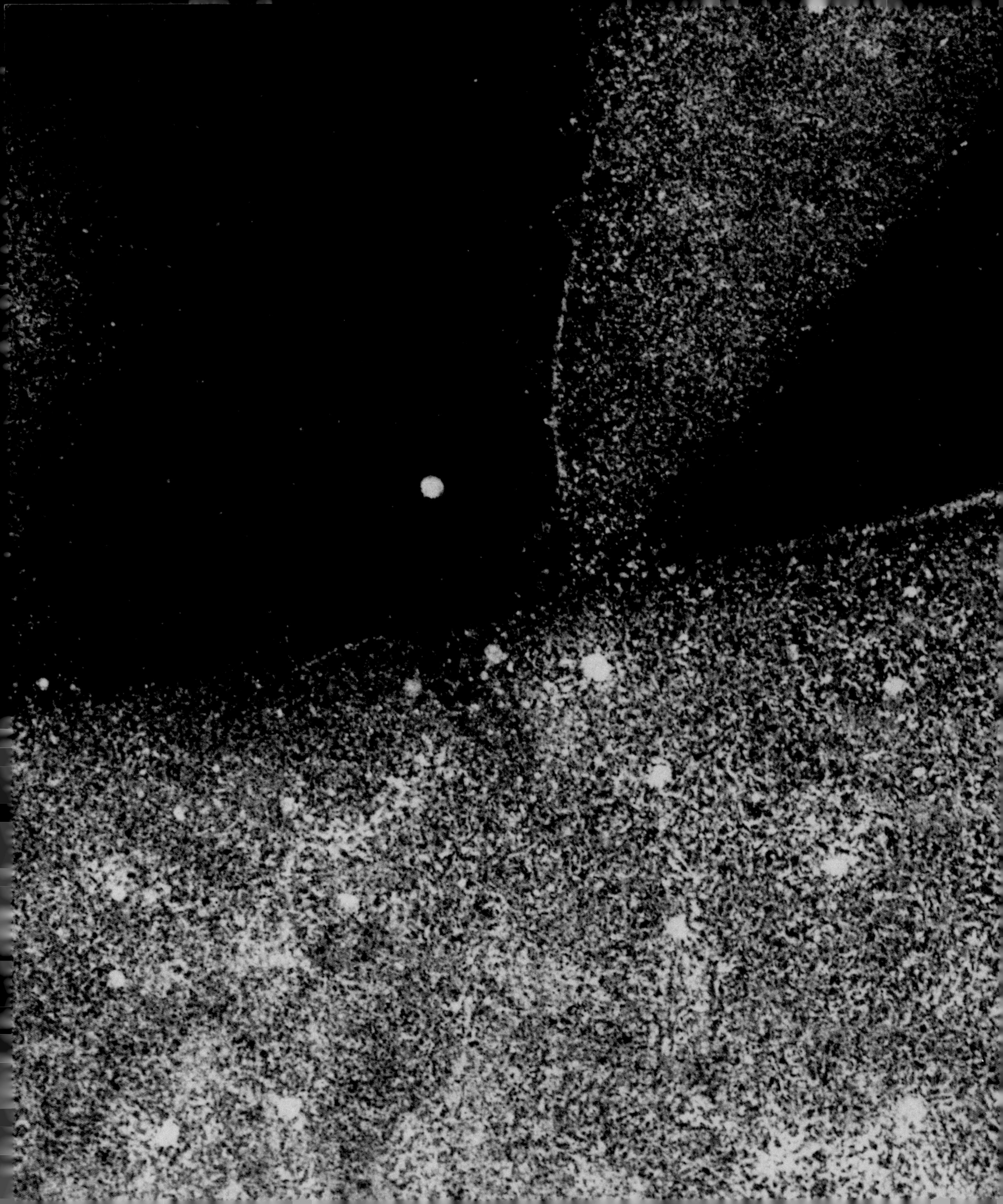

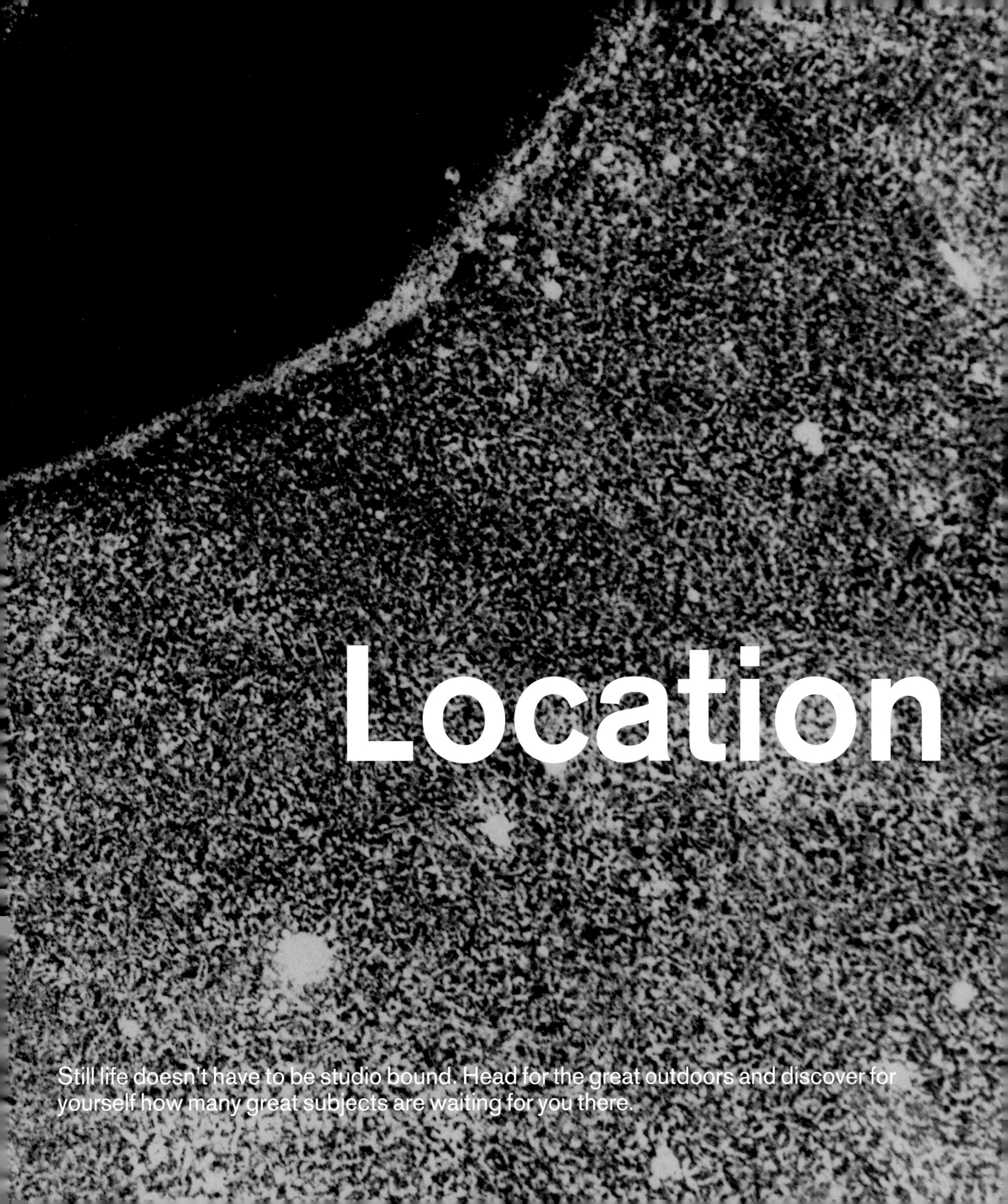

Location

Still life doesn't have to be studio bound. Head for the great outdoors and discover for yourself how many great subjects are waiting for you there.

Submerged Wheel by Gerry Coe
Contax RTS 2 camera, 28mm lens, Agfa APX 100 film.
Exposure 1/30sec at f/16

"I noticed how the clouds were reflecting in the water around the wheel and realised that this was where the picture was."

I find an enormous number of subjects for still life photography outside the studio. Often they're just ordinary objects, but if the way of looking at them is special then great pictures can result. I was out on an expedition to look for pictures with a group of friends, and we decided to visit Fanad Head in County Donegal, the most northerly point of Ireland. We were close to the shoreline, and came across this old wheel that was rusting away in a pool of water. It was a gift for photography, with its decaying structure full of wonderful texture. My friends decided to move in close and to concentrate on close-ups. I decided to walk around it for a little while, however, and thought about how I might come up with something that was a little different. Then I noticed how the clouds were reflecting in the water around the wheel and realised that this was where the picture was.

I decided to compose the picture so that I cropped out the edges of the pool in-camera, a decision that took away the terms of reference for the eye and allowed the picture to take on more of a surreal quality. At first sight the image almost looks as though it's a double exposure, and I enjoy the fact that it takes a little while to work out what's happening here. This was certainly the most successful picture that any of us took at this particular location, and it shows the value of looking for a different angle on a straightforward subject.

Gerry Coe

Technique For this picture to be successful, I needed sharp focus from the edge of the wheel, which was about a foot away, to infinity. I decided to use a 28mm, because a wide-angle lens will naturally offer far greater depth of field, and fortunately the day was bright, and so I was able to use an aperture of f/16 to boost the focus still further. At times such as this the value of a stop-down facility on a lens becomes apparent. Depressing a button on the side of the lens will manually stop the lens down to the taking aperture. Although the image you see in the viewfinder will become much darker, it should allow you visually to check exactly which areas of the picture are going to be sharply registered.

Pointer You don't always require beautiful subjects to make great pictures. This wheel, to most eyes, would have been another piece of junk cluttering up a beauty spot, but it still had enough about it that was interesting for me to get a worthwhile photograph. You need to develop the eye to see the potential for still life in everything: stop and look, and take the time to see if you can come up with an angle that is all your own.

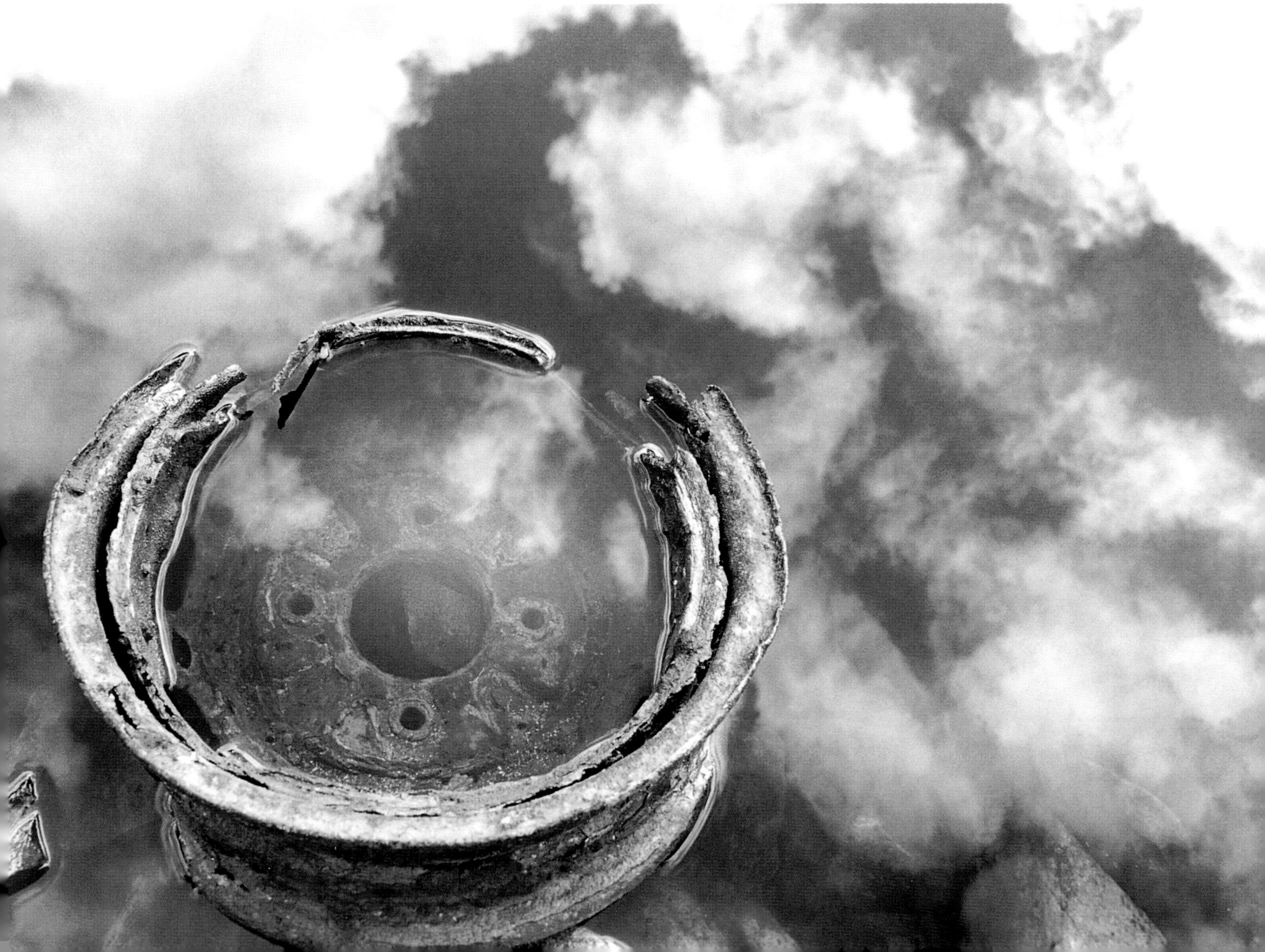

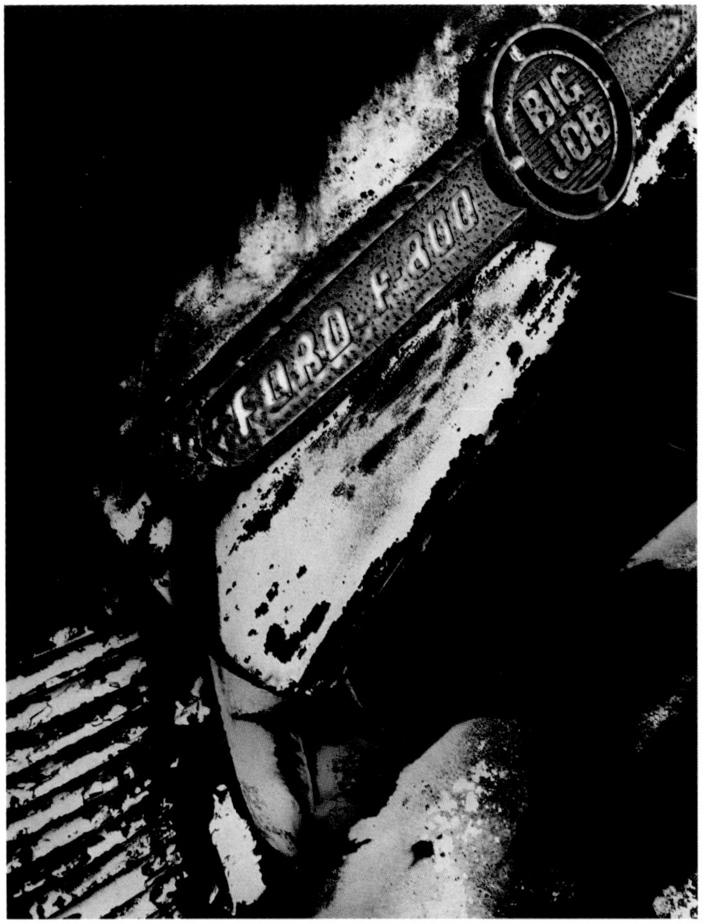
FORD F-800
BIG JOB

Location

If you keep your eyes open for pictures there are things wherever you go that will become subjects for wonderful still life photographs. I found myself on location in the United States, shooting pictures for the Jack Daniels distillery with a small team that consisted of an assistant and an art director. On our way to the shoot we passed a couple of abandoned and decrepit old cars around 100 yards off the highway. The moment I saw them I knew I had to come back that evening when the light would be subtler to try to take some detail pictures.

There's something very special about a once magnificent piece of machinery like this that's been left to decay. It takes on a new kind of beauty, as the rust eats away at its very substance and adds rough texture to its surface. It says much about the transient nature of most things on this planet while, on another level, the pitted badge that the car still wore attracted me because of the typography that it featured and the way it helped to identify my subject, even though I'd moved in to extract just one tiny area of detail.

There was a final twist to this story because, thinking that the cars had been left to rot and wishing to have a souvenir of the occasion, I decided when I'd finished taking my pictures to try to remove this name-plate. As I did so, a pick-up truck full of men arrived from nowhere, and I noticed that they carried guns. One of them asked me what I was doing and, when I replied, he said 'that's my uncle's car'. At this point the art director said, in an accent that couldn't be mistaken for anything but English, 'I don't know who these people are', and then he ran off and left us! Luckily for us the truck departed shortly afterwards, with a 'we'll be back' warning, and we escaped with our pictures, but it was a worrying moment!

John Claridge

Abandoned Big Job by John Claridge
Mamiya RZ67 camera, 140mm lens, Agfa 100 film.
Exposure one second at f/16

Pointer Still life is often mistakenly considered to be a subject that is confined to the studio, but in fact it can be found everywhere, and some of the greatest pictures are discovered on location. Faced with a subject such as the one John Claridge photographed here, the only option is to shoot with available light, and so patience and an eye for the movement of the sun are both key elements to ultimate success. To extract the most detail from this rust-pitted badge John waited until late in the day when the light was hitting his subject from a lower angle and accentuating the rough texture of its surface.

Close-up Although the abandoned car was an interesting photographic subject in its own right, there was far more potential to be explored through moving in close. An eye for detail and composition is vital and, by focusing on the badge the vehicle wore, and by including just enough of the surrounding elements, such as the radiator grille, John saved his image from becoming a pure abstract. A good exercise is to find a subject such as this and to spend time exploring it photographically. Different angles, a change of lens, even the time of day the pictures are taken, will all influence your results, and you'll be surprised how much material you'll shoot.

Location

Trilby Hat by Ralph Gibson
Leica M2 camera, 50mm dual range lens, Kodak Tri-X film, developed in Rodinol. Exposure not recorded

"When you're on location, lighting is always perfect, it's the photographer's interpretation of it that is sometimes lacking."

I saw this hat that had been left on a table at the Café Flore in Paris, and it appealed to me because I like to photograph the least significant aspect of a scene and the hat, just sitting there, was a very insignificant gesture. Something dramatic, such as a scene of a man shooting another man in the head with a gun, would be far too significant for me to photograph: I prefer to leave such things to the photojournalists, and to concentrate on the smaller details of life.

When you're on location, lighting is always perfect, it's the photographer's interpretation of it that is sometimes lacking. Every photograph is a lighting event, and through experience you acquire the ability to read the light that you encounter, so that you can use it to your advantage.

Pictures shouldn't be too obvious: to gain an understanding of what it is that I have responded to in my work, I require the viewer to really look at it. A strong photograph is one that compels the viewer to bring a lot to it.

Ralph Gibson

Tone, Texture and Contrast A striking still life has been created from what was a very ordinary moment, simply through Ralph Gibson's ability to read the way that the natural lighting hitting this Parisian street café was highlighting the texture and form of this everyday artefact. Because it was coming from a low angle, the light has created strong contrast in the scene, throwing a dense shadow around the brim of the hat to emphasise its shape and to echo the dark tone of its band. The shadow has also revealed the texture within the hat, something that would have been lost had the light been falling more directly on this scene, and this has become a vital element of the picture. It's a remarkable exercise in how to achieve a dramatic photograph from an unpromising situation, while the use of black and white has taken away the distraction that colour would have brought and allowed the image to be reduced to a simple series of tones.

Pointer Don't be afraid to crop tightly in-camera, so that you concentrate attention fully on the subject you're interested in. One of Ralph Gibson's great strengths is his ability to strip away the unnecessary elements within a scene and to focus only on what is important, and this allows the image that he produces to become far more powerful.

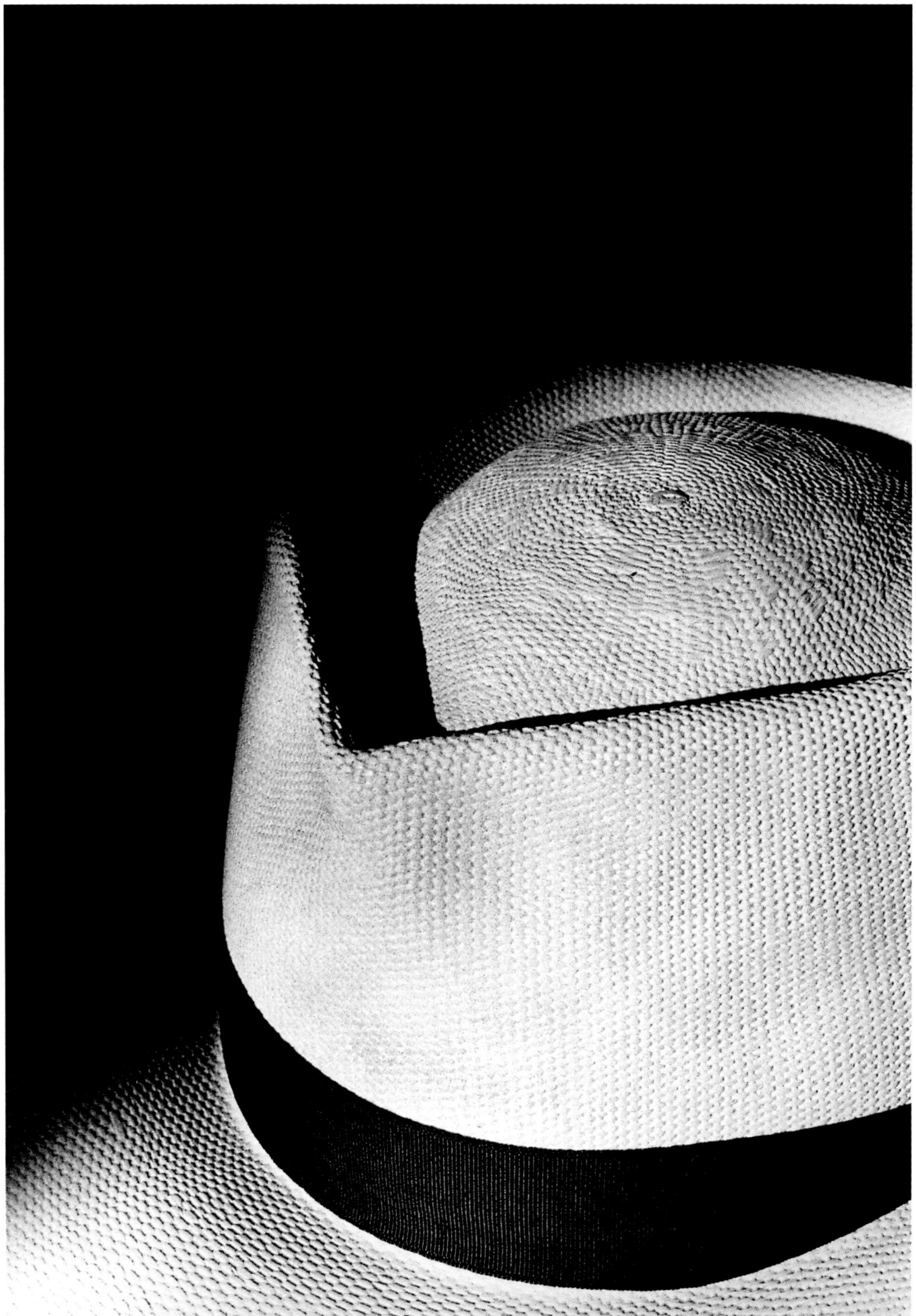

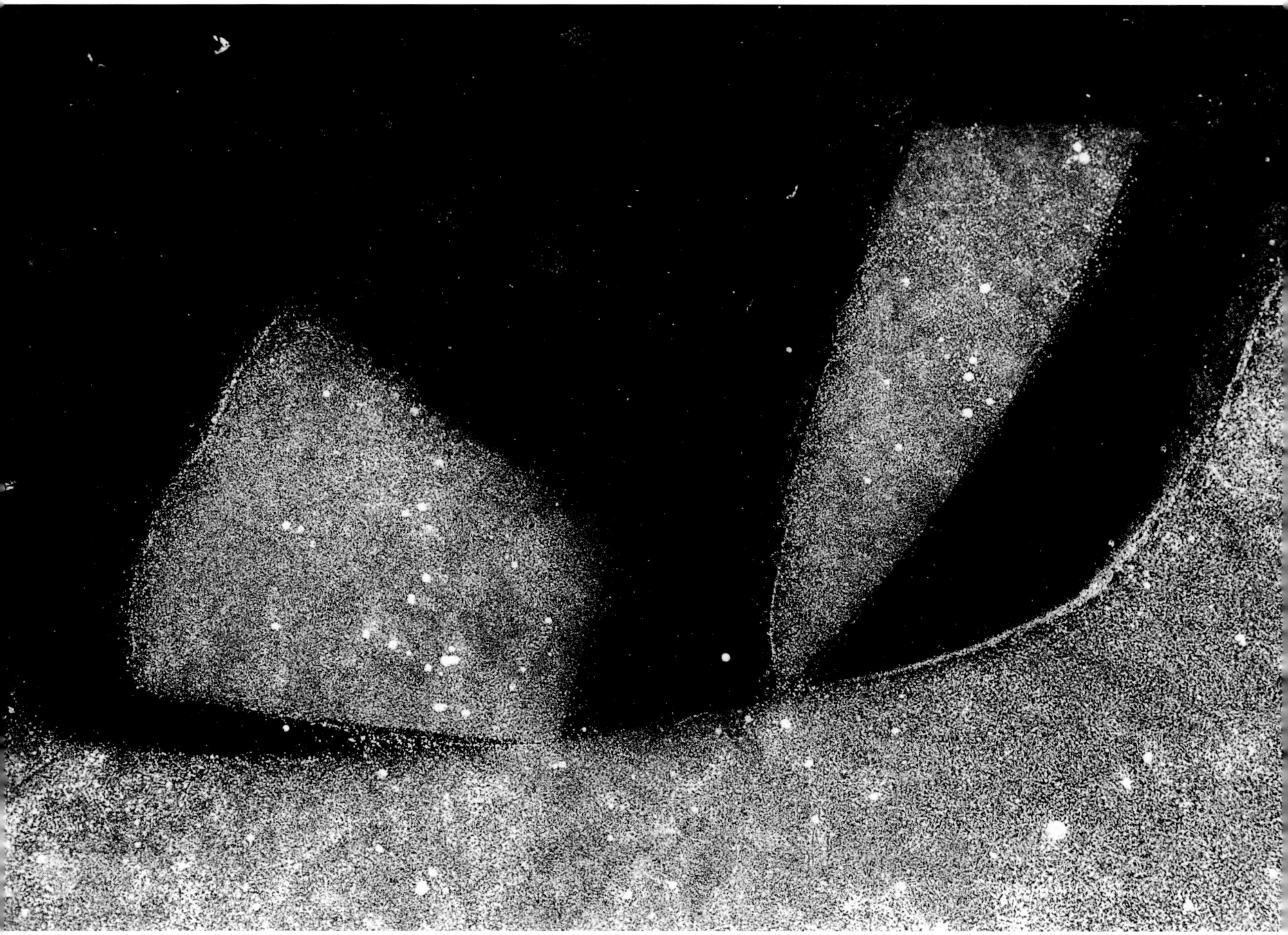

Location

William Blake, the poet and visionary, famously claimed to be able to see 'the universe in a grain of sand'. I found it frozen into the surface of a Scottish loch, Loch Baile Mhic Chailein, near Appin. It was the middle of winter, and when I arrived for a family visit the weather was fairly normal for the time of year, cold but nothing dramatic. Overnight, however, everything changed, and the temperature plunged to -16 degrees, freezing the lake very quickly to a depth of around ten inches. The speed with which the water had frozen created amazing forms, textures and shapes, and I knew it was a very special opportunity for photography. All I had with me was my Contax 35mm rangefinder camera with a fixed 45mm lens. Had I had any warning about what was to happen I would have probably been tempted to use 6x6cm or even a 5x4in camera, but as it was the use of one camera and lens, and a choice of ISO 100 and 400 film, gave the project a rigid format. With this equipment, plus the loan of a small tripod from my father's attic, I explored the surface of the lake for two days looking for images, and as I worked my pictures became more and more abstract. This image of two shards of ice was one of the pictures that worked the best: the dark background is clear ice, and the black showing through is the tone of the water in the loch.

Robin Broadbent

Exhibiting I thought immediately that the series worked well, because there was continuity to it, but the pictures were varied enough for the set never to become boring. At the time I had a design company working in advertising, and I scanned in ten of the images and put together a dummy book so that I could show it to publishers. Eventually Browns in London took it on, and the final book, called simply **Minus Sixteen**, is a collection of pictures running without captions, with a small explanation at the back that puts everything into context. I prefer the idea of a book over an exhibition, because it allows you to control the sequence that images are viewed in, and I love the way that there's a feeling of each page leading the reader on to the next.

Close-up When there is no point of definite reference in a scene to give it scale, it's possible to achieve remarkable abstracts simply by moving in close and concentrating on patterns within the scene. Taken at random, it's virtually impossible to tell what this image represents, and yet the area that's been framed has been selected carefully so that a pleasing combination of shapes and textures has resulted, and this has become the focal point of the picture.

Minus Sixteen by Robin Broadbent
Contax G1 35mm rangefinder camera, fixed 45mm lens, Ilford Delta film ISO 400. Exposure 1/2sec at between f/4 and 5.6

I like to spend time visiting locations with my large format camera, and simply looking for details that might become the subject for a still life picture. It's a good discipline: you can't work too fast with 5x4in, and it makes you stop and consider things, and to take time over composing and setting up the pictures you take, rather than working in a more reportage style as is often the way with a 35mm camera.

This is how this study of kelp came about. I was visiting the Isle of Skye, and decided to head for the beach shortly after the tide had retreated, when I reckoned there might be some interesting material left behind for me to photograph. Kelp is hardly rare in such a setting, but I was particularly taken with its luminosity, created of course by the fact that it had just been uncovered by the sea, and was yet to dry out.

It was a very simple scene, and all I did was to see it and frame it, moving in extremely close so that the result I achieved was almost an abstract. You can only achieve a still life such as this on location, it simply wouldn't look the same if you tried to set something up in the studio and to light it by artificial light. It would also be too considered if you tried to make this arrangement up yourself for the camera. There are some occasions when nature is simply impossible to better.

John Claridge

Close-up A large format camera such as the Deardorff consists of a lens panel and a film back, and the distance between the two is made up of a flexible bellows, which will stretch and contract as the camera is racked backward and forward to allow focus to be achieved. In practice this allows extreme close focusing to be achieved, which will also result in magnification of the image, but the pay-off is that the lens will need to be racked out by an appreciable amount beyond the position for focusing on distant objects. In turn this means that the bellows extension may be twice the length or more for close-ups than it would be for a general view and consequently the light reaching the film plane will have further to travel from the lens, and will be reduced accordingly. This means that an adjustment will have to be made to the exposure when employing bellows extension. For this particular image which was close to life size on the original 5x4in sheet of film, John Claridge used his considerable experience of working with large format cameras to calculate that two extra stops were required, and he then shot a Polaroid test to verify his judgement.

My Favourite Tip A mathematical calculation exists to enable the photographer to decide how much extra exposure is required when using bellows extension but, for me, being able to estimate this accurately simply by looking at the scene is all part of the craft of photography. When I started my career in Fleet Street back in the 1950s, the press photographers I met there all had this ability, and you only acquire it through experience with a manual camera. Fully automatic models will deliver the results, but you can't beat learning on a manual if you want to master the basic skills of photography.

Kelp 1 by John Claridge
Deardorff 5x4in camera, 240mm lens, Agfa 100 film.
Exposure four seconds at f/45

"Kelp is hardly rare in such a setting, but I was particularly taken with its luminosity."

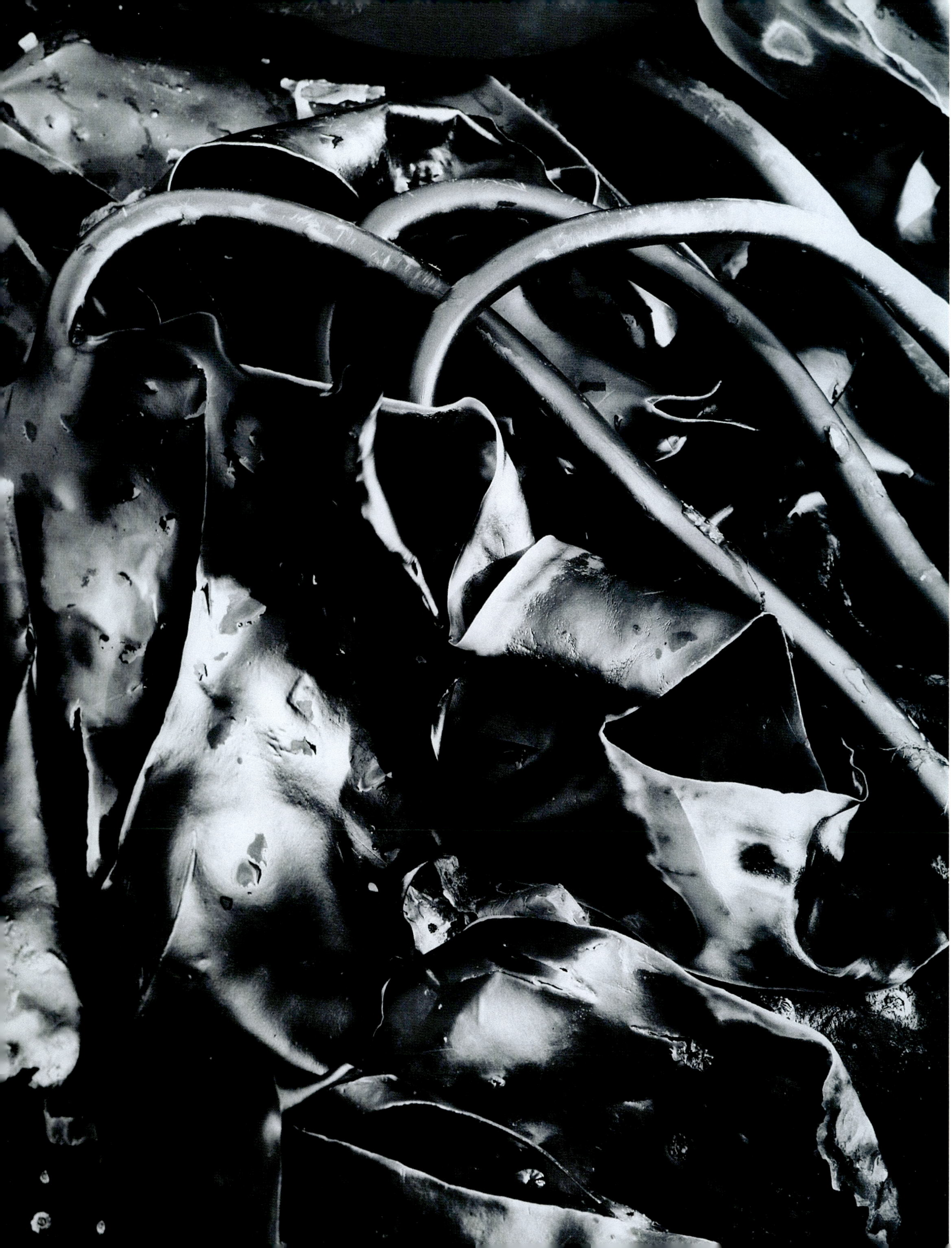

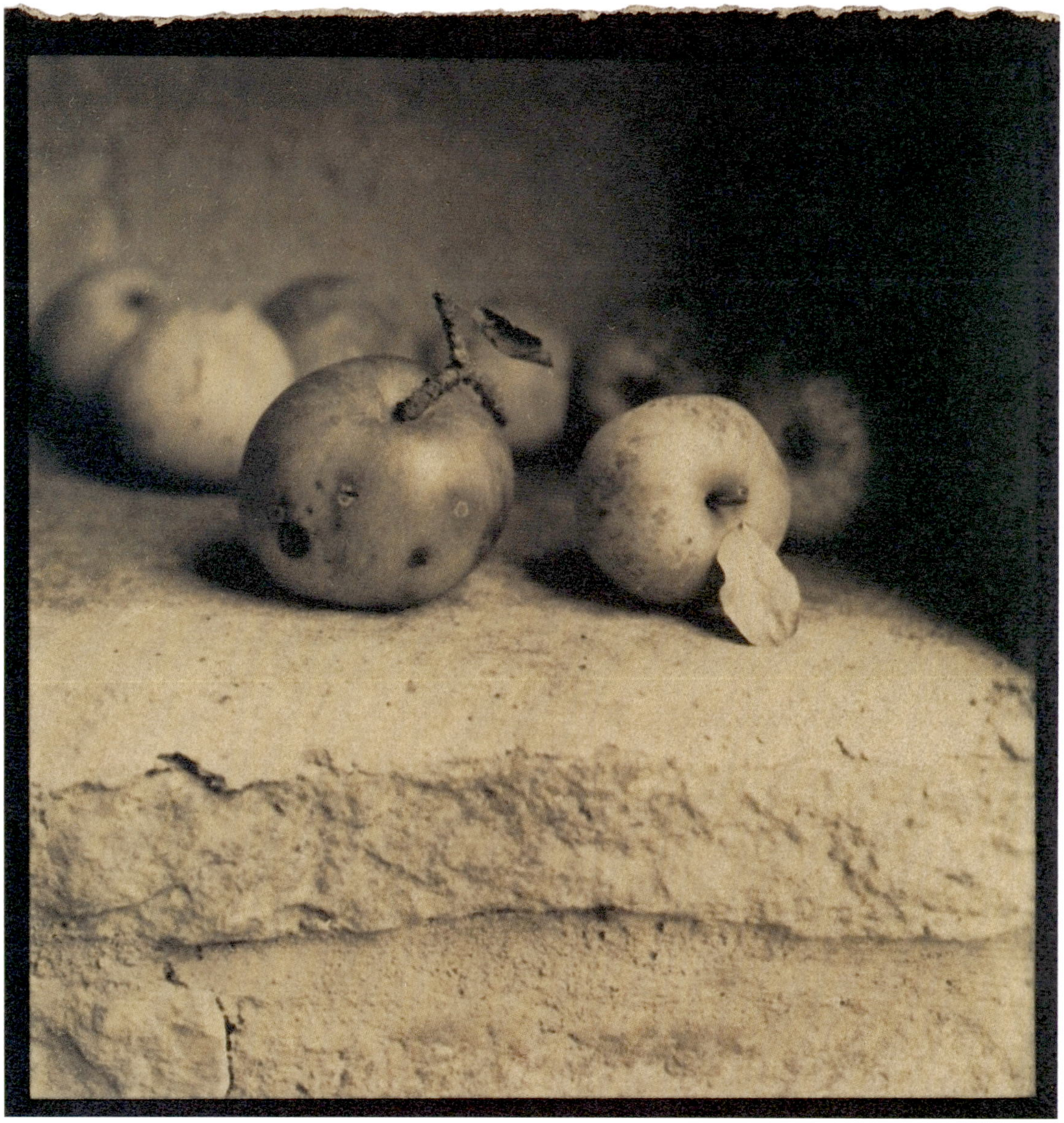

"All I did to achieve the picture that I wanted was to move one of the apples slightly so that the leaf that was still attached to its stalk faced the camera."

Location

Bladon Apples by Allan Jenkins
Mamiya C330 6x6cm camera, 80mm lens, Ilford FP4 film.
Exposure 1/60sec at f/5.6

I spotted these apples when I was visiting the house of a friend of mine, and thought that they made a perfect composition virtually as they were. They were sitting on a ledge inside a stone wall just outside the main door to the place, and the daylight that was hitting them was very subtle and muted, and complemented them perfectly. All I did to achieve the picture that I wanted was to move one of the apples slightly so that the leaf that was still attached to its stalk faced the camera and that was it. It's very much a picture that was found, and the still life photographer should always have an eye for situations such as this, that can yield a strong image. This particular picture is now one of my best selling images.

I took the picture with the camera's standard lens, which is the one I use the most. I don't play around with different focal lengths a lot. I find that photographers will often change a lens when they want a different angle of view, but I prefer to move the camera position instead, and to keep continuity in the equipment that I'm using. I also try to achieve exactly the picture I want in-camera, because I hate to subsequently crop my pictures and, obviously, with the contact printing that I tend to do this would be difficult to achieve in any case. In my view cropping is akin to cheating: if you can't get the picture you want in-camera, then perhaps you aren't taking the right picture.

Allan Jenkins

Technique This is a toned Cyanotype print, and this process requires the negative to be contact printed. With a 6x6cm negative this can lead to the image being rather small: I actually quite enjoy presenting pictures this size some of the time, but in this case I wanted to make a bigger print, and the only way I could do this was to produce an internegative. This is basically an enlarged negative that's been produced from the original, and to get to this point I use a Kodak material known as Direct Duplicating Film. This is an amazing product, because it allows you, under safelight conditions, to make a negative direct from the original negative, and everything works in reverse, so that the more light from the enlarger that reaches the film, the lighter it will become. Previously you would have to make a positive and then a negative from this, and this took everything one further stage away from the original, with all the quality implications that this carries. I made my internegative around 14cm square, and that's now the size of the prints I can produce.

My Favourite Tip Once I've produced the Cyanotype print, I take it a stage further by toning it. I like to experiment at this point, and will use all kinds of different methods to achieve a result. The brown tone that I came up with here was the result of putting the print in a bath of tannic acid, which is effectively a stain similar to one that you might achieve using tea. I also play around with hot water to get different results. If you plunge a print that's blue-toned into boiling water, for example, it will turn purple. This can be highly effective, and to find out exactly what you can achieve you have to be prepared to experiment extensively, and to keep a careful note of results.

Location

Baskets, Singapore by John Claridge
Deardorff 5x4in camera, 180mm lens, Agfa 100 film.
Exposure four seconds at f/32

I happened across this shop that was selling baskets while I was in Singapore, and I was struck by how beautiful this scene was. I find it hard to say exactly what the attraction was but, as a photographer, you just learn to look for details such as this, and I hope this instinct that I have never goes away.

The basic shapes, the structure of this pile of baskets and the textures that have been revealed by the lighting are the elements that make this picture so special, and the final telling touch is provided by the two brushes casually positioned in the centre of everything. It's the first thing that the eye goes to, and then you take everything else in. The whole picture is an exercise in simplicity, and I didn't change a thing. This is the scene exactly as I found it, and that's what I love about it. It's imperfect, but it's considered in another, more naïve way, and I think that's brilliant. It would be great to be able to create something like this in a studio and then to photograph it, but you would simply lose the essence of the picture. Someone has put this arrangement together, not from any aesthetic point of view, but because of the love of what they sell, and all I've done is to realise the potential it had to make a found still life.

John Claridge

Composition The art of great composition is to think quickly and to have a natural feel for the way that elements work together. With an image as simple as this, the key is to move in close, to concentrate on where the interest really lies, and then to crop out, in-camera, any extraneous details that will simply serve to distract. So many pictures have their impact lessened by slack composing: don't be scared to be bold, and to reduce your picture to an abstract scene of textures and tones if necessary.

My Favourite Tip What you don't see in an image is as important as what you do see. Here quite a substantial part of the scene is in deep shadow and recorded simply as dark tone. This has served to simplify the picture and to concentrate attention on the main area of interest, the baskets. I happened across this scene at the right time of day, when the lighting was naturally creating the shadows that I wanted, and blocking out detail inside the shop, while highlighting textures. Had the lighting been more direct the picture wouldn't have worked; it's all a matter of timing, and you have to be prepared to return later if a scene isn't working for you.

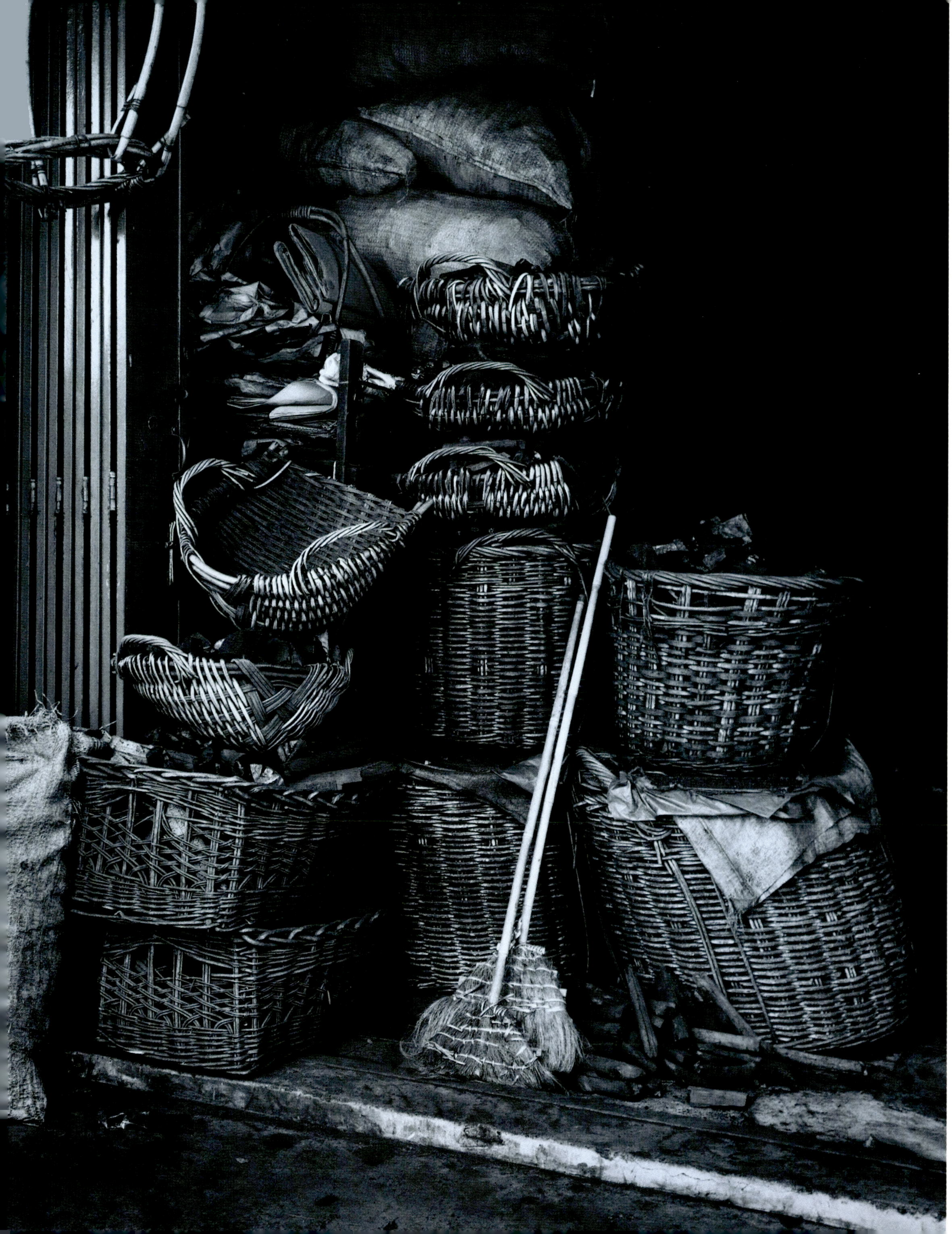

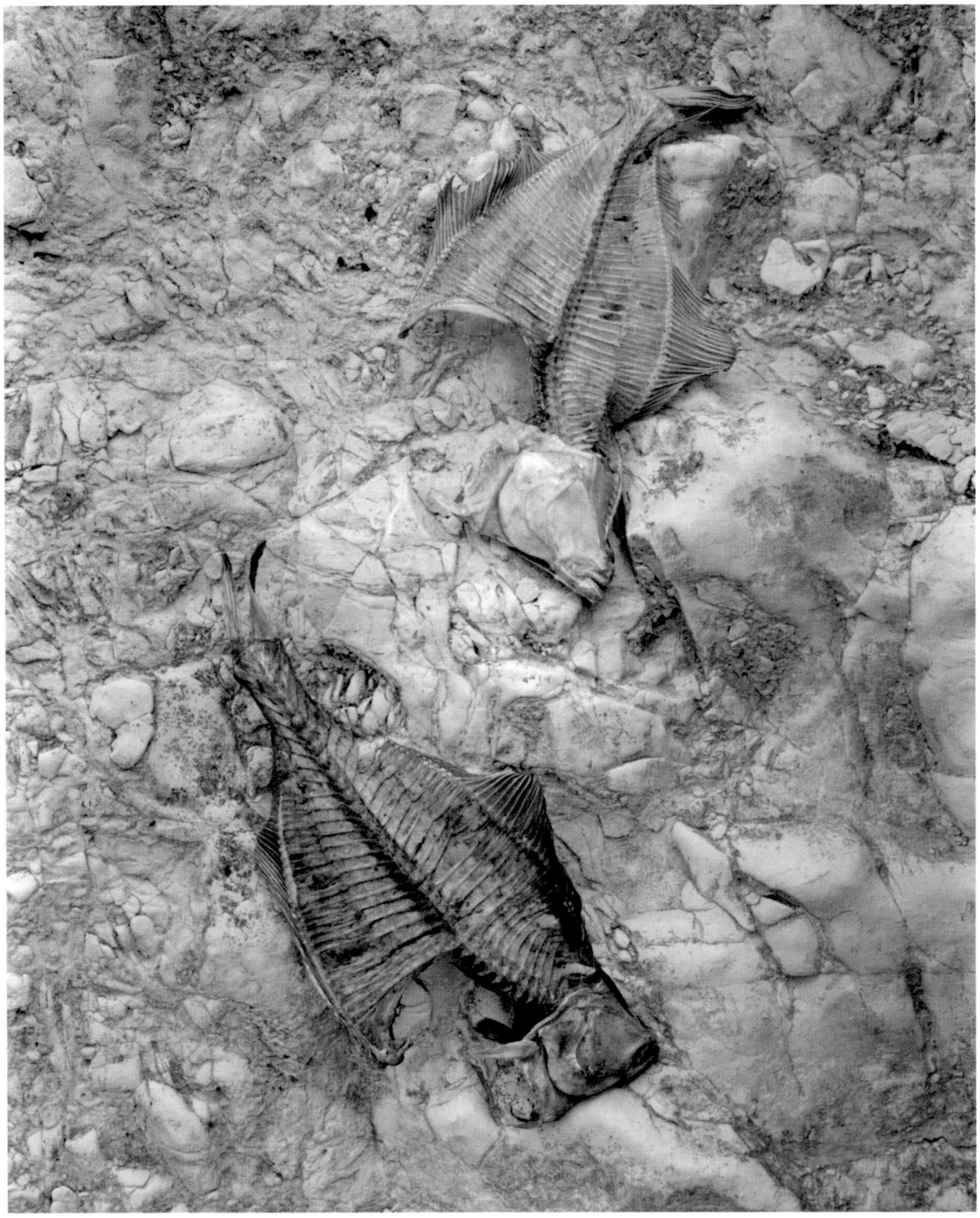

Location

Fossil Fish by Ray Spence
Mamiya RB67 camera, 90mm lens, Ilford FP4 film ISO 125.
Exposure 1/60sec at f/11

I had spent some time photographing genuine fossils around the town of Lyme Regis, where they are particularly plentiful, and then moved on to the Dorset tidal fishing cove of Beer, where I hoped to find some more location still life subjects. While we were there, fishermen were gutting the day's catch, and several of the skeletons that they were left with were thrown on to the beach, where they dried out in the sun. I collected a few together and, still influenced by the fossils that I'd seen, decided to set up my own still life pictures in this style.

At the back of the beach was a limestone cliff, and I arranged the fish there to make this picture. The direct daylight this area was receiving was far too harsh, however, and so to create the soft shadow that I wanted I asked some friends who were with me to shield my subjects with their coats. This gave me low contrast flat lighting, which I always find works well for still life subjects, although our party was rewarded with some very strange looks while we were setting this up!

Ray Spence

Composition I arranged these fish so that they appeared to be in a curve, and this established a relationship between them and worked very well. There were many variations on this theme, which saw me move the fish into different positions, and I also took some multiple exposures to attempt to make the fish blend into the rocks more, but this was the image that worked the best.

Pointer I like to photograph the smaller details of nature, and I'm perfectly happy to manipulate and to arrange the things that I find on location if that helps me to obtain a stronger image. It's one stage removed from pure found still life subjects, but it's still got more immediacy than a straight studio set-up.

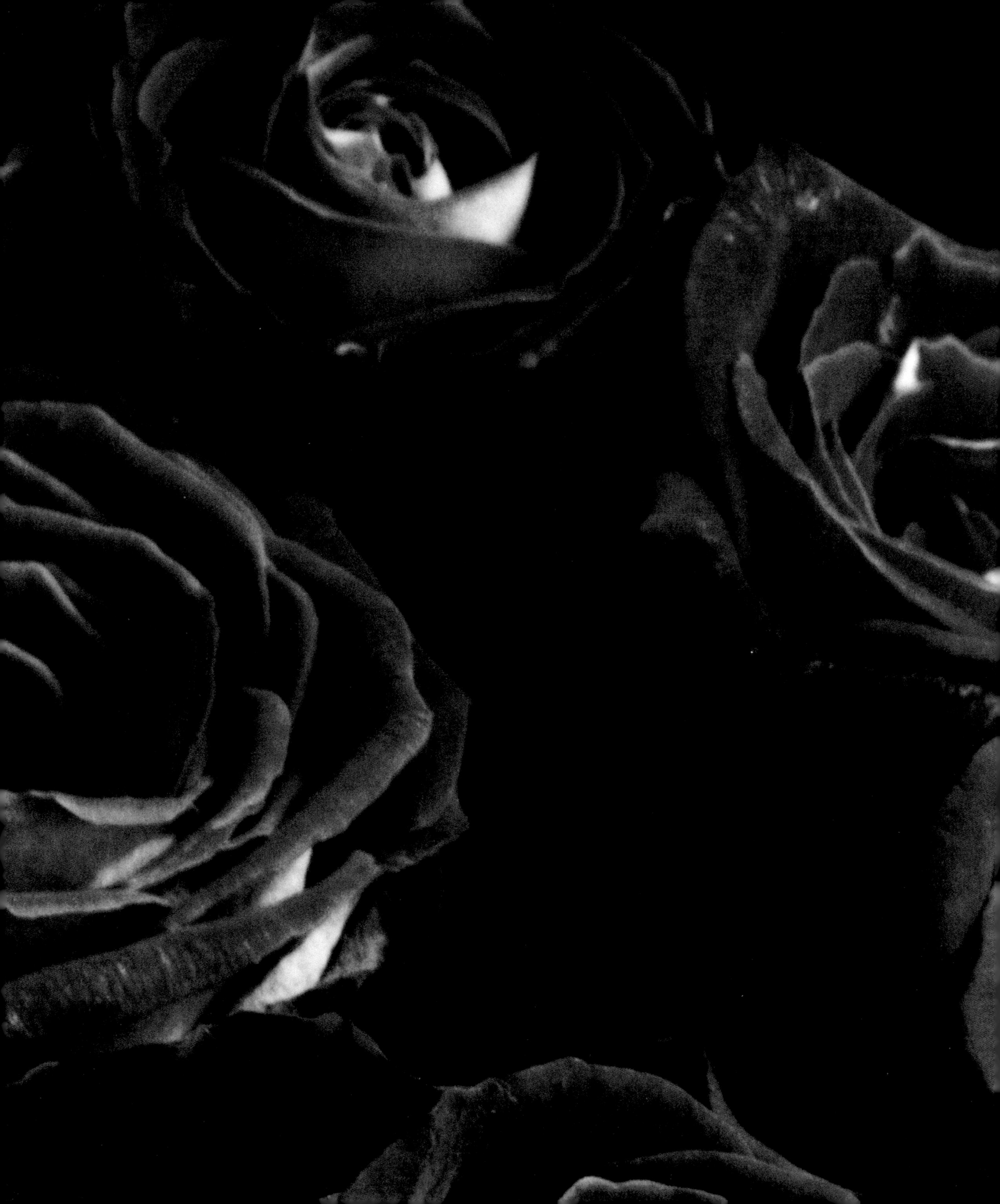

Gallery

It's time for a treat. Sit back and enjoy this collection of wonderful pictures, from a selection of great still life photographers.

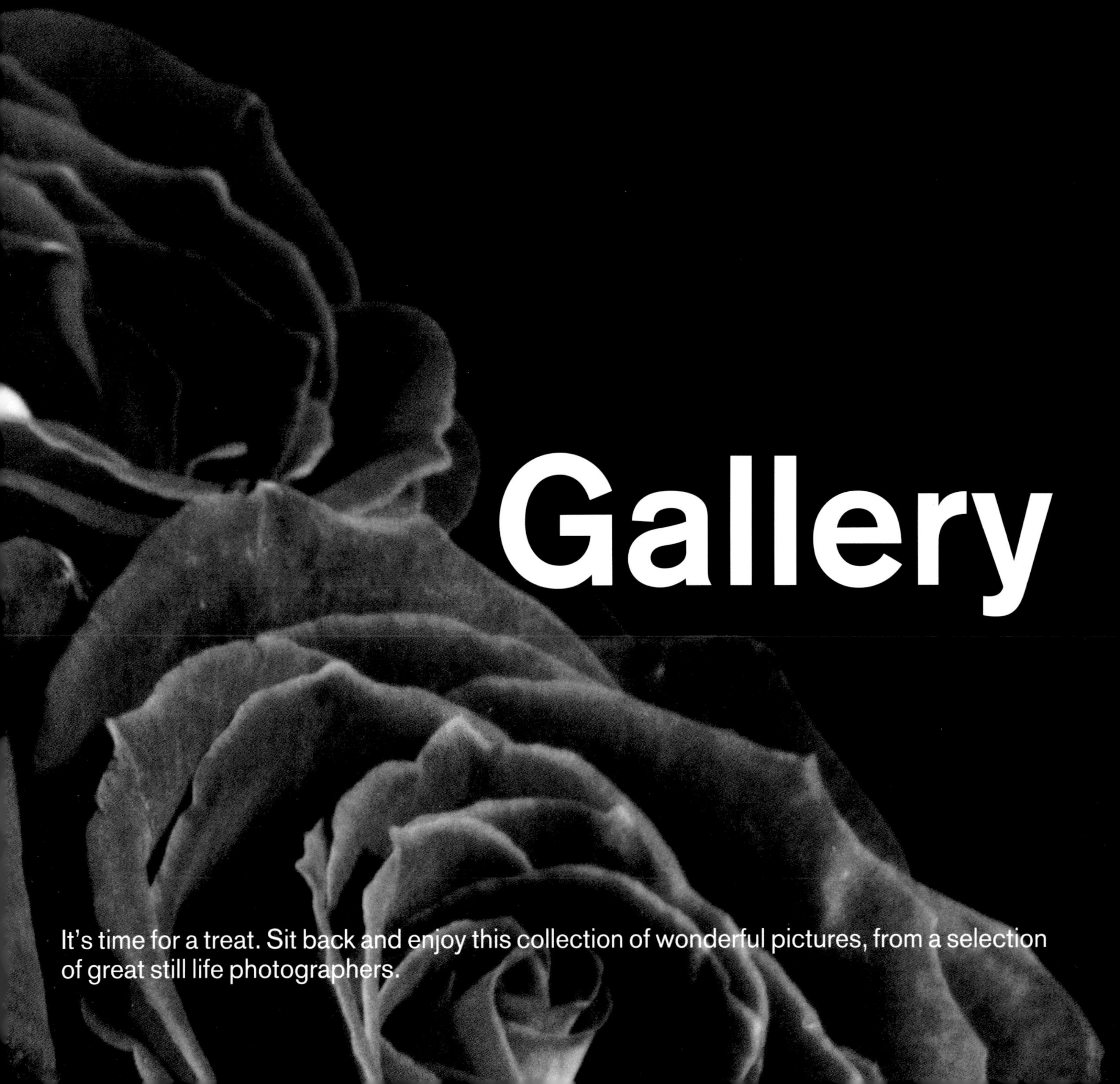

Still Life by Ralph Gibson
Leica M6 camera, 50mm lens, Kodak Tri-X film, developed in Rodinol.
Exposure not recorded

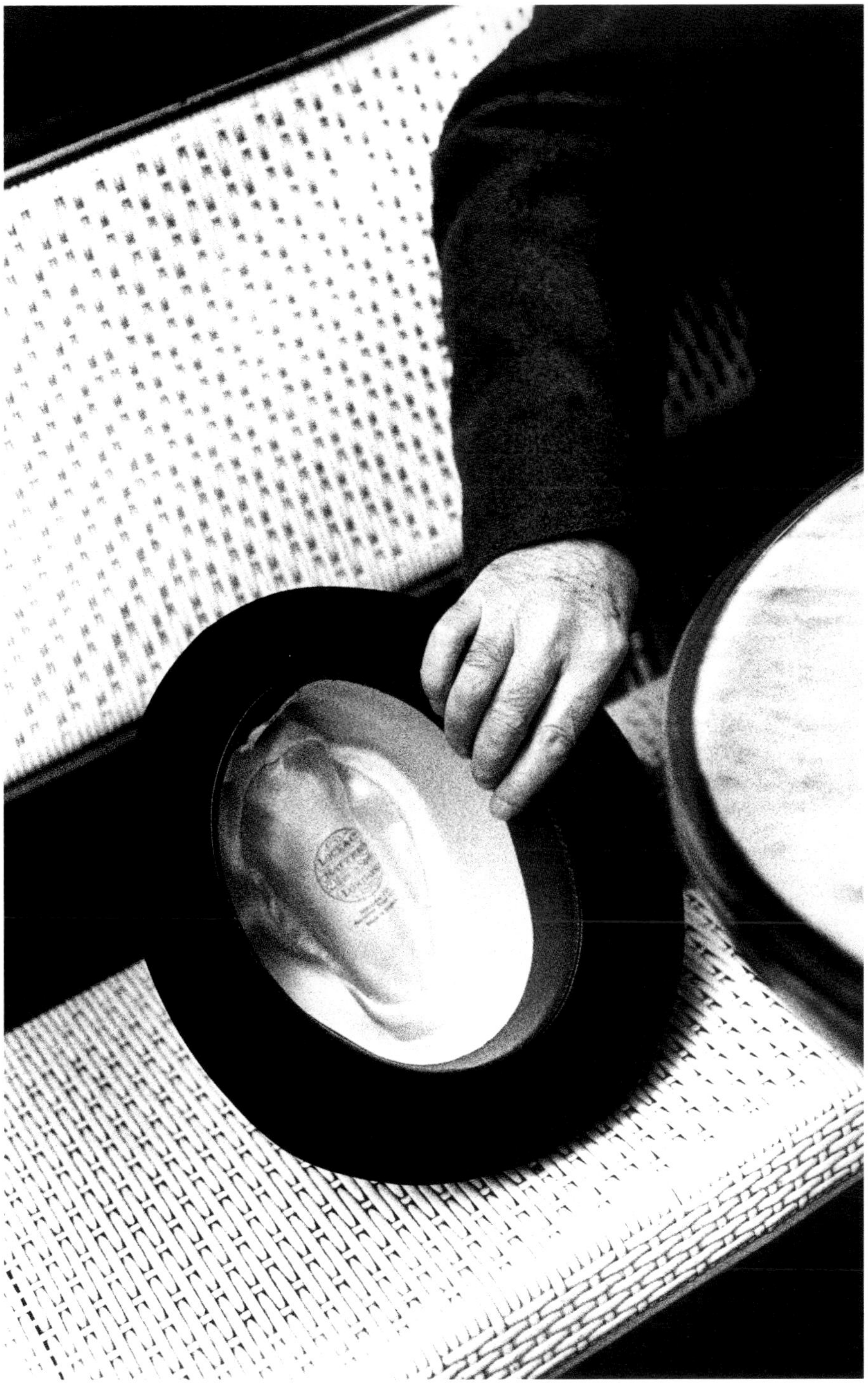

Teabags by Manuela Höfer
Photogram from the Contemporary Packaging Series

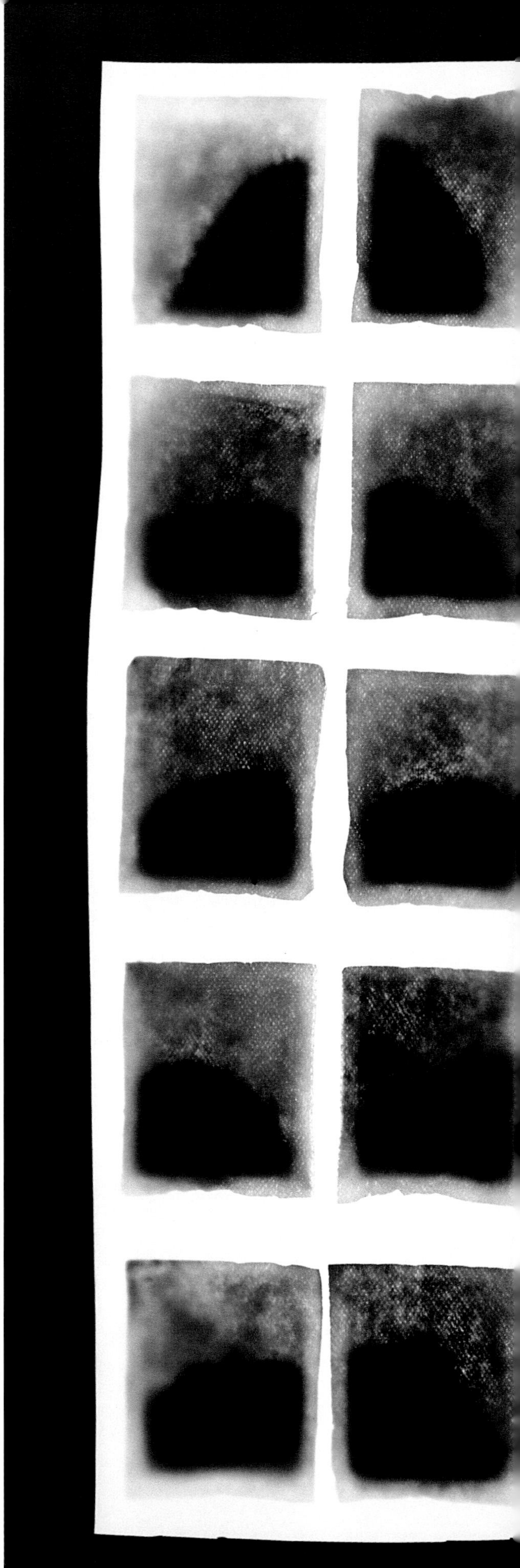

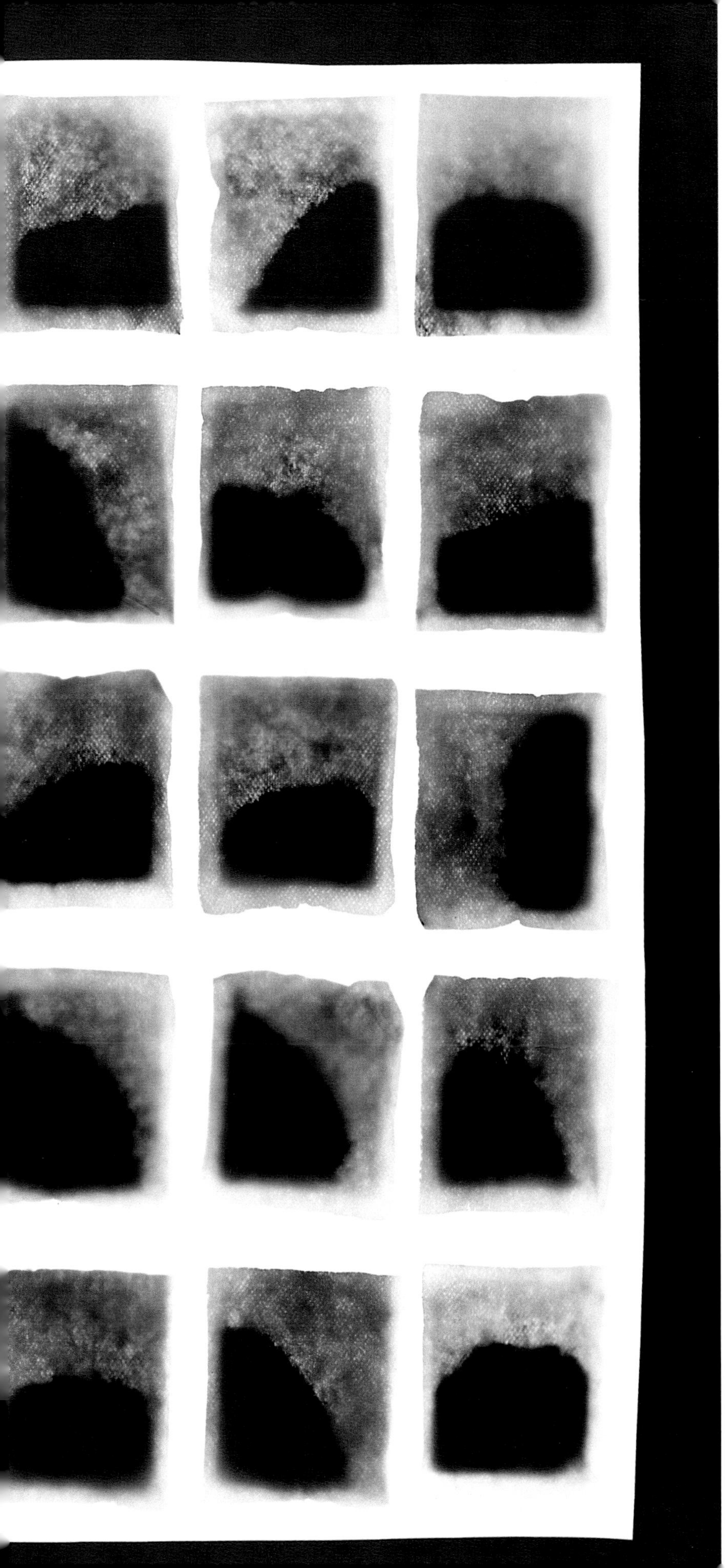

Gallery

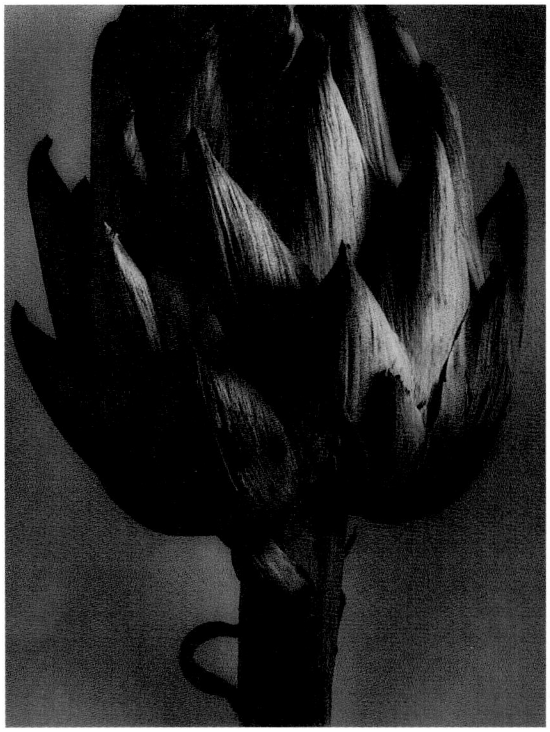

Artichoke Study by Patrice de Villiers
Sinar P 5x4in studio camera, 210mm lens, Agfapan 100 film.
Exposure eight seconds at f/45

Teazels by Joseph Ortenzi
Horseman LPL 5x4in camera, 210mm lens, Polaroid Type 55 film.
Lit by strobe, exposure 1/60sec at f/45. Printed on Kentona Grade Two, developed in lith developer.
Picture: The Michael Trevillion Picture Library

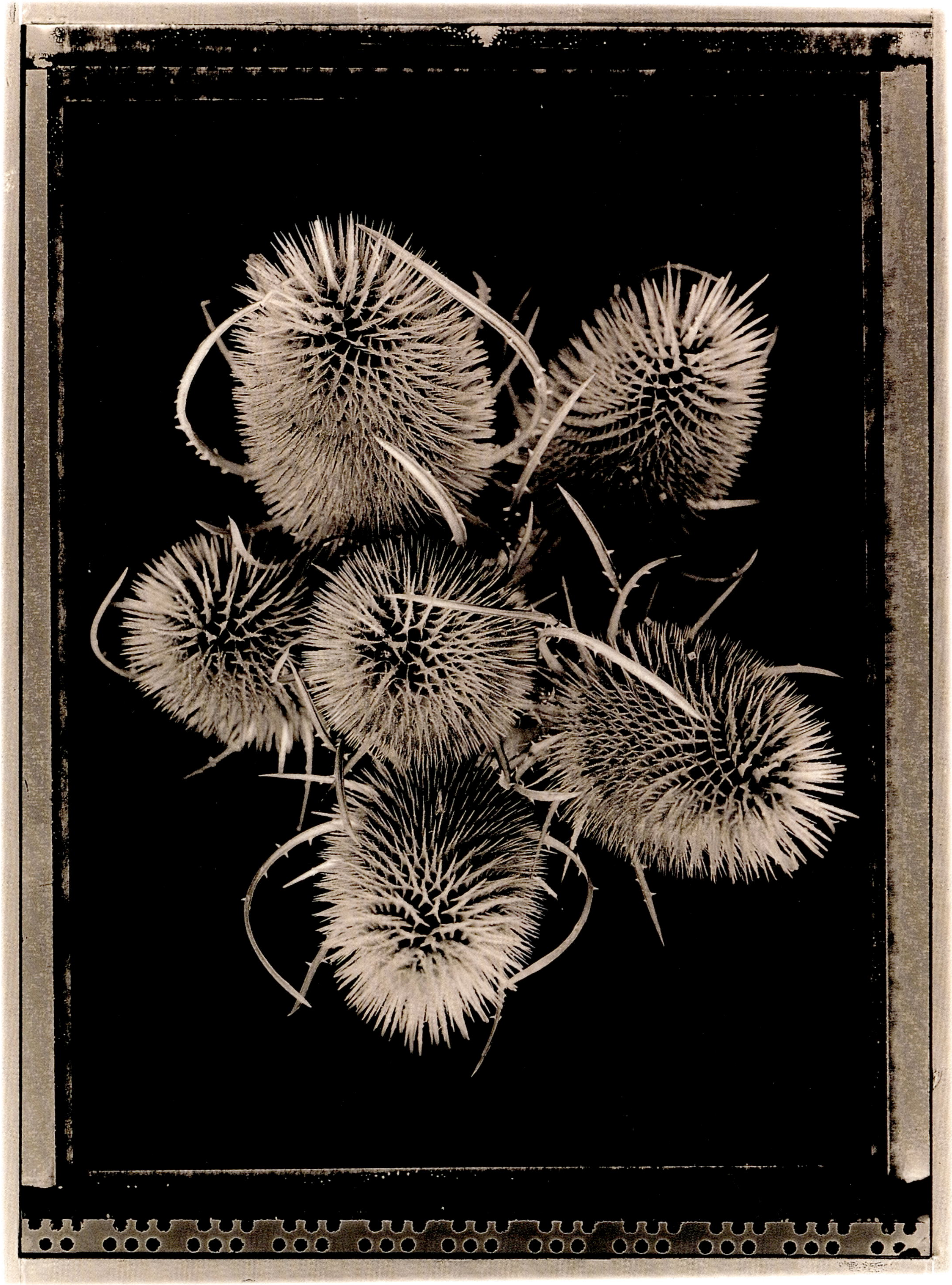

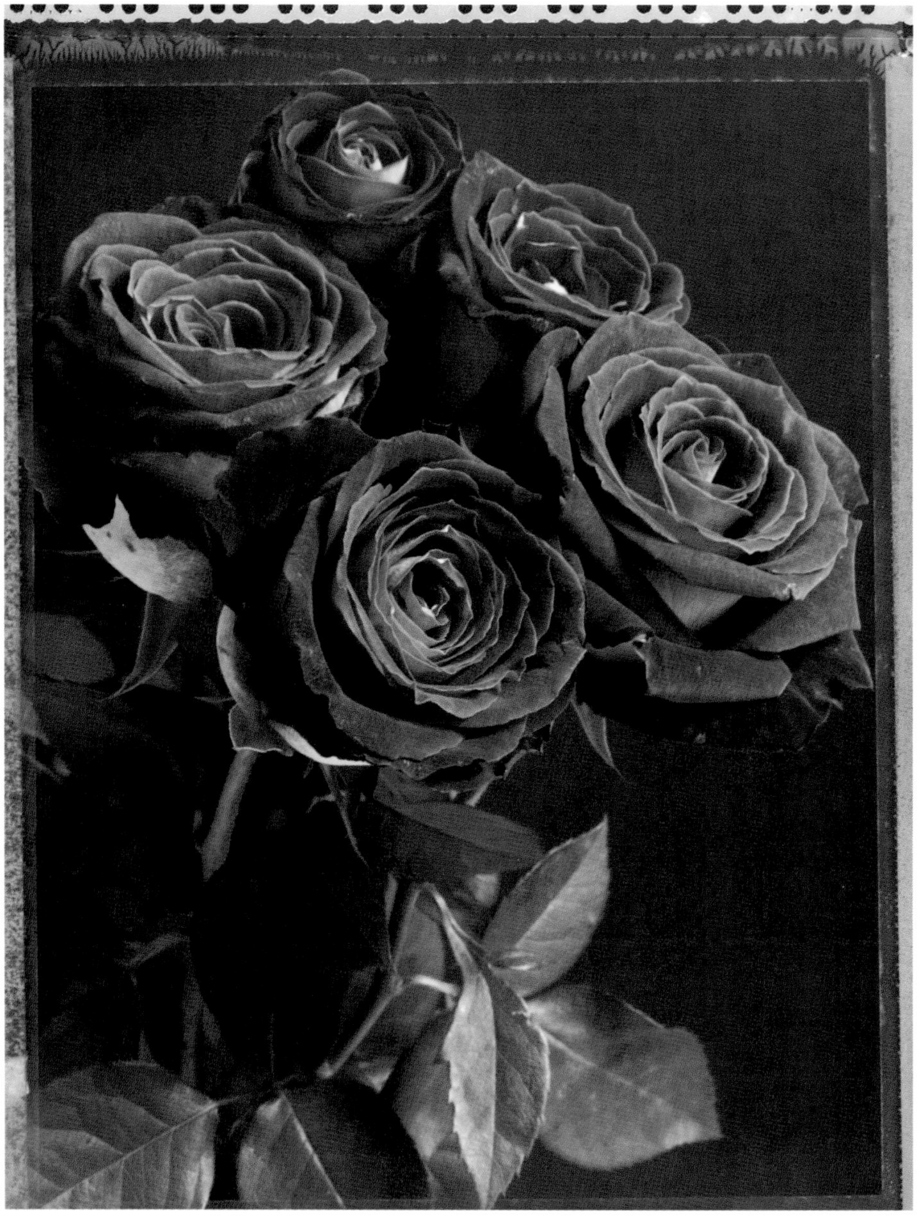

Roses by Seamus Ryan
Horseman LX 5x4in camera, 150mm lens, Polaroid Type 55 film. Exposure not recorded

Pear by Kenro Izu
Deardorff 10x8in camera, Plus X film. Printed on hand-coated platinum/palladium paper.
Copyright Kenro Izu, courtesy of Howard Greenberg Gallery, New York

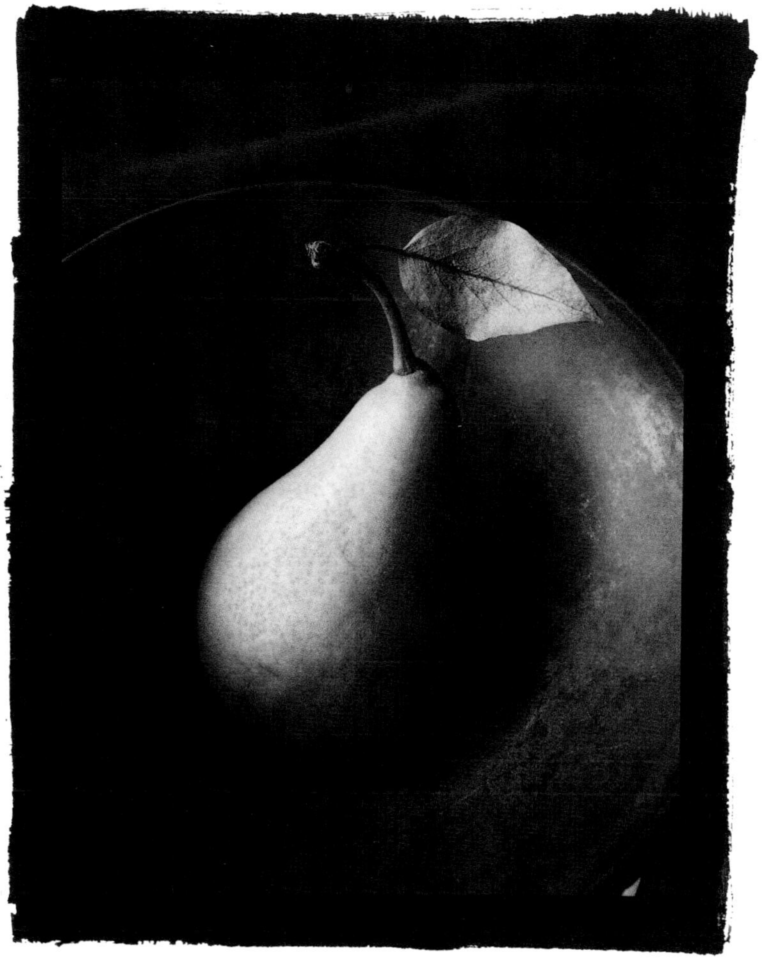

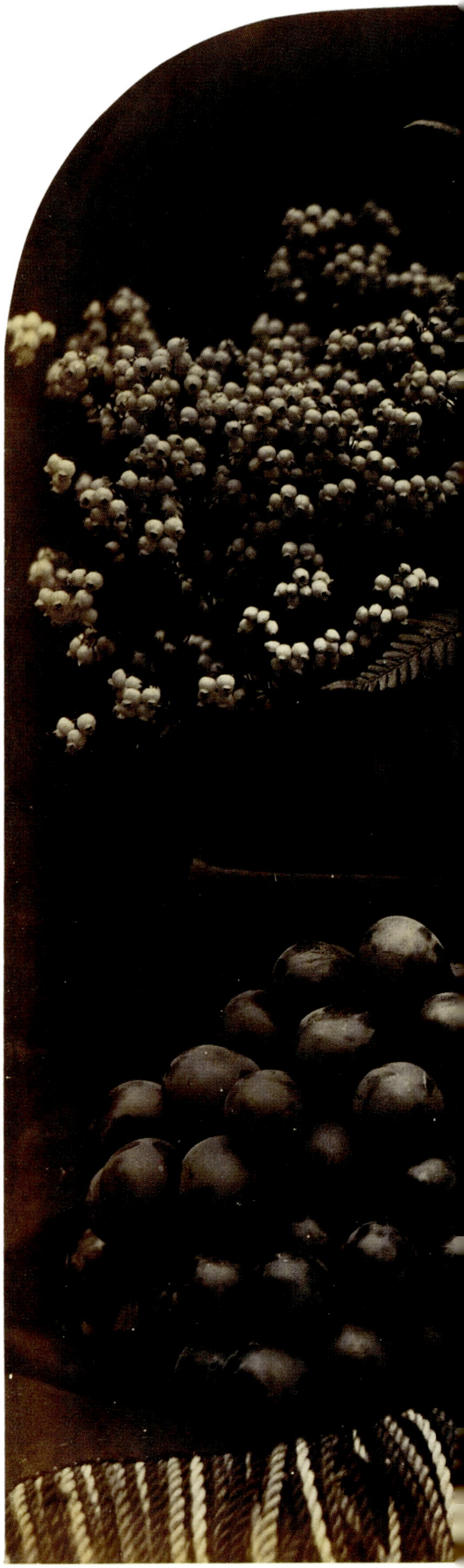

Flowers and Fruit by Roger Fenton, 1860
Albumen print from 20x16in glass wet collodion negative, taken by daylight and arranged outside on a table.
Picture: The Royal Photographic Society, Bath

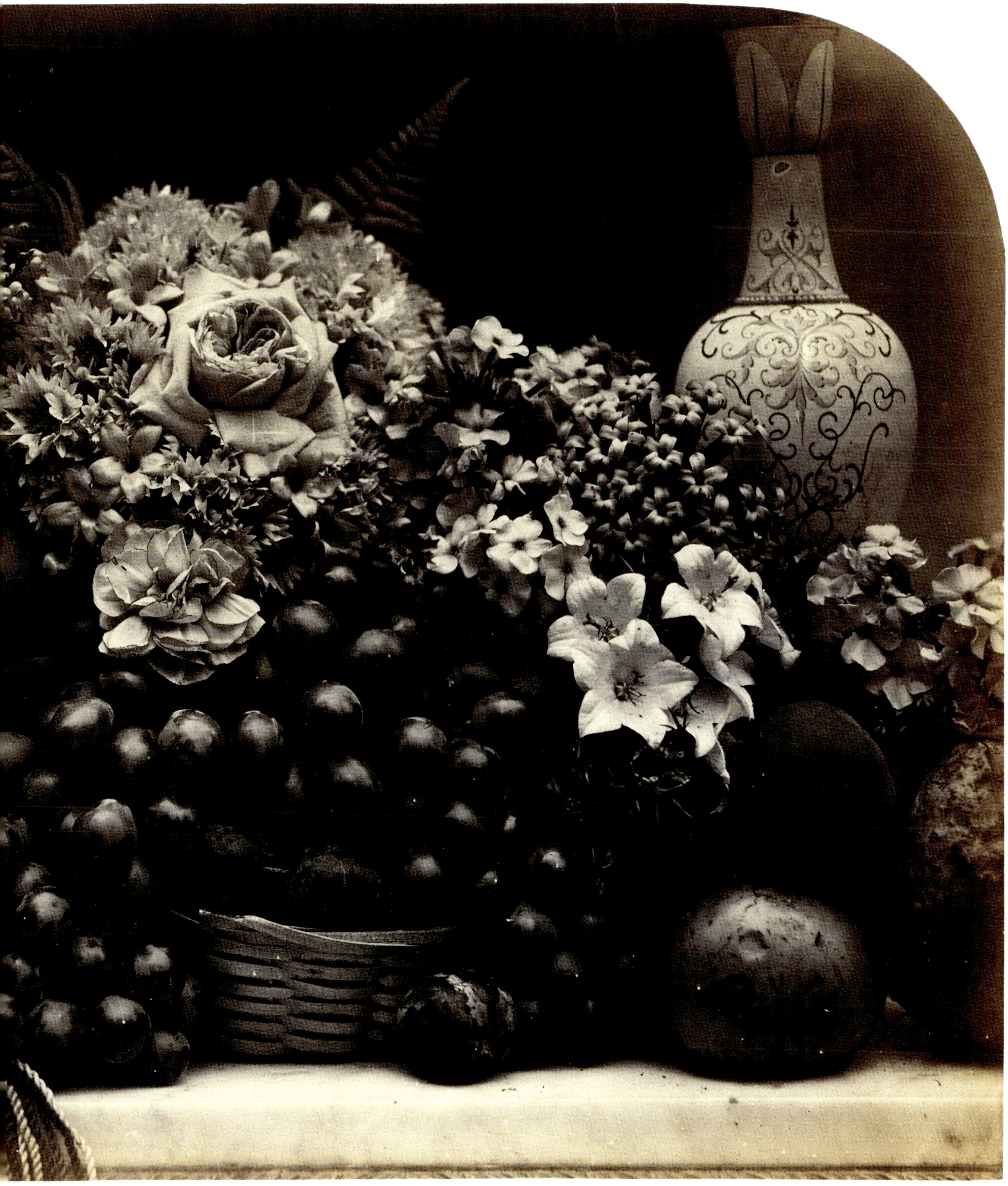

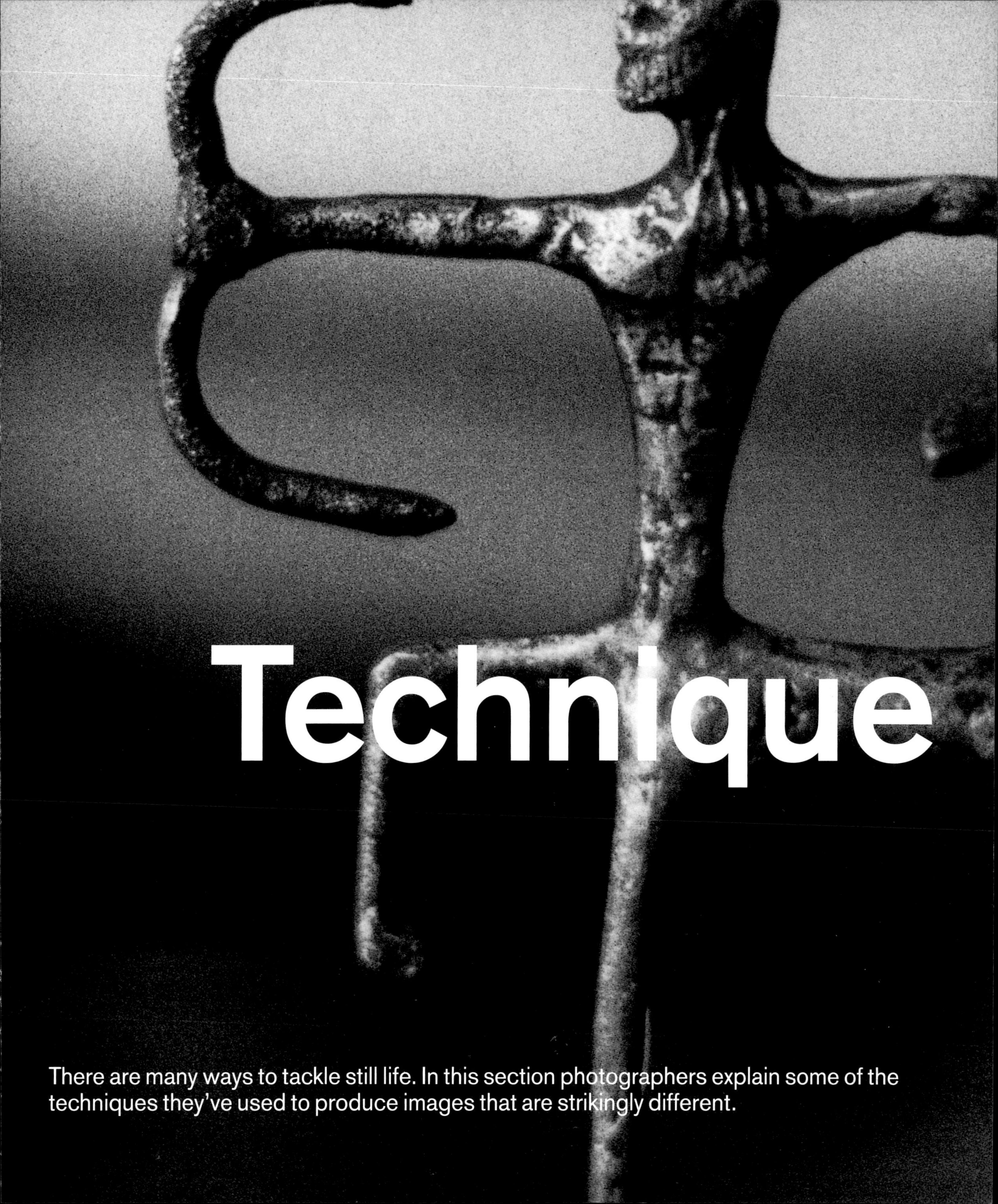

Technique

There are many ways to tackle still life. In this section photographers explain some of the techniques they've used to produce images that are strikingly different.

Country Pursuits No 2 by John Blakemore
MPP 5x4in camera, 180mm Symmar lens,
Ilford FP4 film developed in ID-11. Double exposure

I have used the multiple exposure technique in my work for many years, and first developed it when I was working with landscapes. Some of the pictures I produced at that time were extremely complicated, and could involve anything up to 48 exposures on a single sheet of 5x4in film. For me, multiple exposure became more than a technique, it became a way of working through ideas, and it opened up a lot of visual possibilities at a time when I was looking for different ways of interpreting my subject. This image is a straight double exposure, and I produced it in 1995 as part of a series of images that I was working on that went under the title 'Country Pursuits'. It was taken in Ambergate, Derbyshire, a location that I've photographed many times before, and my intention was to make a statement about the general misuse of the countryside. I wanted to show how, even in a beautiful place, when you peel back the veneer you will find the detritus that man has left behind.

When I arrived at the location, my first move was to look around and to gather together all the bits of rubbish that I could find in the vicinity. I was particularly interested in things that contained references to nature because this said something about its commercialisation, and added strength to the image. Once I'd gathered together enough items, I selected the ones that I wanted and arranged them as a still life on a rock to be photographed. Once I'd taken a selection of pictures I then looked for a suitable subject to act as the partner in the image, and eventually chose a section of fern leaves to do the job. Working with a 5x4in camera, producing a double exposure is quite straightforward, because as a matter of course with a camera such as this you expose each sheet of film in the dark slide on an individual basis. With a double exposure the process is simply carried out twice, and further exposures can be made just as easily if required.

John Blakemore

Pointer When shooting multiple exposures, you must be aware of the relationship between the elements you're including. It shouldn't be a random process, and the most successful multiple exposures will have been planned so that the overlap of images is complimentary. A light object, for example, will produce greater density on the negative and effectively block out any subject that is behind it. A darker object will be less distinct and, if you want it to register, it will need to fall against an area of mid to darker tone.

Composition The placing of the lettering and objects within the picture here was carried out with great care by John Blakemore to ensure that everything fell where he wanted it. The dramatic graphics of the word 'Lion' grabs the attention near the centre of the picture and draws the eye into the frame, from where other elements then become distinguishable.

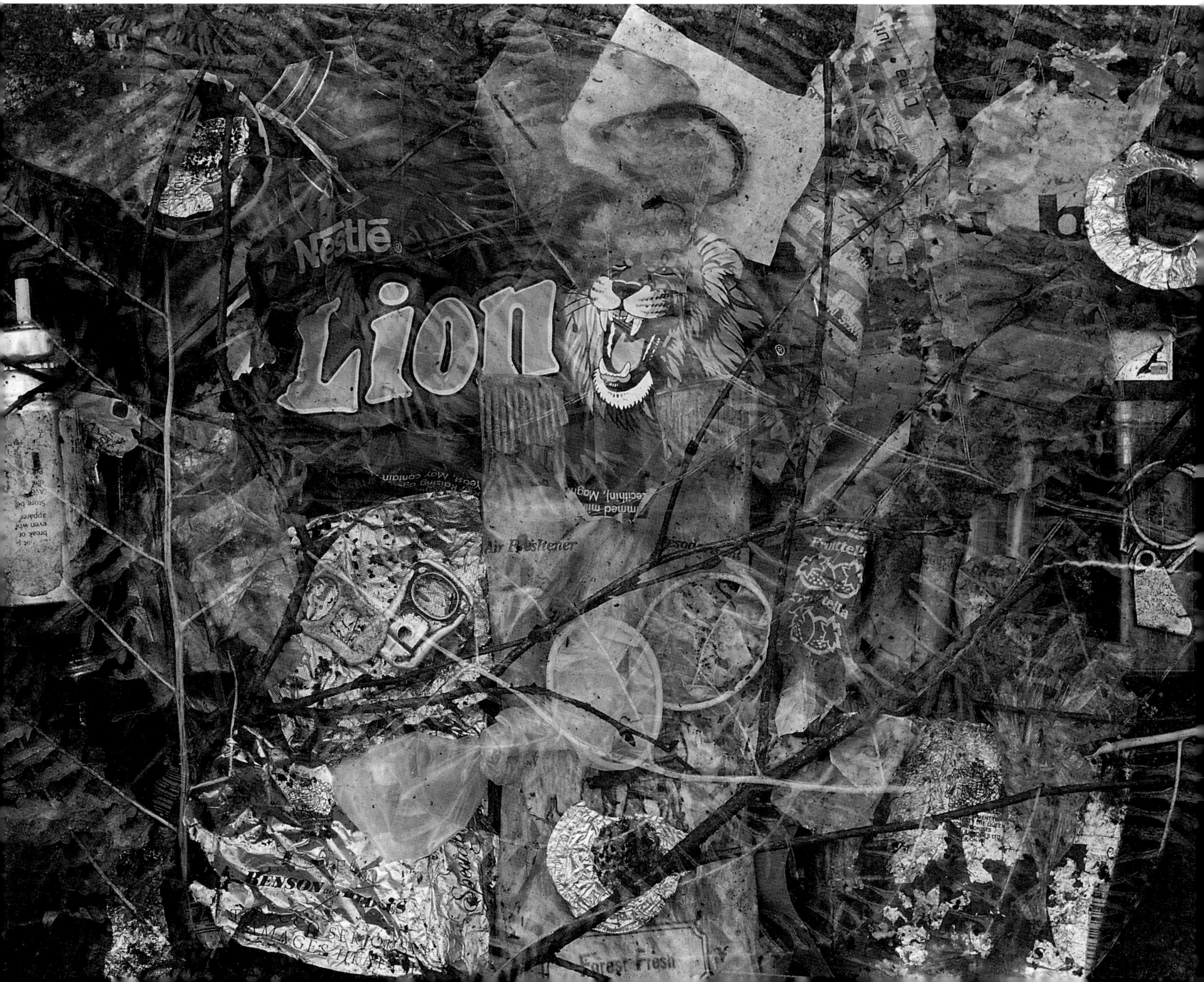
Nestlé
Lion

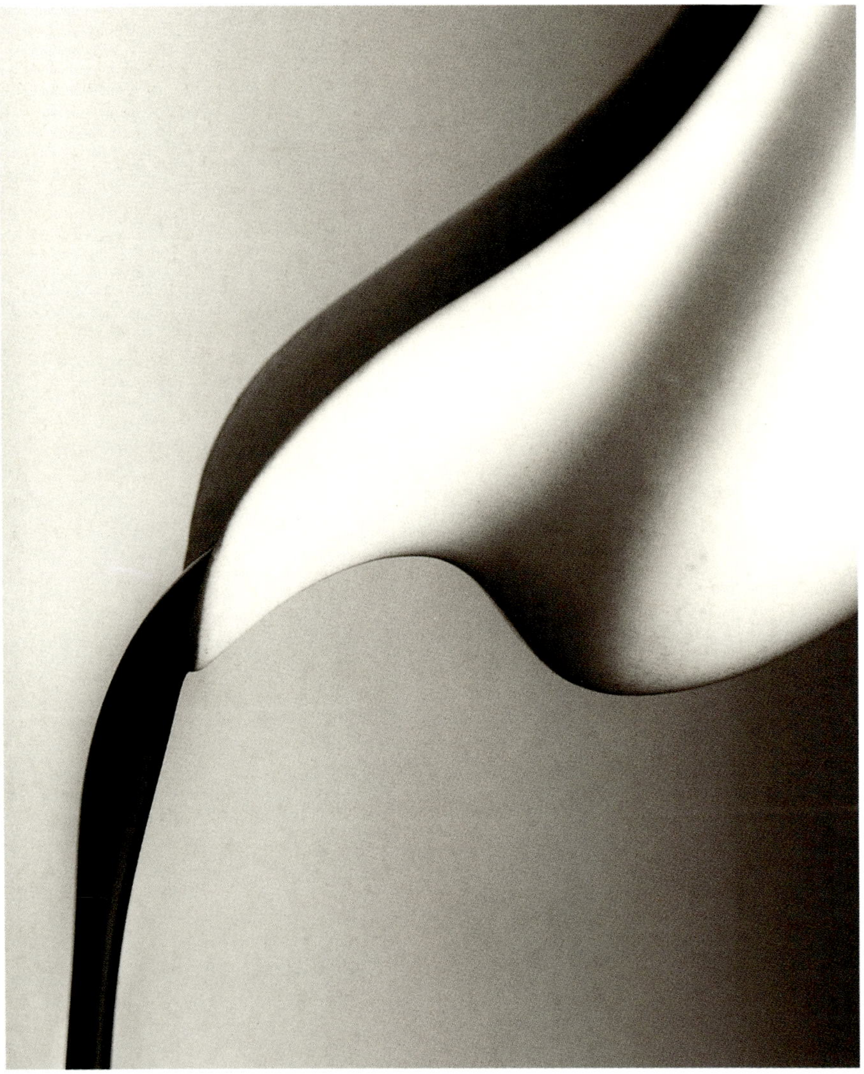

Gravy Boat by Patrice De Villiers
Sinar P 5x4in camera, 210mm lens, Agfapan 100 film.
Exposure 1/250sec at f/16

I was asked to produce this picture of a gravy boat pouring gravy for a **Sunday Times** editorial piece, and I decided to shoot in black and white because I thought this suited the subject. In the studio we had to devise a way of setting the picture up that would allow the pour to be consistent. Our solution was to hold the gravy boat in a clamp at a 45 degree angle and to hide inside it a 3/4in diameter pipe through which gravy could be poured on cue.

That was as technical as it got, and I counted down with my assistant and on three he poured the gravy and I pressed the shutter when I thought the moment was right. I couldn't look directly through the camera, so I placed my head low down and as close to the lens as possible so that I got some idea of what the camera was seeing, but a picture like this is always a little hit and miss. You might get the picture on the first sheet of film, or it might not happen until sheet 20.

By holding the gravy boat in position, however, we ensured that at least one element was stable, and that was vital, because it meant that we could line the camera up on that, something that would have been impossible had someone been pouring by hand.

The liquid pouring from the gravy boat is the real thing, because we had to make sure that its viscosity looked right, and it was easier not to have to fake anything. We may have made it a little stronger than usual, but otherwise this part of the picture was completely straight.

Patrice De Villiers

Pointer The gravy boat was a beautiful shape, and I was very anxious not to lose its curves, so I had to take care with the lighting to ensure that some shadow was thrown to emphasise these. The light I used was flash, because I needed the fast speed to ensure that the pouring liquid was frozen, and I went for a type known as a 'fish fryer', so called because of its rectangular shape. This was positioned at 45 degrees to the gravy boat, from above and to the left of the camera position, and a white polystyrene board was used opposite this to throw a little light back into the shadows to allow some detail to register there.

My Favourite Tip I wanted some graduated tone on the background, and yet I didn't want to have to light this area separately. The solution was to use a device like a flag, known as a Gobo, which directed light from the fish fryer very precisely into this area, and it helped to set the gravy boat off perfectly against its background.

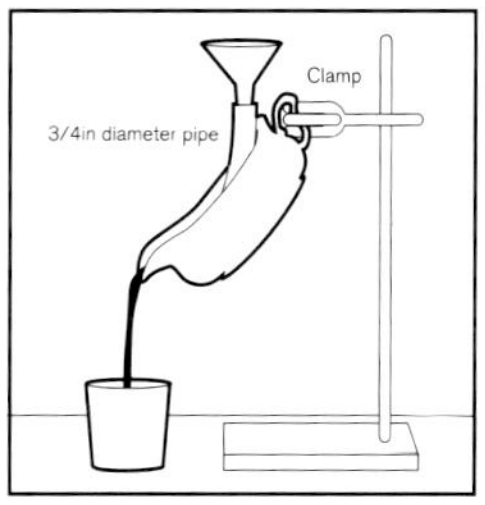

"I set the lily up against a plain white background, and placed it close to a window so that it was receiving plenty of non-directional light."

Technique

Curves by Gerry Coe
Contax RTS 2 camera, 50mm lens, 21mm extension tube, Agfa APX 100 film. Exposure one second at f/22

I've developed a technique for portraiture that gives me an effect that resembles a pencil drawing, and I decided to apply this to my personal still life work. This picture of an arum lily is the result, and I think the delicate nature of this print has ideally suited the subject matter.

I set the lily up against a plain white background, and placed it close to a window so that it was receiving plenty of non-directional light. A card reflector helped to bounce some illumination back on to the scene, and this gave me all the modelling that I required. I was looking to produce a negative that was quite dense but which wouldn't give me a contrasty print, and I bracketed to achieve a perfect result, ending up with one that was ideal for the purpose at around two stops overexposed.

I printed this on Kentmere's Document Art Grade Two paper – Grade Three would have taken away the subtlety – and, by making several exposures on a test strip, I was able to judge how much exposure to give to achieve a result where the tones were only just registering and there were no blacks.

For me the result proves that you don't require a full range of tones to make a perfect picture. I love the effect that this technique gives me and, by varying the exposure given at the printing stage, it's possible to produce a range of different looks to suit all kinds of tastes.

Gerry Coe

Close-up To achieve the kind of close-up that I wanted, where I could really move into the flower and explore its curves and textures, I used the middle of my three extension tubes. The extension tube is a tube of similar diameter to the lens mount with suitable fittings for attaching the lens to one end and the camera body to the other. They can be used individually or in combination with each other to achieve greater magnification. Although easy to fit and use, there is a price to pay, in that there will be an increase in exposure times, typically of a stop, and the focusing range is affected, which is why I needed to stop down to f/22 to keep the flower in focus. For still life, however, a long exposure is rarely a problem, and extension tubes offer one of the most practical and cost-effective ways of achieving close-up pictures that there is.

Printing and Processing I developed the Agfa APX 100 film that I was using in Rodinol developer, a chemistry that I use all the time for the sake of consistency. For a picture of this kind it was perfect because, although I find that it doesn't give me the finest grain, it does make the grain extremely sharp, which helped to emphasise the pencil effect that I was after.

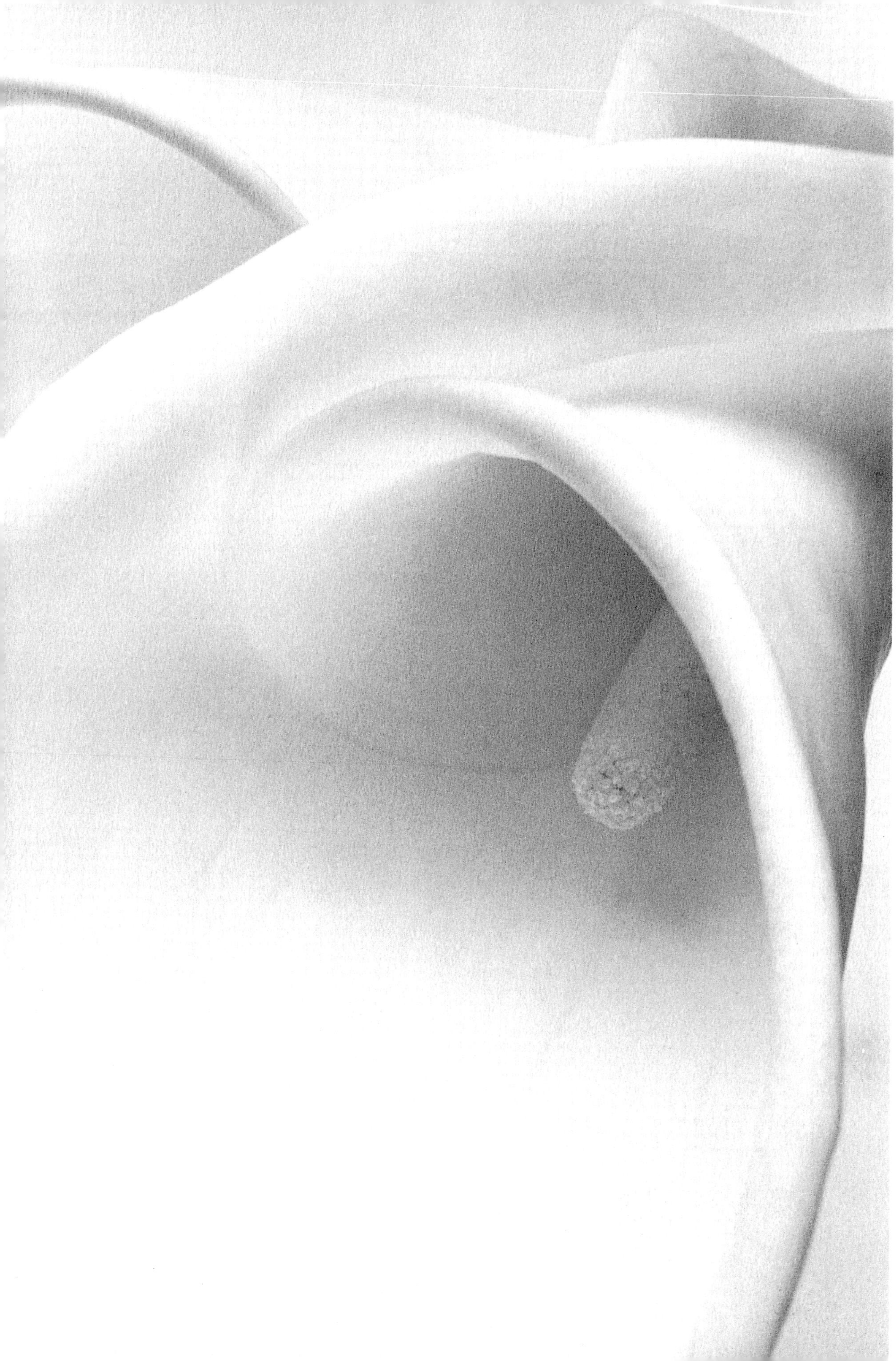

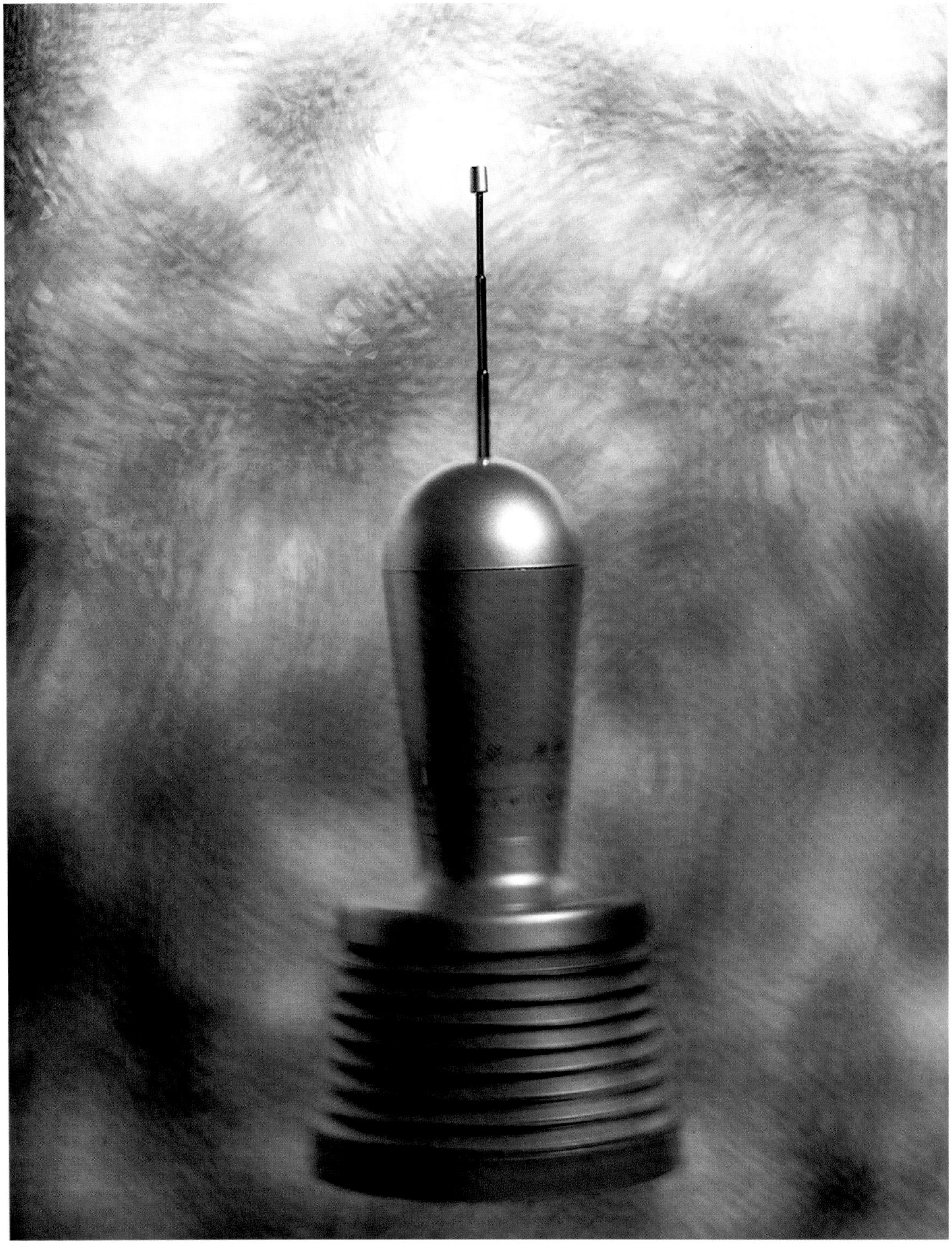

I'm always looking out for interesting objects that I think will make good subjects for still life pictures, and when I saw this futuristic radio I knew that I had to buy it. At the time I wasn't sure what kind of photograph it was going to make, and I put it to one side for a few weeks while I thought about the approach I would take. Eventually I started playing around with it, and initially set it up against a plain background. Although this looked all right, the picture only really started to happen when I placed it against a background of textured silver foil, which caught the light and created all kinds of interesting little highlights.

There was still something missing, however, and my next experiment was to put my lighting, which was a single tungsten head bounced from a reflector to the left of the camera, through a wooden framework, which was designed to break it up and to throw shadows across the scene. Again this didn't really work, but I happened to look through part of the framework with the camera and I suddenly noticed how, when it was close to the lens and completely out of focus, it formed areas of soft focus randomly throughout the picture.

I eventually chose to use a framework that was slightly smaller, and this was the result that I achieved, and I heightened the effect by selecting a wide aperture – f/8 – for the lens, so that the depth of field was kept to an absolute minimum.

Tim Brightmore

Futuristic Radio by Tim Brightmore
Sinar Norma 5x4in camera, 120mm lens, Agfa Scala transparency film ISO 200. Exposure 1/8sec at f/8

Pointer I'm always scouring specialist graphics shops for paper and reflective materials that might make interesting backgrounds for my still life work. There are all kinds of things that work brilliantly: layers of plastic covered in miniature fresnel screens, sheets of highly reflective packaging, highly coloured pieces of card. Everything is filed away in a drawer, where it waits until the day when I find a use for it, and the right background can prove to be inspirational.

My Favourite Tip You can also use a plain background and make it more interesting by throwing a pattern on to it. One of my favourite lighting effects involves directing the light source towards a sheet of frosted glass, and this will then act as a reflector and throw a myriad of highlights and shadows up behind the subject.

Technique

Centaur by Eric Howard
Contax RTS 3 camera, 35–135mm macro lens, Agfa APX 100 film. Exposure three seconds at f/8

An antique dealer in the town of Sherborne in Dorset, where I have a home, acquired this wonderful statuette of a centaur. Its history is amazing: it dates from around the seventh century BC, and it was excavated in Greece in the 1930s by two ladies who brought it back to this country. Just four to five inches high, it's made of solid gold. It was a real privilege to be able to borrow it for the shoot, and I wanted to make it the focus of my picture, while making its surroundings complementary.

I decided to play around with differential focus to try to produce something that was intriguing, and yet still allowed the centaur to dominate. So many images I've seen have featured a foreground that's out of focus, while the background has been sharp, so here I thought I'd turn the principle on its head and focus closely on the figure and allow the background to fall away. My wife Debra took up position around four to five feet behind the figure, and I asked her to lean into her arms so that they effectively created a frame around her face. Although she's registered so softly, you can still pick up on the fact that there is a person there, and I like the idea that this could be a romantic maiden in the background seen against a figure resembling Cupid.

"I decided to play around with differential focus to produce something that was intriguing, and yet still allowed the centaur to dominate."

The fact that I was using quite a wide aperture, combined with the macro setting on the zoom, ensured that the depth of field that I achieved was minimal. I still needed to arrange the figure carefully, however, so that his head fell against an area of light tone, and didn't blend in to the surroundings. On a technical level it got no more complicated than that, with lighting provided by the natural illumination flooding through three large Georgian windows just to the left of the camera position.

Eric Howard

Pointer An added touch has been provided by the reflection of the figure in the highly polished surface of the table. Had I been looking down on the subject from a higher position I would have picked up very little of this. As I dropped down to a position close to front-on to the figure, however, the reflection was revealed, and ultimately became an important element of the composition that I achieved.

My Favourite Tip Whenever I'm looking to use a very slow shutter speed, such as here, I'll always use a cable release to fire the camera's shutter, even if everything is mounted on a sturdy tripod. The cable release, which is a relatively cheap accessory, simply screws into the top of the shutter button, and allows me to fire the camera from a distance of a few inches away with the minimum of vibration. Firing by hand, however, it's virtually impossible not to create a tiny bit of camera shake, which will affect the quality of the final picture.

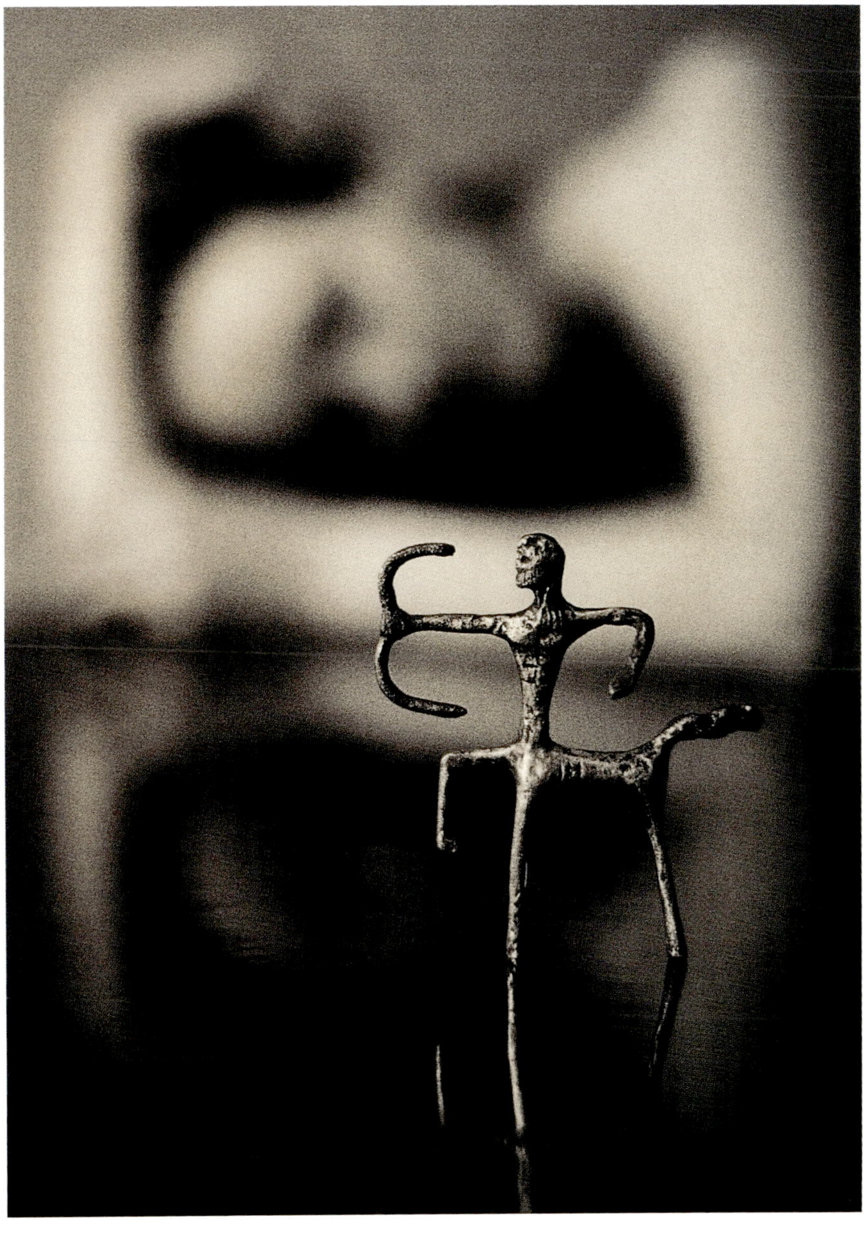

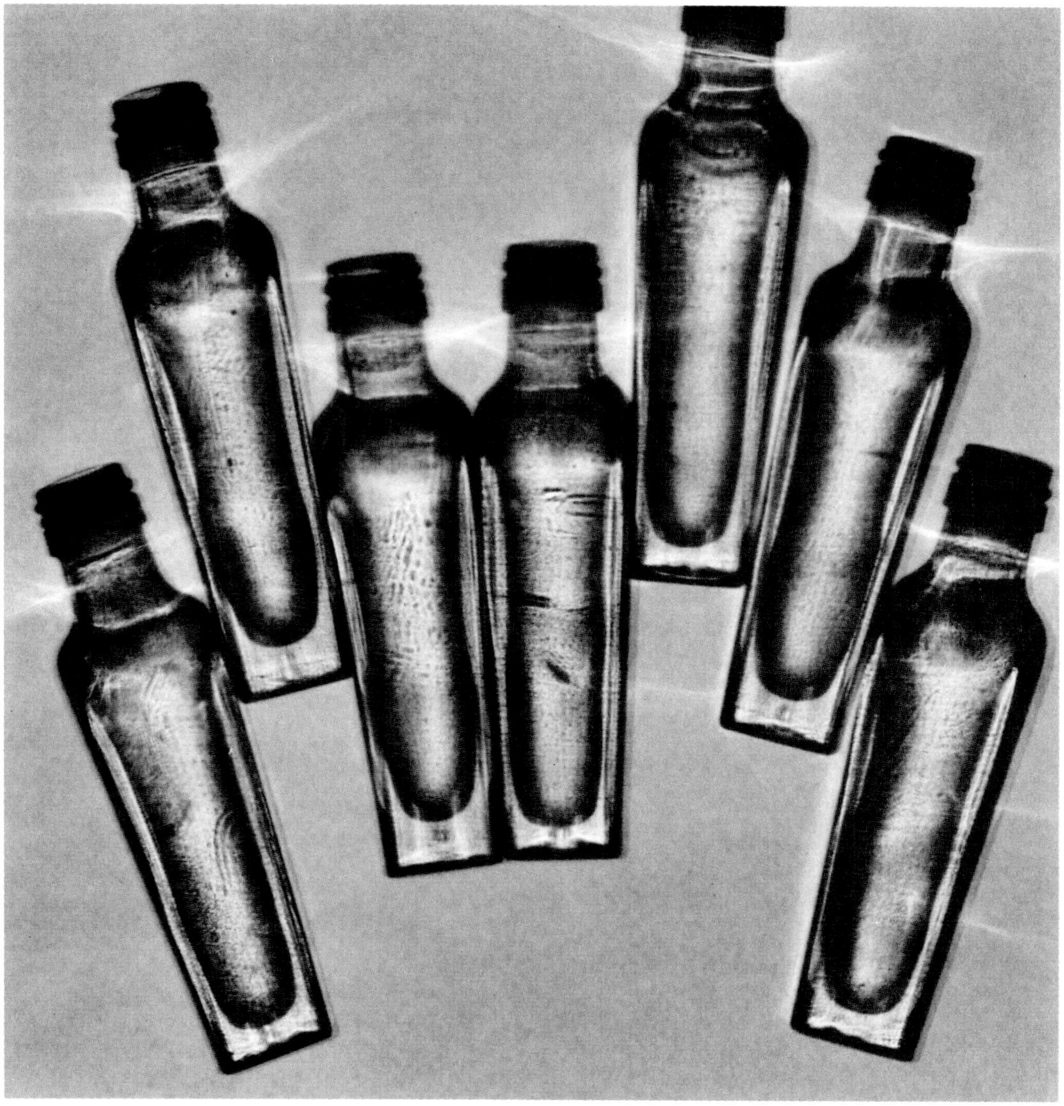

Technique

Contemporary Packaging by Manuela Höfer
Photograms on Ilford Multigrade paper

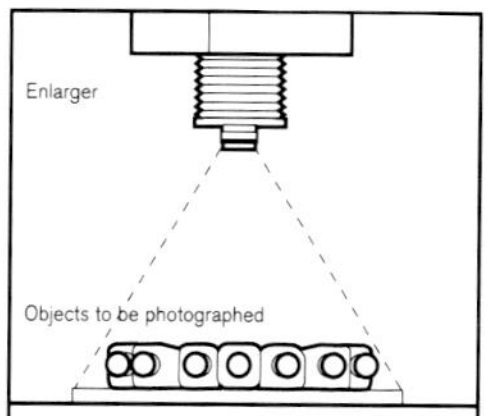

The photogram technique requires no negative as the objects leave their impression directly on to the printing paper

Photograms are not like conventional photographs at all. No camera is involved, and there is no negative as such. Instead the object itself is used to create the picture, and what you achieve is, in effect, a life-size contact print of whatever it was that was placed on the printing paper for the duration of the exposure. It's a technique that dates right back to the dawn of photography itself.

The theory is simple enough: conventional printing paper is sensitive, and will darken, once exposed to light and processed. That's how printing with an enlarger works, with the lighter parts of the negative creating darker areas while the dark areas define where the highlights go. If, however, you discard the idea of a negative and substitute instead an object that's placed directly on the paper under safelight conditions, you will be able to record a negative record of its image on to the paper by flashing it with light and then processing in the usual way. In its simplest form, you could just put your hand on the paper, turn the room light on for a second or so and then process to create a picture of the hand's outline with a solid black background. I decided to take the process much further, however, and used it as the basis for a series I was planning that looked at Western civilisation's obsession with disposable packaging. Even ordinary items, such as the bottles seen here, proved to be the basis for some strong imagery. By experimenting extensively with different light sources for the exposure – such as a torch, coloured lights and room light – I was able to create different effects. I calculated my exposures by using full sheets of paper as test prints. It wasn't an economical way to work, but it was the only way to see exactly what effect I was achieving.

Manuela Höfer

Pointer Because you're recording your image directly on to the paper, what you're producing is a negative photogram. To produce the positive images here, I had to use the original print as a paper negative, and to place it face to face with an unexposed sheet of printing paper and then flash with light again. Once more I found that I had plenty of scope to experiment. Sometimes I would wet both sheets of paper so that contact between the two was very close, while at other times I would expose to make the positive print through a sheet of reticulated glass, to add texture. Even just a straight print would be softened, of course, since the picture would have been exposed through the back of a sheet of paper.

My Favourite Tip Get inspiration from your own circumstances. I was born and raised in the German Democratic Republic, and I grew up in a consumer world very different from the one here. When I arrived in this country and saw the Western way of 'selling through the package', I was amazed by the high level of non-recyclable food packaging that I saw, and used the experience as the basis for a project that looked at society's relentless waste of resources.

Technique

Simple pictures can so often work the best, and when I saw the shape that this particular tulip, one of a bunch that was sitting in a vase in my studio, had naturally taken up, I knew it would make a wonderful still life study. My problem was that I was rushing to a meeting, and yet I knew that the tulip would not be the same when I got back. The tulip won.

I decided that I wanted to play around with the focus in this picture and narrow it right down, and the studio camera that I was using gave me the opportunity to do this through the movements that it incorporated. Basically a studio camera is just a light tight box with a lens on the front and a film container at the back, and by moving the front, or even the back, of the camera from the vertical it's possible to introduce different focusing effects.

Here I swung and tilted the front panel of the camera so that the plane of focus was along a diagonal axis, and this allowed only the tulip itself to be sharp – although if you look carefully you'll see that there's also an area of sharpness on the edge of the table underneath the flower. I used a focus magnifier to examine the ground glass screen at the back of the camera in close-up, so that I knew exactly where my focus was going to fall, and then I took five separate sheets of film, each one utilising a slightly different composure. This was the best study, and it proved to me that I was right to miss that meeting!

Stephen Widdows

Tulip by Stephen Widdows
Sinar 5x4in studio camera, 150mm standard lens, Kodak T-Max 100 film. Exposure 1/125sec at f/5.6

Pointer Lighting here was also kept simple. I placed the flower and vase on a sheet of glass so that a reflection was thrown there, then set up a white background and then lit by bouncing just one flash head from this. It meant that all the light in the scene is reflected – even the front of the tulip head is in shadow – and it gave me just the subtle feel that I was after.

Printing and Processing I decided that I would produce the picture as a bleach print. The start of the process involved me lightly pre-flashing ten sheets of printing paper in the darkroom, all of them at slightly different exposures. This was to expose the paper slightly so that it would acquire a subtle base fog, and lower the contrast. I needed to work with several sheets of paper because it's difficult to know exactly what result you'll achieve until you've undertaken the final processing, and I wanted to give myself a variety of densities to work with. Once I'd made each of my prints I fixed them and then put them into a bath of Farmer's Reducer (a mixture of potassium ferricyanide and sodium thiosulphate that will lighten a print), and pulled each one out when they reached the point I wanted. Only when they were washed again and finally dried did the colour stabilise and I was able to choose the print that I felt had worked the best.

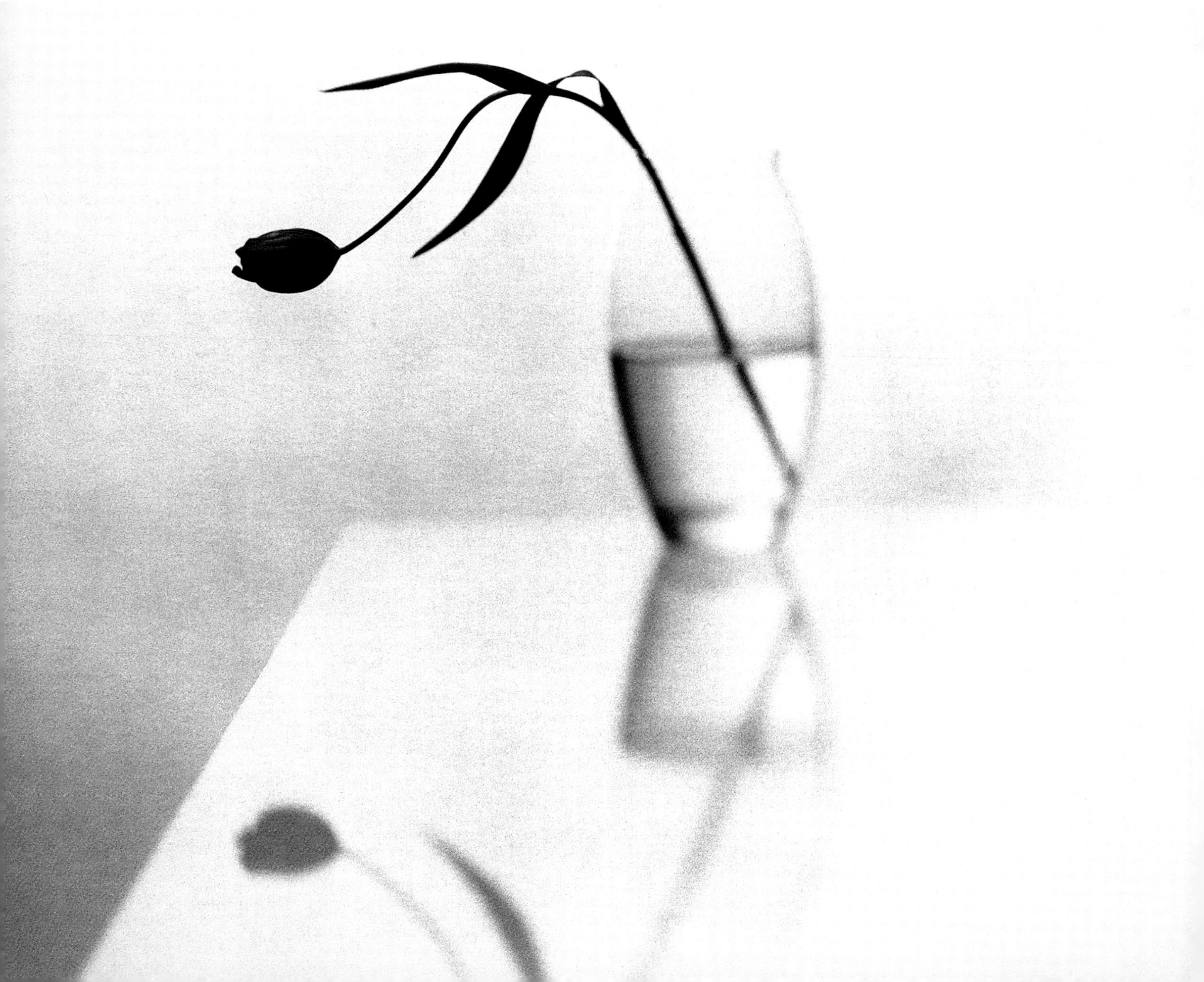

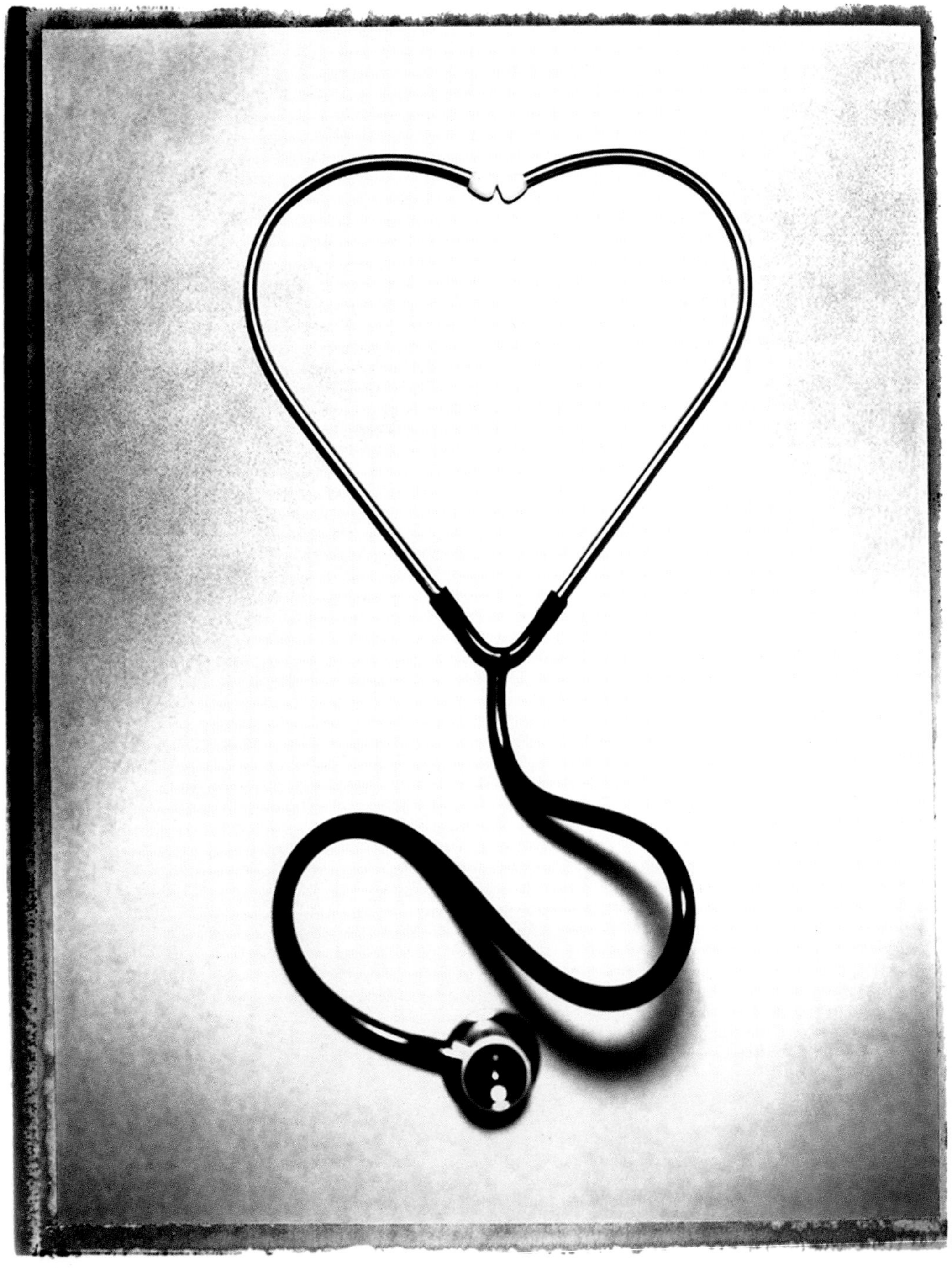

Technique

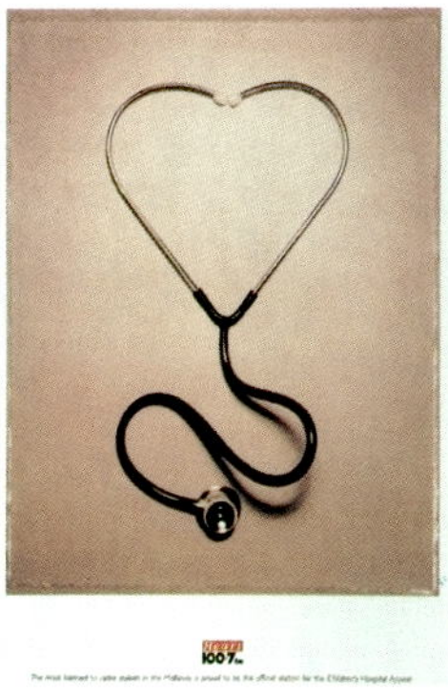

Stethoscope by Stephen Widdows
Sinar 5x4in camera, 150mm lens, Polaroid Type 55 film.
Exposure 1/125sec at f/8

"The starting point was a genuine stethoscope, and I removed the ear-pieces and made new ones from lengths of stainless steel tubing."

I was asked to produce this picture by the Leo Burnett advertising agency to help publicise a charity event that was being held by a London-based radio station, Heart FM, which was aiming to raise money for a children's hospital. The name of the station and the cause it was promoting had suggested this image to art director Mark Tutssel, but I needed to prepare a model to photograph. I had very little time to spare, since the job was given to me on a Friday, and it was required for the following Monday!

The starting point was a genuine stethoscope, and I removed the ear-pieces and made up new ones from lengths of stainless steel tubing that was then given the required shape by being bent carefully around the cylindrical body of a fire extinguisher. Each piece was matching, and together they made the heart shape that I wanted: it was a subtle image, but suited the brief perfectly.

Mark asked me to light this still life so that the steel tubing I'd added would be picked out by a narrow highlight with shadow either side. I achieved this effect, which was similar in some ways to the light provided by a ringflash in that it was virtually shadowless, by using one top light, which was directly over the subject. The added benefit with this arrangement was that the flexible part of the stethoscope, which I'd curled so that it lifted slightly off the paper background, was then able to throw a distinct shadow, which highlighted its shape, and gave the image a little more structure.

I wanted to emphasise the heart shape still further, so I used the movements on my studio camera to achieve the effect. By tilting the front lens panel slightly forward I was able to keep the focus sharp in the top half of the frame while allowing the bottom half to become slightly soft.

Stephen Widdows

Printing and Processing This was a straight print, but I knew that the overall dark tone of the background would detract from the subject. To counter this I decided to apply a very dilute solution – about one tenth of the recommended strength – of the product known as Farmer's Reducer to selectively lighten the area around the stethoscope. Farmer's Reducer is a mixture of potassium ferricyanide and sodium thiosulphate, which will have a greater or lesser subtractive effect on the print depending on the ratio the two are mixed at. By making my solution so weak it meant that the effect took longer to achieve, but I had great control over where and how it was working. Once the area of the print that I was working on had been lightened to the required degree, I simply washed it for ten to 15 minutes to finish the process.

Pointer Large format cameras usually give the photographer the ability to direct a fine degree of control over the image that is produced, through the fact that it's possible for the lens axis to be moved relative to the film plane. These camera movements, which are made possible by the fact that the lens and film panels have the ability to be tilted, moved up and down and swung in different directions, allow focusing to be directed precisely to areas that are required. They can also perform such tasks as correcting tilting verticals, and all the time the photographer will have the ability to see the effect that is being produced by studying the camera's ground-glass viewing screen.

Technique

Acoustic Guitar by Andrew Davis
Pentax ME Super camera, 50mm lens, Kodak T-Max film ISO 100. Exposure 1/30sec at f/8, hand-held

I was playing around with an old acoustic guitar, and was trying to think of a way that I could photograph it that would be interesting and thought-provoking. Eventually this was what I came up with and, in terms of technique, it was relatively simple. Because the guitar had a hollow body, I realised that I could fire a simple hand-held flash in through one of the f-holes, and the light would be picked up through the other one, creating a powerful highlight. Because the light would be contained in just this one small area, however, the surface of the guitar, lit by available light from a window, would still register detail, and the contrast between the two areas would be quite surreal.

I shot the picture unfiltered, but decided that I liked the idea of some soft focus so that the edges of the f-hole would appear hazy, and so I fitted a Cokin 83 diffuser over the enlarger lens to achieve this result. I also cropped in a little at this stage, and tightened up the composition. It's rarely necessary to feature the whole of an object in a still life study for the result to be effective, and here the detail of the guitar that I've concentrated on has told the full story.

Andrew Davis

Printing and Processing To finish my print, which I made on old cadmium-rich Agfa Record Rapid paper, I decided to add some tone. The first step was to mix up a strong selenium solution, and the print was immersed in this – with great care and in a well ventilated room because of the dangers this toner presents – for a short period. When the highlights started to pick up some colour, I removed the print and washed it very carefully for around an hour to remove as much of the selenium toner as I could. The next stage was to immerse the print in the bleach bath of a sepia toner, so that the density of the print was reduced. When it had reached the stage where it had turned a tobacco colour, I removed it but, instead of developing it back up in sepia toner, I washed it and stopped the process there. The result is a print with a very delicate colour, which I'm told is not particularly stable: I like the effect, however, and it's survived for quite a few years now.

My Favourite Tip With still life I like to use found objects such as this, and to experiment with the lighting and the framing I use. I couldn't spend a day painstakingly building up and lighting vegetables in an intricate studio set: in photography you have to play to your strengths and I like to be more spontaneous.

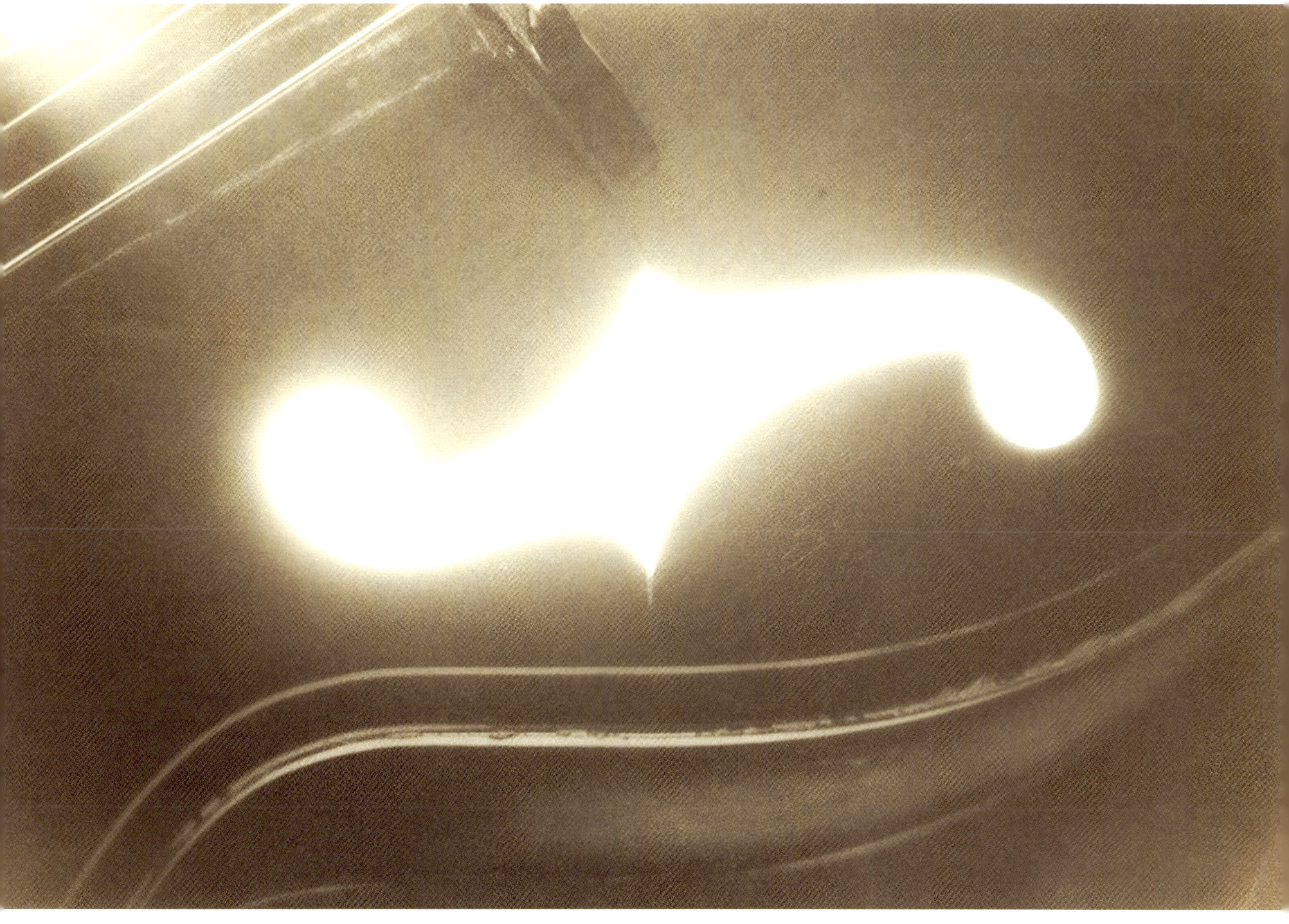

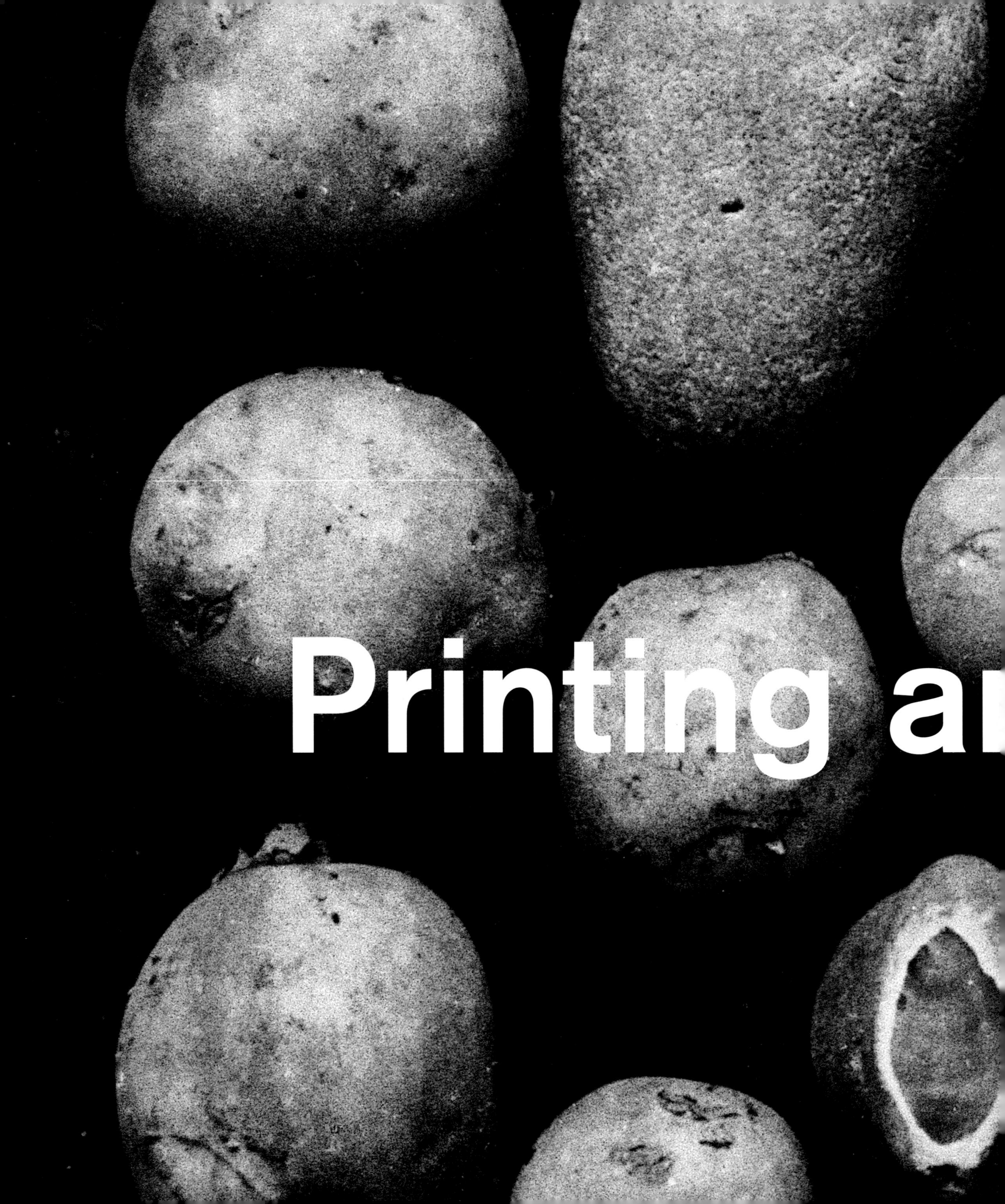
Printing a

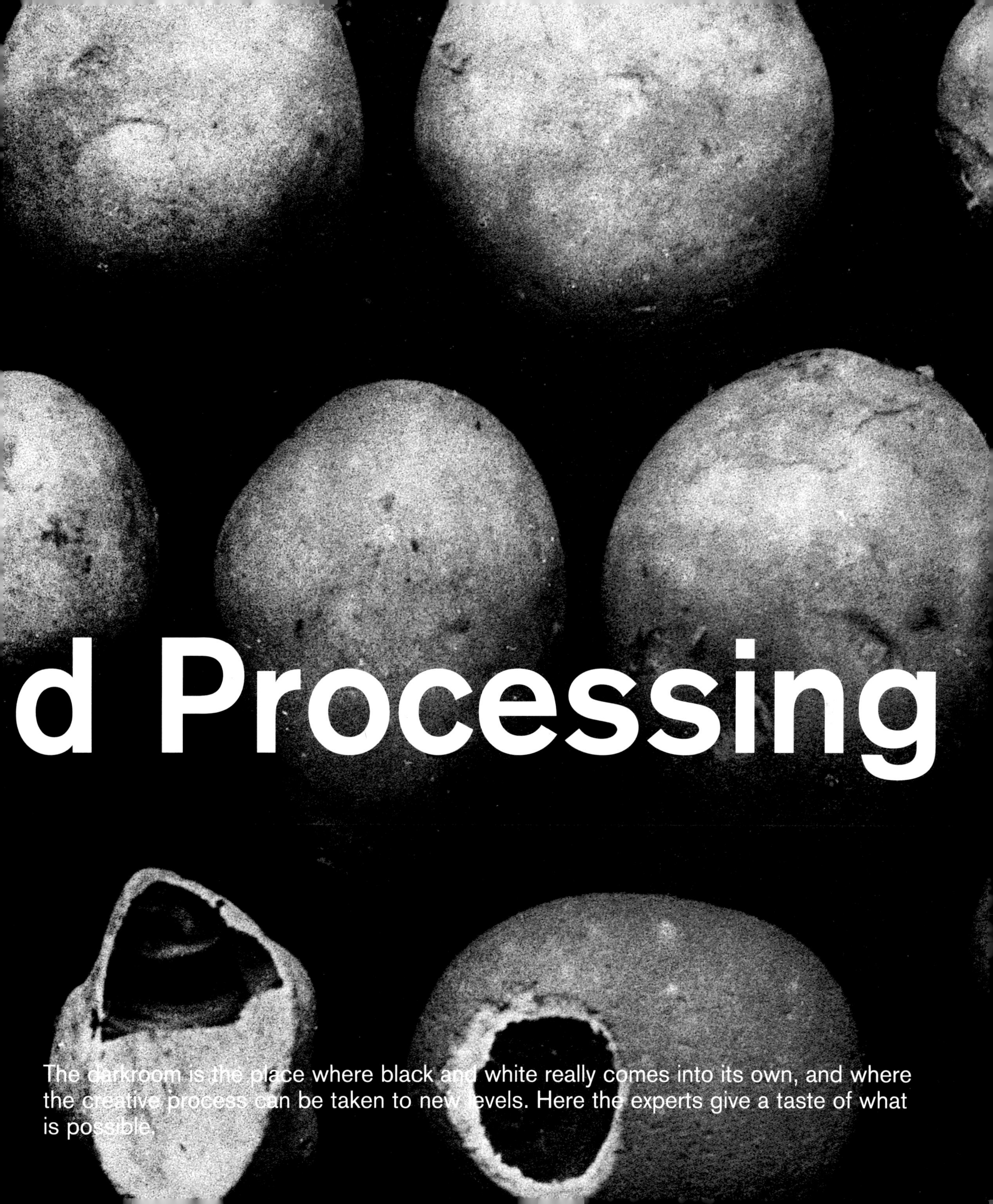

d Processing

The darkroom is the place where black and white really comes into its own, and where the creative process can be taken to new levels. Here the experts give a taste of what is possible.

I don't use an enlarger in my darkroom, and instead contact print directly from my negatives on to platinum/palladium paper that I've coated myself. I've had little interest in silver printing since I became enthralled with the tonality and textures of a platinum print I saw in a Paul Strand portfolio 20 years ago, and all my personal work is now reproduced in this way.

I start with French watercolour paper, which I've found to be the best surface for me to work on. This will have been previously treated with sizing chemicals, however, and so I have to remove all traces of this by immersing the paper in an oxalic acid bath, and then washing thoroughly and drying and pressing the paper to prepare it for coating.

The chemicals I use to make up the emulsion are potassium chloroplatinite (platinum), ferric oxalate, potassium chlorate and sodium chloropalladite (palladium). Because there are heavy metals involved, there are dangers involved in handling, and I always wear a gas mask to avoid inhaling the dust when I'm mixing chemicals.

Although the emulsion is sensitive to ultraviolet light, I can coat the paper by fairly bright (500W) tungsten light in my 'darkroom', which I refer to as 'the light room'. For coating I use brushes that are custom-made for me by a traditional brush maker, and these are made of bristle which won't absorb the solution. They have to be soft enough not to damage the paper, but stiff enough to give an even coating.

Once the paper has been coated, I'll blow dry it with a hairdryer. It's an extremely time consuming business, and I will probably only manage to coat around 20 sheets in a single day, and then these will have to be kept moisture free and used up within a couple of days. I'll need to test each batch that I've made to determine the exact exposure it will require, and to check on the contrast that it will give me.

To expose a print, I'll place the negative directly on the paper's surface and then put this in a printing frame, and expose it to light from a mercury vapour lamp. Eventually the image will start to print out on the surface, producing a faint brown image. This is then developed by using a mixture made up of equal amounts of water and ammonium citrate. The image comes up virtually immediately, and then needs to be left for one minute and washed thoroughly. There's no fixer required, but the print will need to be cleared and then washed for around an hour and dried, using a net screen.

Kenro Izu

Pair of Lilies by Kenro Izu
Deardorff 14x11in camera, vintage lens, Kodak Plus X film ISO 125. Exposure not revealed

Pointer Although it sounds complicated, the platinum/palladium process is quite straightforward, although quality control is all-important, because my prints are designed for the fine art market. An awful lot of them end up in the trash, because anything that is inferior can't be exhibited and has to be destroyed. I'll produce a batch of around eight to nine at any one time, and won't know until they have dried if they are ok.

Technique The platinum/palladium process works best with a negative that is very contrasty and dense. If you were taking a picture in a normal way, you would consider that the picture had been overexposed to the point where it wouldn't print properly even on a Grade Zero silver paper. I've learned over many years the kind of negative that will work for me, and I've had to adapt my exposures to take this 'overexposure' into account.

A full account of platinum and palladium printing methods, plus background on many other vintage emulsions, can be found in the book **Spirit of Salts** by Randall Webb and Martin Reed. The book can be ordered through the Internet at: http://www.silverprint.co.uk, or email sales@silverprint.co.uk

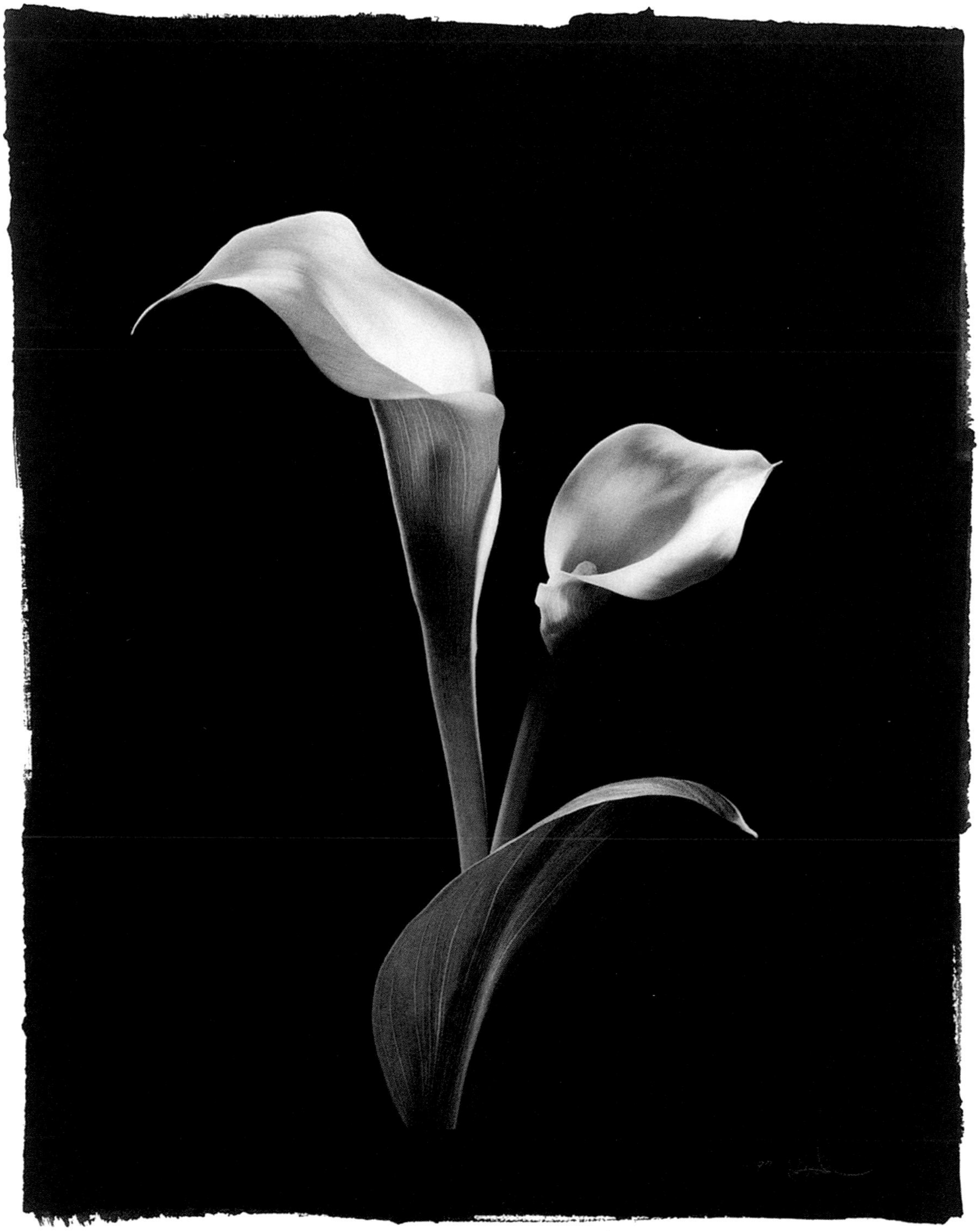

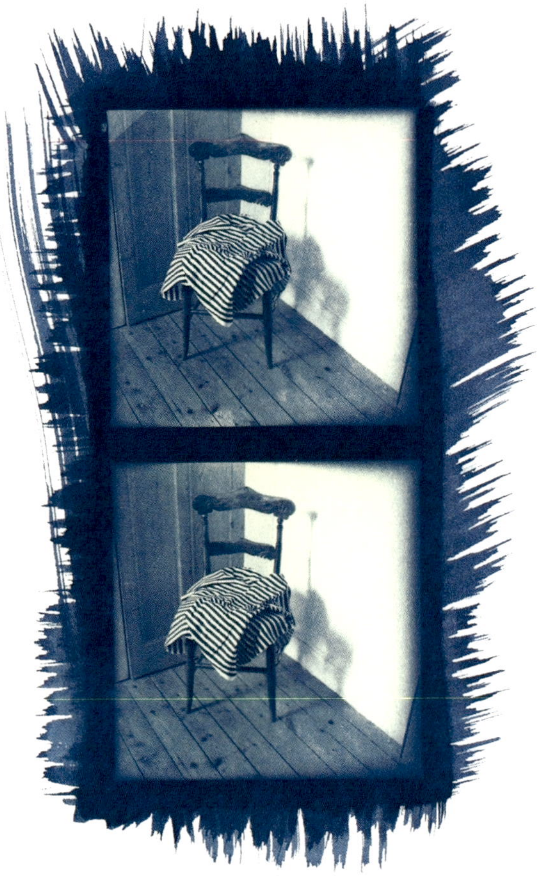

I saw the potential of this scene one morning in my house, and shot it on a tripod using just available light. This simple picture was the perfect starting point for a Cyanotype print. This is a printing process that was perfected by Sir John Herschel as far back as 1842 and which, in terms of being cheap to mix and easy to use, still has much to offer those who wish to produce their own emulsions.

To start with, in normal room lighting or subdued daylight you need to mix ten grams of ferric ammonium citrate (use the green variety, not the brown) in 50ml of tap water, and then pour the solution into a 250ml brown stoppered bottle. Then you need to mix four grams of potassium ferricyanide (not ferrocyanide) in 50ml of tap water. This should then be poured into a second brown bottle. Then you need to mix equal quantities of both solutions, say around ten millilitres of each, in a china saucer, ready to be brushed onto the paper. You can use a wide variety of papers as a base for your Cyanotype print, indeed any cheap cartridge or drawing paper will do provided it does not contain alkali, and has sufficient wet strength to withstand soaking in water for five or ten minutes. When you coat your paper make sure that you don't put too much liquid on at first, because if you create puddles these will eventually dry to form a crust that will peel off later. If you do put too much on, wipe off the surplus with a piece of cotton wool or kitchen roll.

When the paper is covered with a pale yellow-green coating, you should dry it immediately with a hairdryer. Then load the negative and coated paper together in a contact printing frame, or under a sheet of heavy, and clean, glass. This should then be placed under an ultraviolet lamp or sunlight and, in a few minutes, you will see the brushed margins of the print turn from yellow-green to dark green and then to blue.

Open the hinged back of the frame at five-minute intervals to check the progress of the exposure, but resist the temptation to take it out when it 'looks right', because it will still be underexposed at this point. Continue exposing until the shadows take on a gunmetal grey appearance, and only the brightest highlights remain yellow green. It is a fairly slow business and even in bright sun the exposure can take up to 30 minutes. After exposure remove the print and wash it in a dish with frequent changes of water until all the yellow background has disappeared and the image, including the brushed edge, is bright blue. As it is exposed to the oxygen in the atmosphere the iron in the iron compounds present will oxidise and turn a deeper shade of blue. Rinse the print in water, and then hang it on a line to dry or use a hairdryer for speed. You can speed up this oxidisation by rinsing the print in a dish of water containing a teaspoon full of hydrogen peroxide.

Randall Webb

Printing and Processing

Chairs by Randall Webb
Hasselblad Superwide 6x6cm camera, 38mm lens,
Kodak T-Max 400 film rated at ISO 200. Exposure 1/4sec at f/8

"This simple picture was the perfect starting point for a Cyanotype print."

Technique Coating the paper is relatively simple, but will need practice. To brush the emulsion on, as I did here, take your sheet of paper and attach it to a flat piece of hardboard with a strip of masking tape along each edge to hold it flat. Now take the negative, or negatives as here, and place them on the paper and very lightly mark where you want its position to fall. Now take the saucer containing the emulsion, and dip into it with a flat paintbrush (the best are flat wooden handled 'hake' brushes from any good art supplier) about one inch wide, taking care not to overcharge the brush. Then brush the emulsion onto the paper within the area where the negative will fall, taking care to be gentle to avoid abrading the paper's surface. The paper should absorb the liquid to the extent that, when you look across the surface of the paper, no pools of liquid remain. At this stage you can carry the liquid across your markings to give a small margin of brushed emulsion with a ragged edge. When exposed this will give you the brushed edge that is characteristic of so many old process prints.

My Favourite Tip The Cyanotype process, like so many dating from the last century, relies on contact printing, and if you're using a medium format negative, the result you achieve can be rather small. I get around this by often printing more than one negative, almost like a contact strip. Where the subject is the same, as here, the result can be highly effective, and it increases the amount of image you will have in a print.

From Whitstable by Jennifer Bates
Nikon FM2 camera, 50mm lens, Agfa APX 100 film.
Exposure 1/125sec at f/2.8

This picture has its origins in the fact that I found three stones during a visit to Whitstable in Kent, and I was struck by their shape and textures. They were flint, and one of them featured an almost perfect circular chip, while the other two had pieces broken off in a more jagged manner, and the three of them worked well together as a set.

I then had to decide how to photograph them and, continuing the organic feel, I decided to put down a thick layer of soil and to place the stones in there to keep them stable. At this point, I got the idea of expanding the picture and bringing in further elements that would complement the stones: the idea that I hit on was to surround them with potatoes that were of a similar size, and I made them all up into this symmetrical arrangement. Everything was set up indoors next to a pair of double patio doors which gave a natural light, and I took up a camera position directly overhead, and hand-held for the 1/125sec exposure that was required.

Jennifer Bates

Printing and Processing Looking at the picture, Jennifer Bates thought that it would benefit from an unusual printing process, and she decided to try, for the first time, one of the products collectively known as liquid emulsion. This is, as it suggests, black and white emulsion in a liquid form, which can be applied to a variety of surfaces, which can then subsequently be printed on in much the same way as a standard photographic print. This opens up all kinds of creative possibilities, and some photographers have become proficient at printing on surfaces such as rock, wood and fabric, to great effect.

There are several types of liquid emulsion available, including those produced by Rockland Colloid in the US and those from Kentmere in the UK, and the majority of them have characteristics that are similar. They are a normal contrast bromide emulsion with a high silver content, and contain a good concentration of high bloom gelatin, giving them good adhesion. They are also 'blue sensitive', like most black and white photographic papers, and this means that the emulsions can be used under orange or red safelight conditions.

Jennifer used Silverprint's SE1 emulsion, and decided to make her first liquid light print on a sheet of textured watercolour paper, because its fibrous content allowed the emulsion to bond well. Using a brush and working under safelight conditions, she applied the emulsion to the centre of the paper, creating a roughly square area that was sensitised, but which featured brush marks around the edge. When the paper had been dried (with a hairdryer if necessary) and was ready to expose, she could place it on the baseboard as usual and then use a red filter over the enlarger lens to allow her to frame her negative correctly. It was important that the image was enlarged enough to continue beyond the sensitised edges. This was to avoid the edges of the negative creeping into the picture, because this would have introduced a straight line, which would have ruined the effect she wanted.

Liquid light is processed like standard printing paper, and standard developers such as Agfa Neutol, Kodak Dektol and Ilford PQ Universal are all good to use. Stopbath and fixer are likewise similar to those recommended for normal paper, and the final result should have a similar life span to a bromide print if the emulsion has been correctly applied and developed.

Pointer Coat a separate sheet of paper with the liquid light, and use this as a test strip under the enlarger before introducing the item that you want to print onto. A full run through of the properties of liquid light, and its applications, can be found in the book **Silver Gelatin** by Martin Reed and Sarah Jones, (Working Books, £19.99), which can be ordered through Silverprint at www.silverprint.co.uk or email sales@silverprint.co.uk

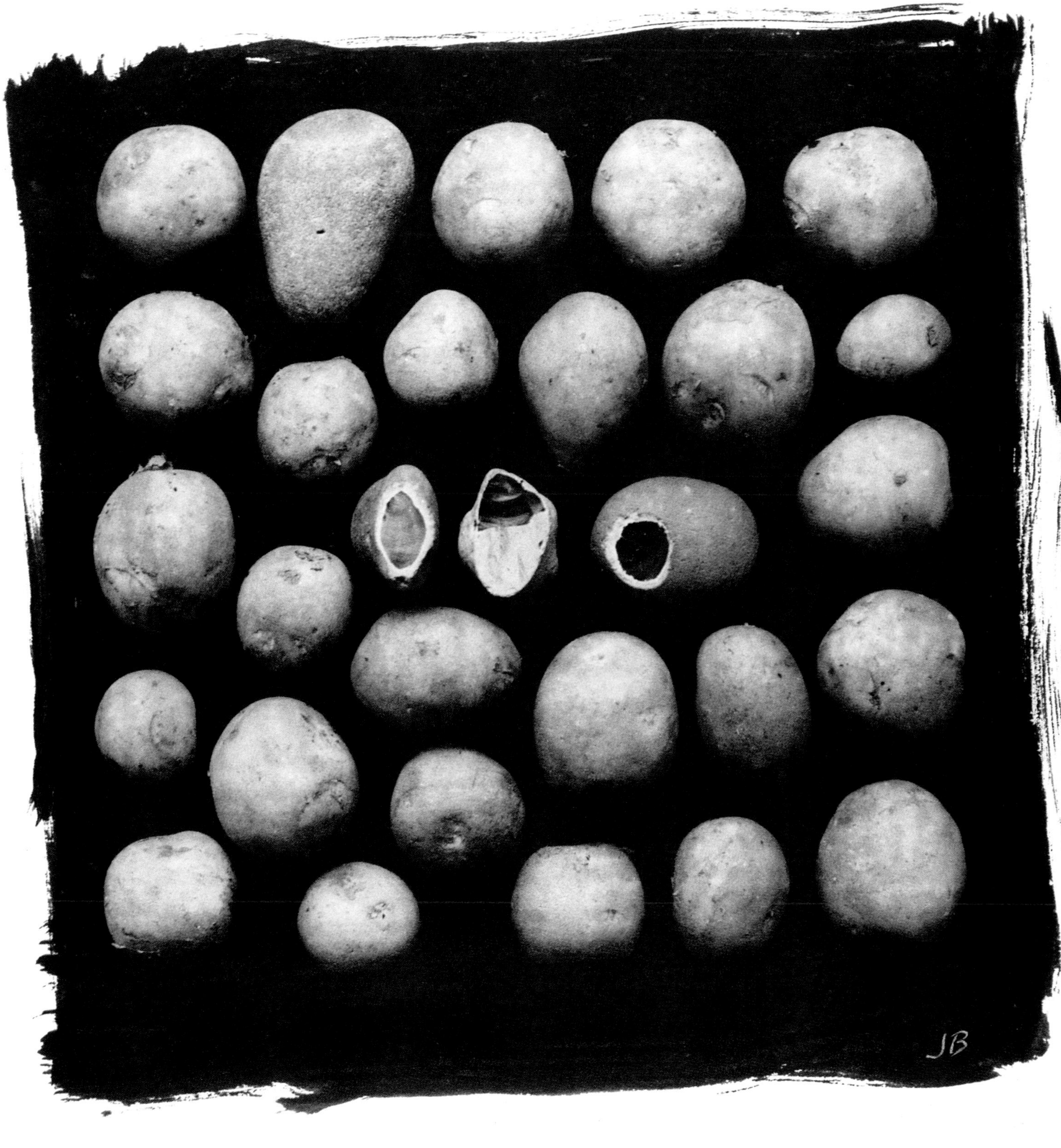
JB

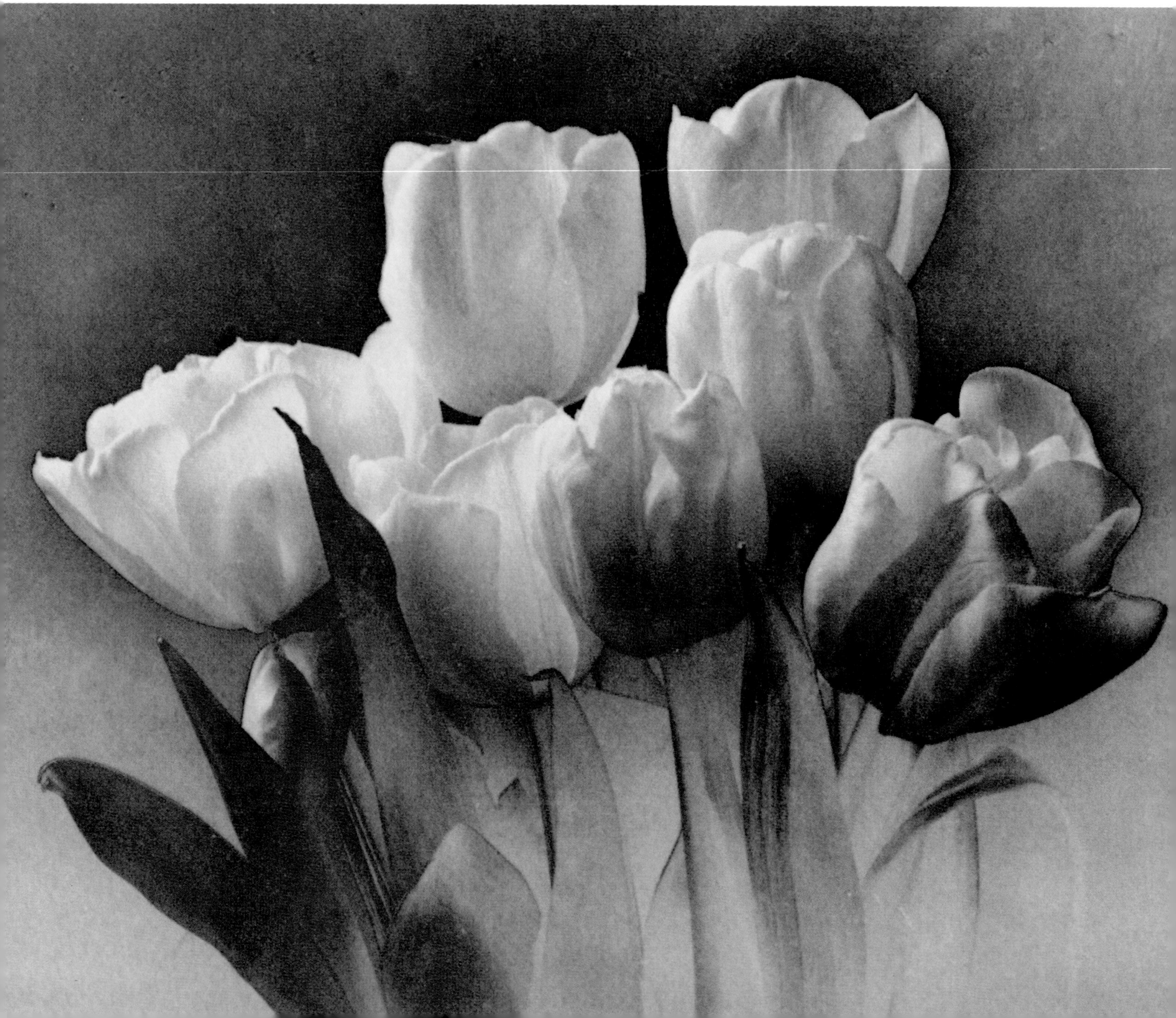

Tulip Study by Randall Webb
Raj 10x8in studio camera with a half-plate reducing back, vintage 12 inch Goerz lens, Ilford FP4 film. Exposure 20 seconds at f/22

This delicate tulip study was enhanced through the partial solarisation of the negative, a technique that involved switching on a 100W white light in the darkroom for around one second about halfway through normal negative development. The effect of this was dramatic because, as development continued after this point, a picture was created where the dark tones of the background had been broken up in a random and ultimately pleasing way. A fine line had also been formed around the edges of the subject. This is particularly noticeable here around the tulip on the right, and it almost appears to be seen in relief against its surroundings as a result.

Strictly speaking, solarisation is reversal, or partial reversal, of the image due to gross overexposure. Also known by some as the Sabattier effect, it's characterised as here by the reversal of weakest densities and the formation of a thin contour line around strong tone boundaries.

This print was made on Kentmere Art Classic paper, and the pink tone that was achieved here was created by developing this chlorobromide paper in Kodalith developer, diluted one to one. Exposure under the enlarger was one and a half minutes and processing time was ten minutes.

Although the technique itself is simple enough, judging precisely how it will affect the picture you're working on is pretty much impossible. Every image that you produce by this method will be unique, which is an attractive thought for photographers who want to achieve something that is very special, but it does mean that results are unpredictable and not repeatable to any exact degree. There is often a high degree of wastage also, because negatives may not always react in the way that you want.

Randall Webb

Technique The picture was set up in my dining room, and I used just window light that was coming from the left-hand side of the tulips as my illumination. To even things up a little, however, I also bounced light back into the scene from the right, using a polystyrene board that had been covered with kitchen foil. The background was the painted wall of the room, which was a deep red. Normally this would have given a background that featured a dark tone, but solarisation has broken this up and lightened the effect.

My Favourite Tip The camera I use was hand-built in India, and I purchased a selection of vintage lenses that were adapted so that they could be used with it. These are beautifully made, but they're so old that they don't feature a shutter, with the result that every exposure has to be over two seconds in length to give me time to complete it by hand! I have a leather-covered lens cap that I could attach and detach to make the exposure, but this could create camera shake, and so I use the black focusing cloth, which is folded up and held over the lens and removed for the necessary exposure time.

Printing and Processing

Still Life 1 by Allan Jenkins
MPP 5x4in camera, 150mm lens, Ilford FP4 film ISO 125.
Exposure one second at f/22

I set this still life up on the top of an old wooden cable reel outside my house, and used a second reel behind to serve as a background. I love to include a mixture of organic things, and to feature textures and shapes from a variety of sources to make my picture. Here I filled a glass container with water, and floated bananas and an artichoke head in this, and also placed lengths of metal rod half-in and half-out to pick up some diffraction. Bubbles formed on the inside of the glass, and this has been picked up by the camera and has become part of the composition too. Other items in the picture were either found – the weathered piece of carved wood, for example, is the front of a drawer that I found in the forest – or borrowed, as in the case of the pair of scissors. I attached the spoon on the left of the picture to a piece of thick string to link it to the composition. I've been heavily influenced by the way that painters such as Juan Sanchez Cotan (1560–1627) and Luis Melendez (1716–1780) use this visual device in their work, and it's something I do quite a lot. I may spend several hours piecing together a composition such as this, to make sure that everything flows and has a reason for being there. Smaller details, such as walnut shells and sunflower seeds here, help to complete the scene. I don't try to make the elements that feature in my pictures too perfect: often a certain amount of decay makes such things as textures more pronounced, and adds to the interest.

Allan Jenkins

Printing and Processing Allan Jenkins regularly uses vintage photographic printing processes, and this picture was produced as a Van Dyke print. The chemistry for this is relatively simple, and to begin you need to mix up solutions in three small measuring jars. Solution A is 35ml of distilled or purified water and ten grams of ferric ammonium citrate (green). Solution B is again 35ml of water, this time mixed with two grams of tartaric acid powder. Finally solution C is 35ml of water again, mixed with four grams of silver nitrate. Care should be taken not to spill the crystals, since they are highly corrosive and will stain everything brown. Solution A now needs to be poured into solution B and mixed thoroughly. Then silver solution C needs to be added a few drops at a time to this, stirring all the time until it's mixed. Pour this mixture into a brown bottle to keep it fresh, and it should have a life of several months.

Now you can coat your paper with this liquid in roomlight conditions, making sure that it's well brushed into the paper and that no puddles are left. Dry this with a hairdryer, at which stage the emulsion will be a pale yellow green colour. To make a print, place your negative – which should ideally be slightly contrasty – dull side down on the paper, tack it to the paper in one corner with a small strip of sticky tape and place it in your printing frame. This will then need to be exposed in the sun or under an ultraviolet lamp: after a few minutes the brushed edges outside the image will turn a deep orange colour, and a few minutes later you can check a corner of the image carefully. When the print has reached the right density, remove it from the frame and wash it under a cold tap for around five minutes. While the print is washing, make up your fixer solution. This consists of 250mls of warm tap water and 25 grams of plain hyposulphate, and this then needs to be added to 250mls of cold tap water and poured into a dish.

When the washing is complete, place the print into the fixer and leave it for around five minutes. The image will change colour to become a rich chocolate brown. The print then needs to be washed for around 30 minutes in running water, and then hung up to dry. When completed, it will have changed to a slightly deeper shade of brown.

Further reading For more information on vintage processes refer to **Spirit of Salts** by Randall Webb and Martin Reed, available from the Internet at http://www.silverprint.co.uk or email sales@silverprint.co.uk

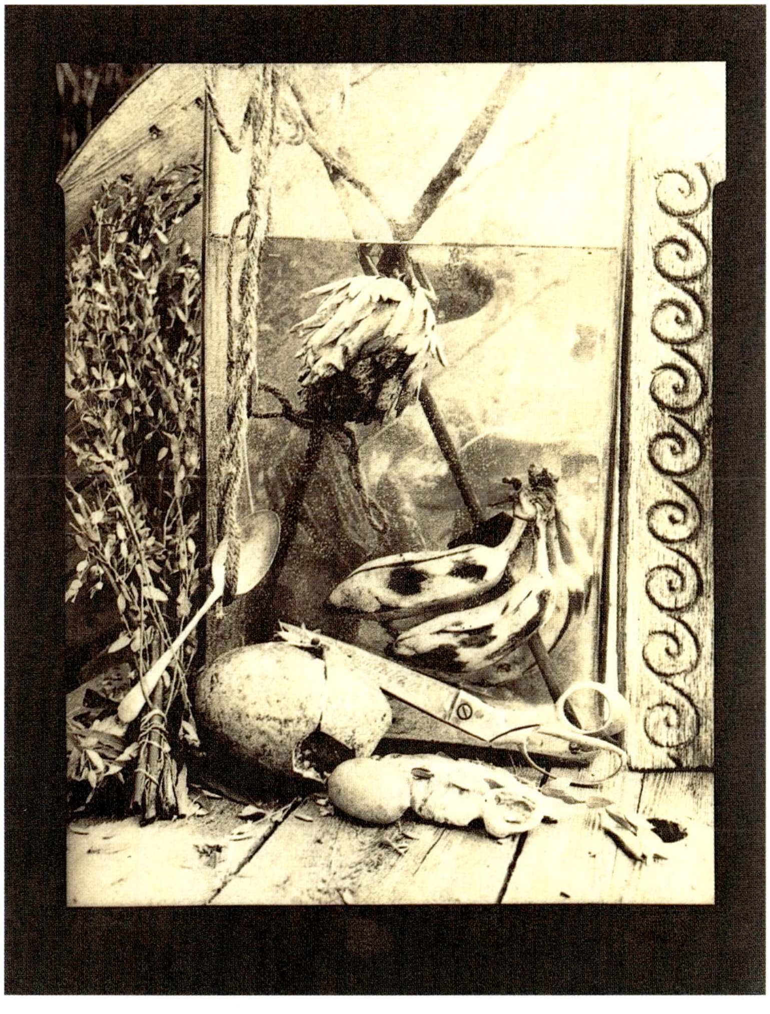

"Bubbles formed on the inside of the glass, and this has been picked up by the camera and has become part of the composition."

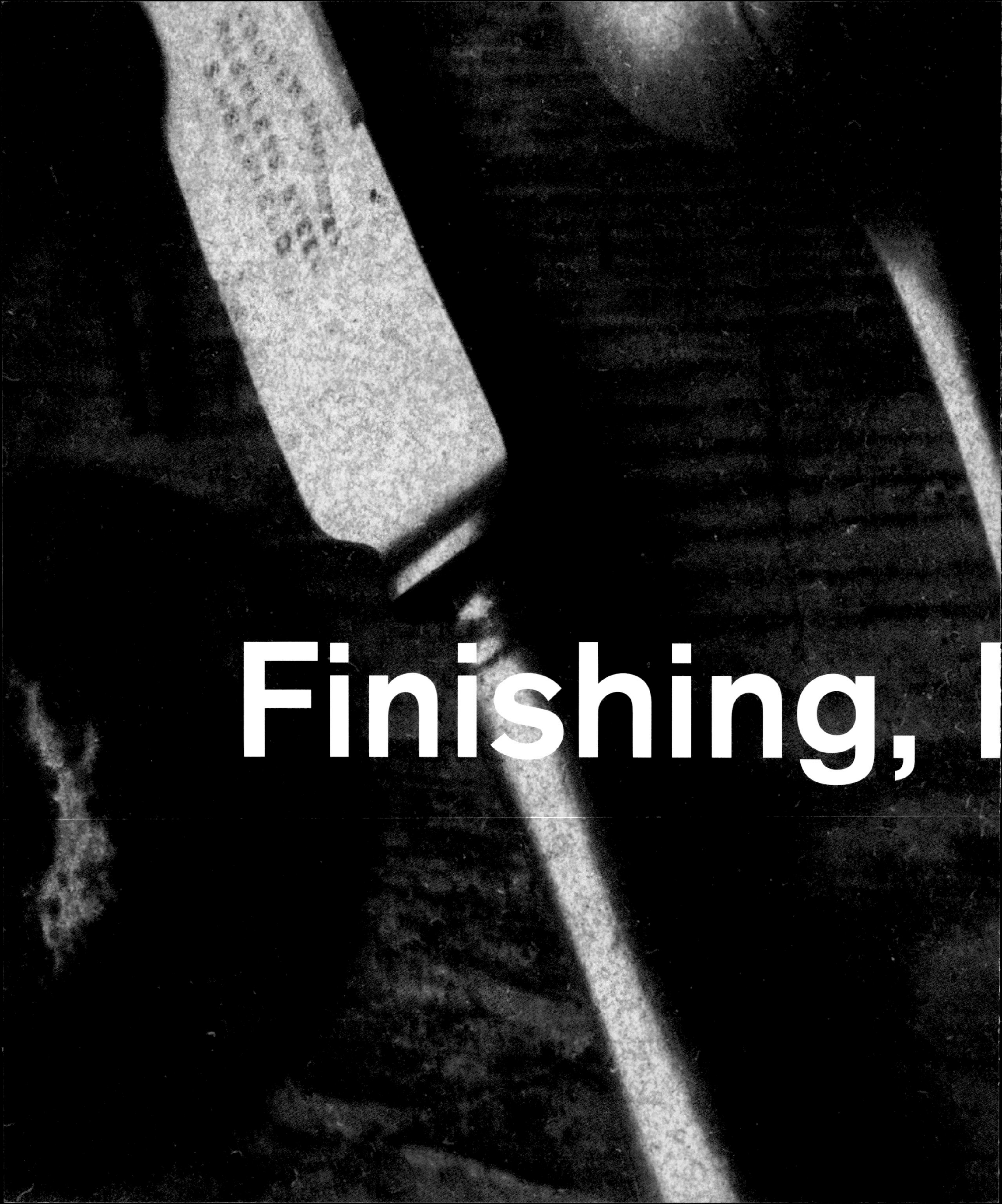

Finishing,

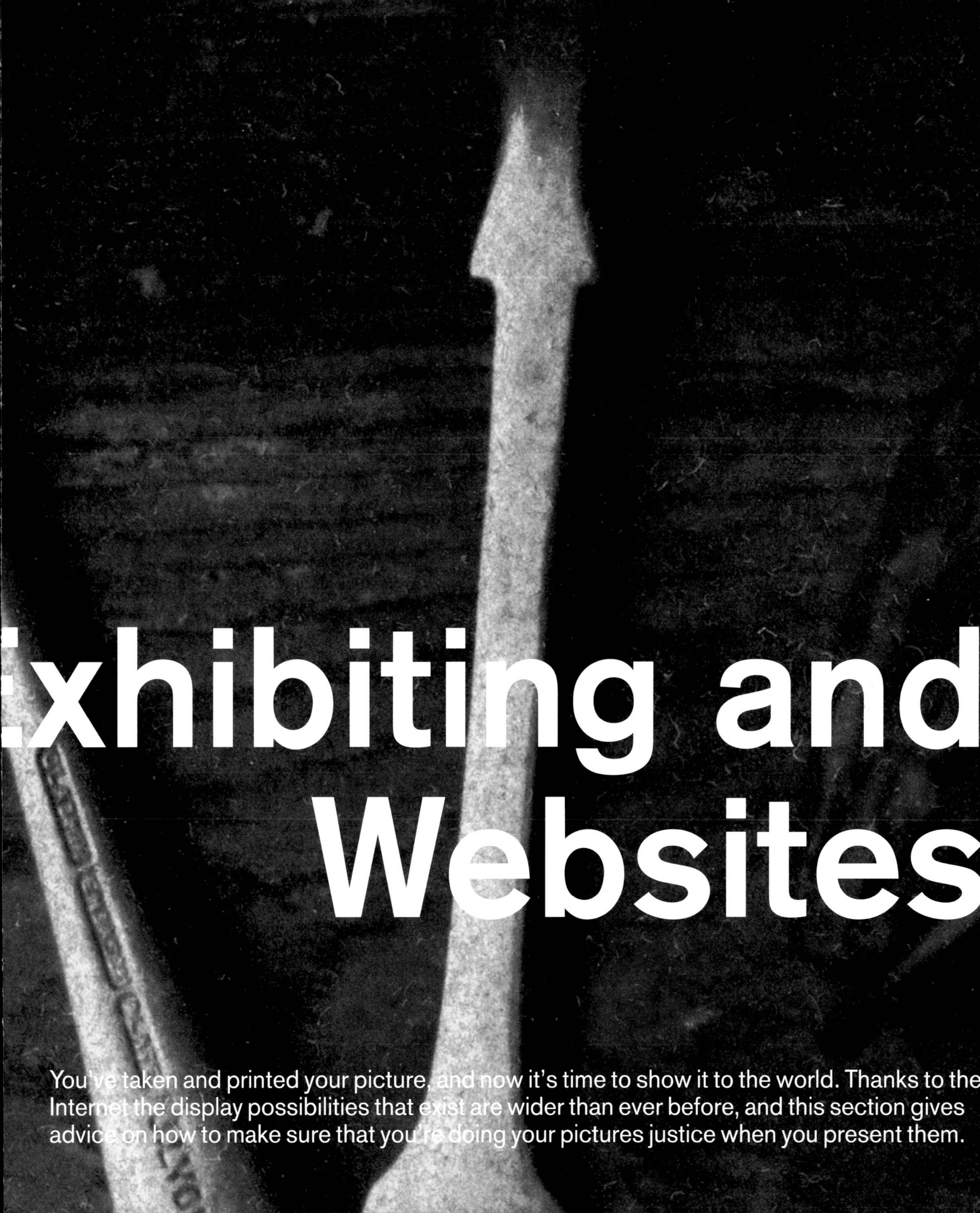

Exhibiting and Websites

You've taken and printed your picture, and now it's time to show it to the world. Thanks to the Internet the display possibilities that exist are wider than ever before, and this section gives advice on how to make sure that you're doing your pictures justice when you present them.

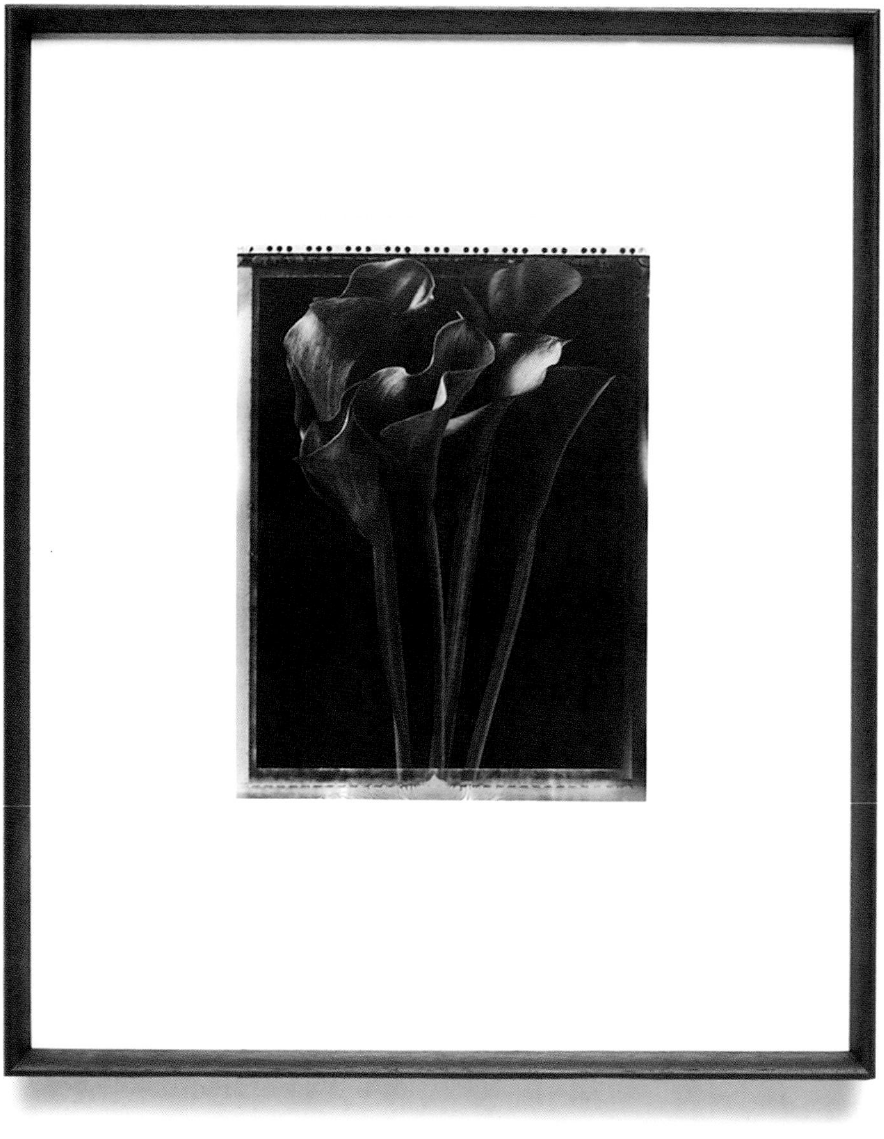

Lilies by Seamus Ryan
Horseman LX 5x4in camera, 150mm lens, Polaroid Type 55 film.
Exposure not recorded

It's amazing how often photographers put maximum effort into the production and printing of a picture, only to neglect the final framing and mounting stage. And yet the presentation of a picture is a vital part of the whole process, and it's entirely possible that a picture could lose much of the impact that the photographer has worked so hard to achieve simply through lack of care in its finishing.

If you want your picture to last and to be shown off to best effect, there are certain key steps to follow. At the printing stage it's important to ensure that fixing and then washing is extremely thorough. Toning can also add to the permanence of an image: a light selenium tone is used by many printers, because this has little effect on the normal black and white tones, but helps to make them more stable. Tones such as thiocarbamide and sepia will also add to a print's archival qualities, and the colour they add to a picture is often beneficial as well.

Once a print has been washed and dried, it should be carefully spotted with archival inks to make sure that there are no dust marks or hairs visible. The picture is now ready for mounting.

Mounting The job of the mount is to set the picture off, and to create an area around it that is plain and unlikely to distract. The width of this mount is down to personal choice, though some pictures that are printed as miniatures often benefit from a wider surround in ratio than prints that are larger. Keep the colour of the mount neutral – with black and white images white or light cream is the usual choice – because it will then be able to carry out its job efficiently and well, and the picture itself will remain the centre of attention. Great care needs to be taken over the cutting of the mount: generally specialist tools are required to ensure that a smooth bevelled edge is created. If you try to cut a mount using just a scalpel and a steel edge, the chances are that it will look messy and that you will slice through at least one or two fingers. Visit an art shop and ask for advice from the staff there, and they will recommend the equipment that you need.

The Print Room at the Photographers' Gallery in London handles thousands of valuable photographic prints every year, and often arranges the framing and mounting of pictures for purchasers. Print Manager Fiona Duncan explains the policy on mounts: "Generally when we sell a print", she says, "we mount it in archival acid-free board. One board is used as the backing board, and on this we create three small pockets from archival tape, and these hold the print gently in place. The print doesn't need to be fastened any more securely than this, and this method allows it to be removed easily at a later date if required.

"Then a window mount needs to be cut so that it frames the picture, and this is connected to the backing board along one long edge using archival tape. This means that it's effectively hinged and can be brought across the picture, and then the picture is ready for framing."

Framing Once again frames are a matter of personal choice, but often it's those that are the simplest in terms of design and colour that work the best. A black frame, for example, can look stunning when it's surrounding a classic black and white picture, whereas one that features a strong colour or an intricate design will start to fight the picture. "The only other colour apart from black that might work on occasion, particularly with vintage black and white prints, is gilded silver leaf", says John Dawson, a Director of John Jones Frames, who carry out much of the framing for the Photographers' Gallery Print Room.

"We would normally suggest that frames shouldn't be more than half an inch wide for pictures up to around 20x16ins, while above that size the width can rise to three quarters of an inch without becoming too dominant. The mount should ideally be around three inches in width increasing to three and a half inches at the bottom for prints up to 20x16ins, and again this can rise a little, to four inches perhaps, for larger prints."

The final stage of the framing process is the selection of glass and, for archival purposes, you should select a material that offers protection from ultraviolet light, because this will give your print a longer life, particularly if it's going to be hung in a room that attracts a lot of daylight.
John Jones Framing Department can be contacted on 020-7281 5439

Habitat 1 by Jennifer Bates
Nikon FM2 camera, 80–200mm zoom, Agfa APX 100 film.
Exposure 1/250sec at f/5.6

This is a classic found natural still life that I took at Lake Annecy, a beautiful clear lake which is located on the approaches to the French Alps. It is a very serene and lovely place and this picture, featuring a detail I found as I walked along its shores, is intended to be a celebration of nature.

I had no idea when I took the picture how I would ultimately present it, but my discovery of liquid light emulsion, which can be coated on to just about any surface to allow it to become a photographic print, opened my eyes to a huge range of possibilities. I decided that I would try to print the picture on to glass, and then mount it in such a way that the glass itself would become part of the overall picture.

To this end I decided to use bathroom glass that had a mottled texture, because I wanted to simulate, if possible, the effect of water. The first step was to have a piece of glass cut to size, and then to have the edges ground so that they were round and safe to touch. Then I had four holes drilled so that the glass could later be mounted. These are things that could, in theory, be done at a later stage, but you then run the risk of losing a completed picture.

The glass itself has to be completely clean before you start, and this is one of the most important stages. A small amount of household or industrial detergent and a thorough drying with clean paper towelling can be enough, while it's also possible to add a layer of subbing (see Pointer) to the surface of the glass to ensure that the emulsion is accepted.

I wanted my picture to have hard edges, so I stuck strips of sticky tape on the front of the glass so that the emulsion was contained in a regular area. Then, under darkroom conditions, I put the bottle of Silverprint SE1 liquid emulsion that I was using in a jug full of hot water. As the emulsion warmed up in the bottle it became runnier, and when I judged it to be ready, I picked up the sheet of glass in one hand and, holding the bottle in the other, I carefully poured some of the emulsion into the centre of it. Then I moved it around so that the emulsion spread to the edges of the tape and beyond, taking care to get as even a coating as possible.

The emulsion soon solidifies into a jelly, and then it's safe to place the glass down on to a very flat (check it with a spirit level) surface to dry completely. Any excess emulsion, providing it's been collected on a clean surface, can be returned to the bottle.

At this stage, I also made sure that I had a few off-cuts of spare glass that I could coat to act as test strips. These are important, because you need to make tests on a piece of the same material as the object that's being printed on, so that exposure and focusing is accurate.

Once the emulsion is fully dry, the tape can be peeled off, and the glass can be exposed and developed in much the same way as a conventional black and white print. Handle and leave the print to dry carefully, as the emulsion layer is very delicate until completely dried down. The effect I achieved changes as the light and the shadows move around, and the whole thing has now become the picture, taking this still life on to another stage.

Jennifer Bates

Pointer Because glass can be a difficult surface to coat, it can be beneficial to add a layer of what's known as subbing solution. The principle involved is to apply a thin layer of a substance that has physical and chemical properties intermediate between those of the base, and the emulsion which is to be applied. This allows bonding between the base and the subbing layer, and also between subbing and the emulsion, providing much better adhesion than would be found by coating the base directly. It may be possible to provide a good subbing layer by applying a coating of a suitable varnish, although a better option would be a gelatin subbing solution, usually a dilute solution of gelatin hardened with chrome alum. A ready-made pack is Silverprint Hardening and Subbing Solution.

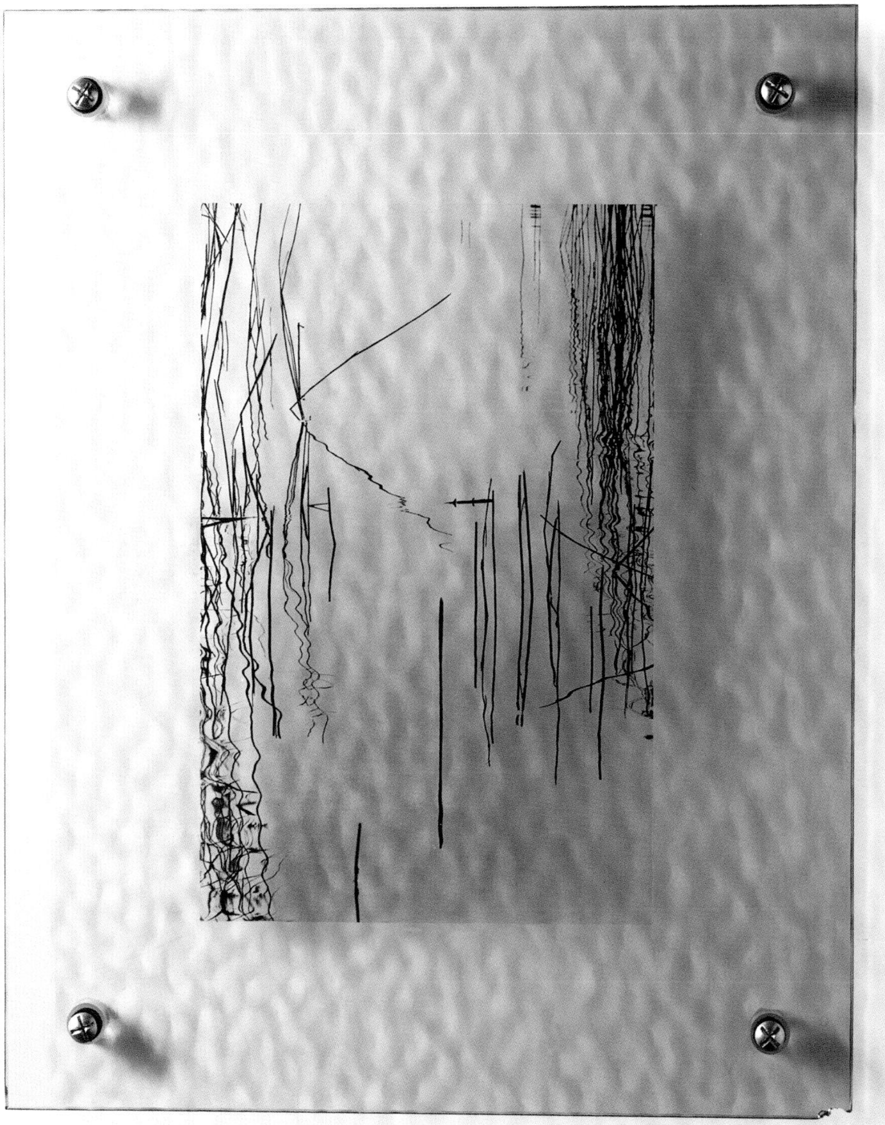

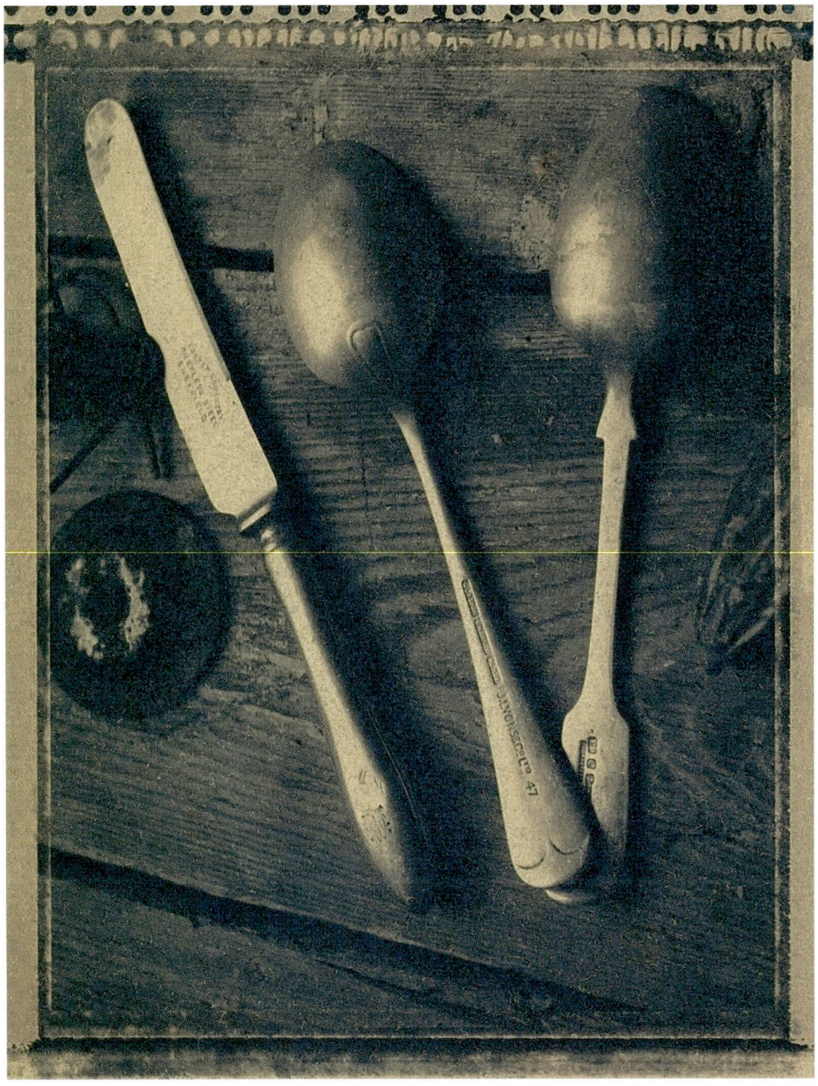

Exhibiting

Having my first major exhibition was an amazing experience. Up until that point I'd been working for around six to seven years to develop an individual style, and I'd been taking pictures largely for myself. Seeing my photographs mounted, framed and hanging on a wall was a great moment of realisation for me, the point where I suddenly understood why I had been doing everything. It was extraordinary to see people's reactions to my work: I had my own favourites, but people would invariably go for others that I would see mistakes in, and they either didn't see or didn't care about what I thought were failings.

You can get absorbed in your work, and then it's difficult to step back, so the input I got from other people on my choice of pictures to display was invaluable. It was particularly useful to hear the opinion of the owners of the gallery who were mounting the show, and who obviously had to come from a more commercial direction than me. I had around 200 pieces of work to select from, and they told me which pictures they thought might be too provocative, and helped me make a selection that we all were happy with. They also undertook the framing and mounting of the pictures, which were displayed in very classical frames with plain white mounts. The mounts gave an important area of clarity around the picture, something that was really needed because they are very low key and quite dark.

Allan Jenkins

Spoons VI by Allan Jenkins
MPP 5x4in camera, 150mm lens, Polaroid Type 55 film.
Exposure one second at f/5.6

Technique I love working with Type 55 film, because there's so much that you can do with it. You can even peel it apart before the print has had time to develop fully, and create a result that's solarised: the potential is amazing. Here I arranged the spoons and the knife, and then introduced other elements in the form of a rusty piece of metal and some old cable, things that had texture and complemented the composition. I used the spoons upside down, which is my favourite way to use them because the light will then catch all the indentations on their surface. By placing all these objects on to a wooden background, I was able to utilise the grain of the wood as part of the picture, but its surface didn't pick up any of the window light that the spoons did, and so it didn't distract. The negative I achieved was then contact printed using the Cyanotype process, and I then toned this to achieve this cold blue finish.

Pointer Putting together an exhibition is one of the most satisfying ways of using your pictures, whether it's a show at a major gallery that you're putting on or a small display at your local library. Before you even start you have to make sure that you're really ready to go public: a theme for your work is essential, and, like Allan Jenkins, you must be sure of your own style, because work that's too derivative will be found out immediately. Making the right selection is the next problem: making rough prints will help you to see how your pictures work together, and it will give you the chance to get feedback from those whose opinion you trust. In the final analysis, however, you must have the confidence to make your own decisions about what to include, otherwise the exhibition will end up being selected by committee.

Websites

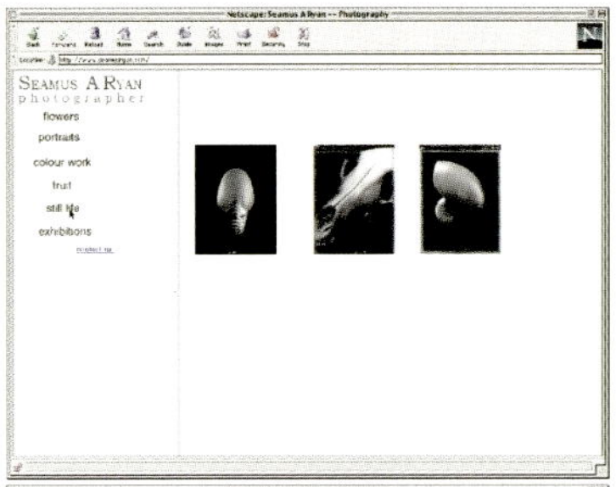

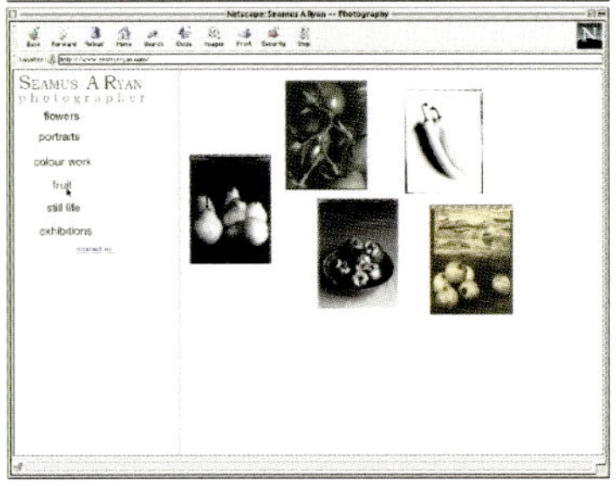

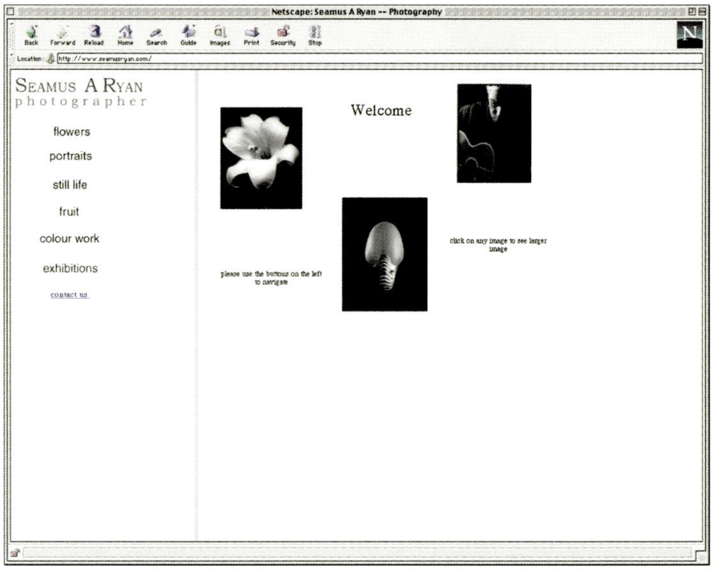

www.seamusryan.com

Introduction Set up a personal website and you've established an exciting and cost effective way of showing your photographs to a potentially unlimited worldwide audience. Best of all, you'll be in charge of the content and the presentation, and so you have far more freedom to express yourself than you would normally expect from a conventional exhibition outlet. All you need is around ten megabytes of web space from an Internet Service Provider (ISP), usually your Internet provider. This service is generally free, and you'll be able to show a large selection of your favourite images, together with any accompanying words you want to include.

What you will need The first essential piece of equipment you require is a computer. The very minimum would be a Pentium 160 with Windows 95. Whatever computer you decide on should have at least 32 megabytes of RAM. (Do remember though, your hard drive i.e. amount of space on your computer, will slowly be eaten up the more programmes you load, which will in turn slow down each action you do). You'll find this extra RAM really useful when scanning and editing.

Next you will need a scanner. There are lots on the market and most will do the job. Please note though, the image that will appear is only as good as the resolution of the computer screen displaying it, so it's no good scanning at the highest resolution of your scanner thinking you will get a better displayed image. Typically, screen resolution is 72–96 pixels per inch (ppi). Also, the greater the size of the image, in megabytes, the slower it will take to appear (download) on the Internet. The good news for those working in black and white is that mono images will download approximately eight times faster than a colour one.

Once pictures are scanned, you can alter them on an image-editing programme, and PhotoShop is widespread. The capabilities of such programmes are vast, but at a simple level, you could create electronic frames and borders, lighten, darken, change image sizes or add a tone. Additionally, you could watermark your images i.e. give them an electronic signature that says they are yours. Although you cannot stop people copying your images from the Internet, at least if they appear again, they are watermarked. Remember to save your image: the Internet supports gif or jpg, e.g. yourimage.jpg.

As previously mentioned, the time it takes an image to appear over the Internet is a function of its file size. For a benchmark, colour images should be approximately 80 kilobytes in size, while black and white should be 1/8th of the file size, when based on an image measuring about 5x3cm. It can also be useful, however, to show very small images, known as thumbnails, because these will download in a fraction of the time. Then, if people are more interested and want to see more detail, they can click on the thumbnail, by use of a hyperlink, and a larger version will download. People will be more prepared to wait for something they asked for, but for this system to be effective you'll need to put a meaningful title against the thumbnail.

Now you need to add some text to your pages. If you want to bring text and images together, but don't want to learn pure HTML, you can use programmes such as Front Page or Page Maker, which are simple drop and drag web-editing programmes.

Each page you complete needs to be saved as an htm file, e.g. mywebpage.htm, and the first page of your Internet site has to be called home.htm, i.e. your home page.

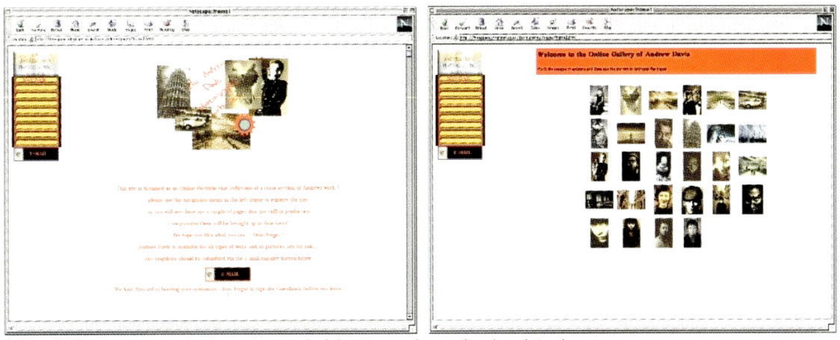

http://freespace.virginnet.co.uk/davis.andrew/index.html

cityart.net This successful web site, currently getting over 2000 visitors a day, was created by web developer Debra Palmer, and was considered so innovative and attractive to use that it was runner-up in two categories in a major competition for web sites held by **The Times** newspaper. The site, which was created on less than 10 megabytes of space, contains 45 examples of investment art in a series of galleries, complete with essential details such as price, condition of picture and so on. It also has links to several other sites of interest to photographers and investors, such as The Royal Photographic Gallery and Photographers in New York, a listing of dozens of top photographers, several of whom have their own links to other sites.

How do I transfer my files to the Internet? First you need to register with an Internet Service Provider (ISP). These are widespread now, and normally free. As well as providing you with an email address, they typically supply an amount of web space, e.g. ten megabytes. You will want to give your website a name, so people could find you. If you register your website name with your ISP, invariably their name will be the prefix to your site, i.e. www.ispname/your name.com. You could, however, register a unique name, without the mention of your ISP. This will cost around £50 for two years, i.e. www.yoursite.com. This was the case with www.cityart.net, which was registered to give our website a professional-sounding name.

Having got your site name registered, you need to transfer your files to your web space. This may sound complicated, but it is actually quite straightforward. You will probably use 'ftp', which stands for file transfer protocol. Basically, all you need to do is dial up your ISP, and via a program for 'ftp-ing', transfer your files to your web space. This is protected by your password so only you have access to editing your site.

How will I advertise my site? How will I get visitors? Difficult one! Just type in 'photography' into any search engine and see how many sites exist. So how do you get ahead of the competition? Placing adverts in journals can cost an arm and a leg, but there are electronic ways around the problem. For example, you could find a popular site that would complement your own, contact them and then ask whether they will include a link to your site; www.cityart.com is one such site that is developing such links. If you feel like writing some web code (HTML), you can also incorporate the META Tags, which are key words that define your web page, in terms of HTML.

Finally, remember to include your email address on your web site, so that if anyone sees your pictures and wants to contact you about them, all they have to do is to click on your address.

Debra Palmer

Biographies

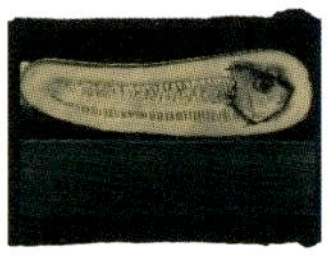

36

Jason Bate comes from an illustration and fine art background, and his aesthetics are firmly based in fine art photography. He usually prefers to work on one project or theme at a time, producing a series of images that confront the subject matter through a progressive study. He uses only natural light for his subjects, since he feels that a certain mood and ambience can be captured by soft lighting, while by calculating long exposure times detail can be rendered in the shadows. Since graduating from the University of East London with a BA (Hons) in Visual Communication in 1998, he's been developing a personal project to study the forms and textures of plants, vegetables and natural objects. The old-fashioned printing processes that he uses are an alternative to conventional silver gelatin prints and create an image that is almost as painterly as it is photographic. These qualities help to create images of harmony and balance, a mixture between the old and the contemporary.

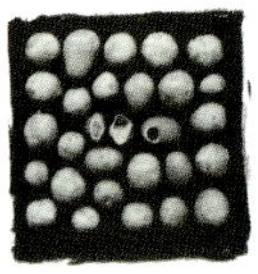

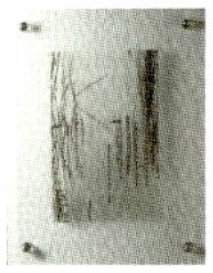

119 129

Jennifer Bates graduated from the London College of Printing with a BA (Hons) in Visual Communication in 1981, and since that time has worked as a freelance photographer specialising in location work, including people and events, landscape and environment for commission, stock and exhibition. She's had her work featured in several group shows at venues such as the Royal Photographic Society in Bath, the Canon Photography Gallery at the Victoria & Albert Museum in London and Brixton Art Gallery and also had a solo show at Surrey University and Guildford House Gallery. Her work also featured in the book **Silver Gelatin – A User's Guide to Liquid Photographic Emulsions** by Martin Reed and Sarah Jones (Working Books, ISBN 0-924346-1-X).

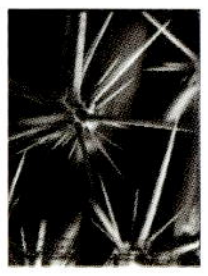

47

Allan Baxter was born in Swindon in 1969 and originally studied photography A' level at the age of 17 at Chippenham Technical College. He moved to London in 1990, and spent four years working as a black and white printer/processor for Tony White. In 1995 he left to study for a degree at Blackpool and The Fylde College, and during his stay there he won the Fujifilm/BIPP, the Mitsubishi Digital Imaging and the Polaroid/KJP Student Awards. He graduated with a degree in photography in 1997 and has assisted and worked in London since that time. Among the photographers he's worked for are Desmond Burden, Spencer Rowell and Eitan Lee-Al. Over the last few years he's worked and travelled in places such as the Maldives, China, New York and the US, Singapore, Sri Lanka, Cuba, Hong Kong and Malaysia. He recently achieved the runner-up slot in the 2000 Fragrance Awards and he's started to receive his own commissions. Influences include William Klein, Ernst Haas, David Lynch and David Carson. He currently lives and works in the Kentish Town area of London, and examples of his work are held by the Michael Trevillion Picture Library, website: www.trevillion.com, tel: 020-8740 9005.

39 40 43 95

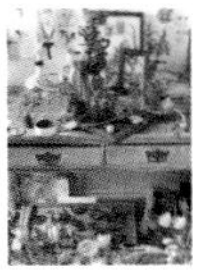 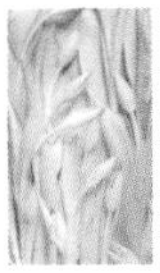 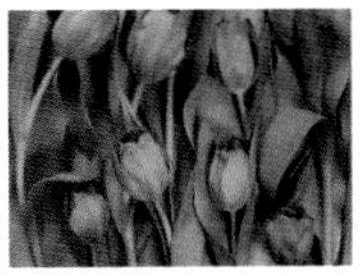 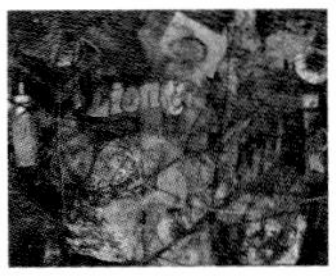

John Blakemore is one of the world's most respected still life and landscape photographers. For many years he's taught both the aesthetics and practice of photography to the students at the University of Derby, a much admired and respected degree course, where he is Reader in Photography. He holds an MA in film studies, is an external assessor for the Royal College of Art and in 1998 was awarded an Honorary Fellowship of the Royal Photographic Society. Recipient of numerous Arts Council awards, John's work has appeared in many publications and been exhibited all over the world. Starting as a freelance photographer in 1956, John soon moved through his personal work, to become England's leading landscape photographer, then transferring his unique and elegant photographic style into areas as diverse as still life, documentary, portraiture and Polaroid colour. He has been involved in photographing a nuclear waste dumping site in Lincolnshire for the C.P.R.E. and has featured in the TV programmes 'Exploring Photography' and 'World Photography'. **Spirit of Place** was published in 1979. 1991 saw the publication of **Inscape**, a major retrospective monograph. **The Stilled Gaze**, based on his Tulip series, was published in November 1994. Recently he has been making exquisite hand-made books, with both black and white and colour photographs. John is much in demand as a teacher of photography, and along with his university work conducts annual workshops at Duckspool and Inversnaid Photography Centre.

100

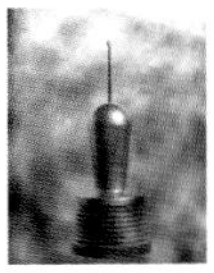

Tim Brightmore has been working in photography since 1986, and originally trained in still life advertising. More recently, however, his work has been dedicated to the photographing of people, again within the realms of advertising. His non-commissioned work involves still life and portraiture, and he is currently developing a series of images which concentrates on people adorned with tattoos. Any enquiries regarding Tim's work, or requests to see his portfolio, should call 020-7278 4747, or email him at timber-b@msn.com.

32 66

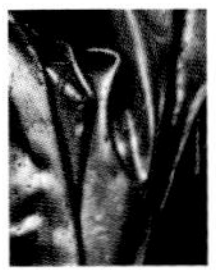 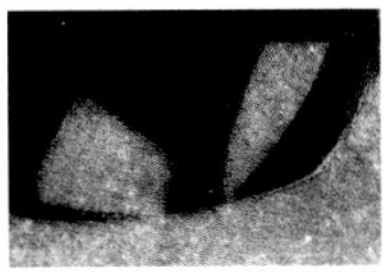

Robin Broadbent was born in 1960, and studied photography at Salisbury Art College from 1979 to 1982, moving to London to assist on completion of the course. After two years he started to work for himself, specialising in still life photography, and he found that his personal black and white abstract work helped him to fine tune the way that he looked at things. He's published two books – **Marmalade** and **Minus Sixteen**, both in 1998 – and he's had solo exhibitions of his work in Smiths Galleries, Covent Garden, the Untitled Gallery in Sheffield and The Studio in London. Awards have included being named a finalist in the Association of Photographers 16th Annual Awards and being named Visual Category Winner in the Glenfiddich Awards. In the summer of 1999 he left London to go and work out of New York, and to concentrate on his still life and fashion work.

Biographies

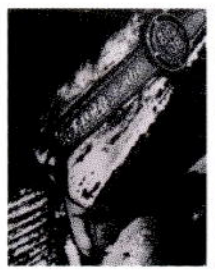
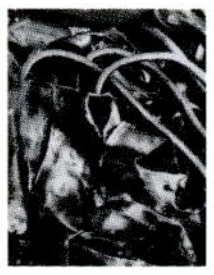
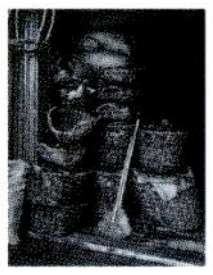

62 69 73

John Claridge was born in 1944 in London's East End and, from the age of 15 to 17, he worked in the photographic department of a London advertising agency. He decided early on that photography was his vocation, holding his first one-man show at the age of 17, and then working as assistant to American photographer David Montgomery for the next two years. He opened his first studio aged 19 in London's City area, and since that time he's worked for most leading advertising agencies and clients in Europe, the USA and Japan. His work has been exhibited worldwide, and he's been presented with over 500 awards for photography, both editorial and commercial. Selected pictures have been auctioned at Christie's in London, and his work is also held in the permanent collections of the Victoria & Albert Museum in London and the Arts Council of Great Britain Archives. He's published three books: **South American Portfolio** (1982), **One Hundred Photographs** (1987) and **Seven Days in Havana** (2000).

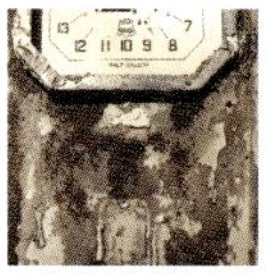
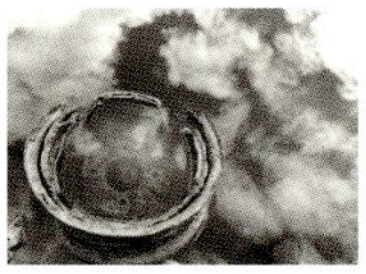
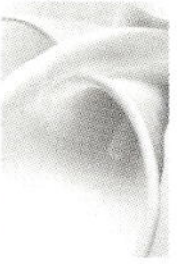

28 61 99

Gerry Coe works out of The Lasting Image Studio on Belfast's Lisburn Road, and has achieved international recognition for the quality of his work. In 1999 he won the Agfa UK and Ireland Portrait Photographer of the Year Award, a first for anyone from Ireland. He's recently followed this up with a further three of professional photography's highest honours, Fellowships of the British Institute of Professional Photographers, The Master Photographers' Association and The Royal Photographic Society. The BIPP also awarded Gerry the rare and very sought after honour of The Peter Grugeon Award for the best fellowship panel of the year. The judges in the MPA accorded Gerry with the accolade of having shown the best fellowship panel submitted in the past ten years, and he went on to win the title of the Illustrative/Pictorial Master Photographer of the Year for 1999, beating over 900 other professional photographers, another first for an Irish photographer.

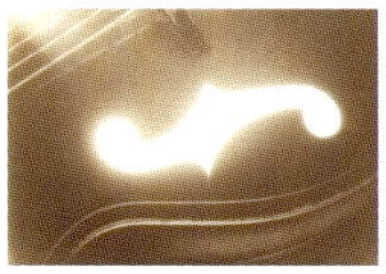

111

Andrew Davis was born in 1963, and is entirely a self-taught photographer. Based near Bath, he shoots primarily in black and white, and develops and prints all his own work, subsequently using toners such as sepia and blue tone to enhance the final effect. His favoured films are Ilford's FP4 and HP5, and he prints on Ilford and Kentmere papers. His regular camera is a Bronica ETRS, used with 40mm, 75mm, 100mm and 150mm lenses. His professional work to date has included CD covers for artistes such as Hazel O'Connor and the Grimthorpe Colliery Brass Band, plus book covers, and he's been taking pictures seriously now for over 20 years.

91

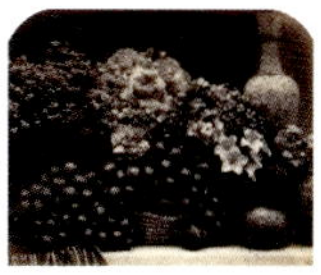

Roger Fenton (1819–1869) was the founder and first secretary of The Royal Photographic Society, and he terminated his photographic career in 1861 after which his equipment and negatives were purchased by Francis Frith. Prior to this he had a varied photographic career, and was one of the first photographers to photograph scenic views, stately homes and art works with a view to selling copies to the public. A perfectionist in all things, Fenton worried about his photographs fading, but some of his prints in the RPS Collection are still in near mint condition.

35 48 51

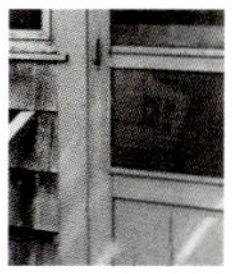
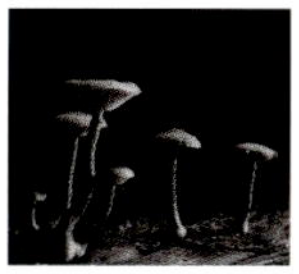
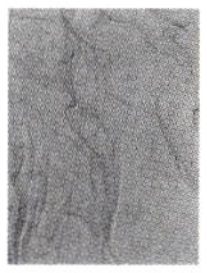

James Flanagan has a minimalist approach to photography, being strongly influenced by the works of photographers Edward Weston and Eugene Atget, which he was exposed to at a young age. Viewing a great photograph leaves him with a feeling of desire. This desire , which compels him to pursue black and white photography, has continued for 30 years so far, and he considers it a beautiful thing that a colourless sheet of paper can dramatise a subject to an importance greater than its reality. In March 1987, realising that the TV programme 'Live Your Dreams' could come with a pay cheque, James opened a commercial studio in New York City. With accounts like Clinique, Chanel and Revlon, he quickly established a name in the cosmetic industry while also pursuing editorial projects. His work appears in the book **Perfume Legends: American Feminine Fragrances**, and for the first time his personal work will be available at both the Catherine Street Gallery in New York and at paintingsdirect.com.

15 65 79

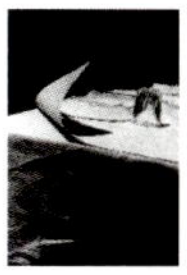
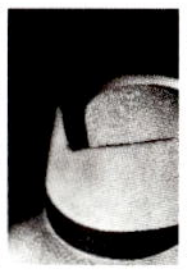
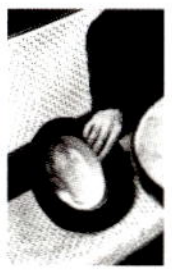

Ralph Gibson is without question one of the world's greatest photographers. Born in Los Angeles in 1939, he assisted photographic icons Dorothea Lange and Robert Frank, before making his own name as a photographer of rare insight and clarity. His work has appeared in numerous books, such as **The Somnambulist** (1970), **Days at Sea** (1975), **Syntax** (1983), **Tropism** (1987) and, most recently, **Overtones** (1998) and **Deus Ex Machina** (1999). Awards have included a Doctor of Fine Arts Award from Ohio Wesleyan University (1997), a Grand Medal of the City of Arles in 1994, a '150 Years of Photography' Award from the Photographic Society of Japan (1989) and a Leica Medal of Excellence Award (1988). The work of Ralph Gibson has been exhibited in some of the world's leading galleries, and his work is held in the collections of international institutions such as the Museum of Modern Art in New York, the Metropolitan Museum of Art in New York, the Whitney Museum of American Art, the National Gallery of Art in Washington DC, the National Museum of Modern Art in Kyoto, the International Centre of Photography in New York, the National Gallery in Ottowa and the Bibliothèque Nationale in Paris. His work is represented in the US by the Howard Greenberg Gallery in New York, email: howard.greenberg.gallery@worldnet.att.net

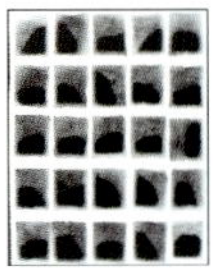
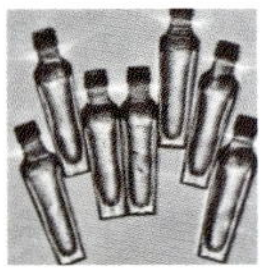

80 104

Manuela Höfer, who was born and raised in the German Democratic Republic, is one of only a handful of photographers selling fine art photography direct to the British public, as well as achieving success selling her images commercially. She has also achieved a worthy reputation as the organiser of the London Contemporary Photography Fair, an annual event that has been held since 1997. In its short lifetime the Fair has already gained European recognition and it attracts photography collectors, curators, agencies, photographers and media journalists from across the world, while also giving unprecidented exposure to many young photographers. Manuela has had her work exhibited in England, France, Germany, the Czech Republic and Hungary, and she has also been published in many photography and art journals across Europe. Her interest in photographing packaging began in 1994 and, after she moved to Britain the following year, she was inspired to continue the series, stunned by the high level of non-recyclable food packaging from supermarkets to sandwich bars. The Manuela Höfer Workshop and Gallery is now established next to the Business Design Centre in London's Islington at 29/30 St Alban's Place, N1 0NX.

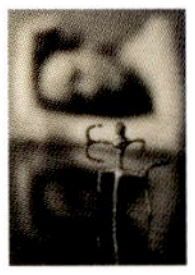

103

Eric Howard was born in 1951, and became an assistant to photographers Michael Legge and Peter Barry on leaving school at 16. In 1969 he decided to turn freelance, and in the period up to 1983 he worked for many of the biggest newspapers and magazines in the UK and abroad, and also sold original prints through Sotherby's and The Photographers' Gallery. From 1983 to 1986 he worked as Creative Director at Photobanc, overseeing calendars for such names as John Swannell and Bob Carlos Clarke and even producing one featuring his own work. In 1987 he returned to selling original fine art prints, including among his clients Lord Palumbo, Sally Cadbury, the **Financial Times** and the Royal Photographic Society. In 1991 he was approached by Mary Gibson, the founder of a fund for Romanian orphans, to take pictures in Romania to raise awareness of the crisis there, and his work eventually raised £20,000 for the charity. Two years later Eric was the Project Director involved in setting up and launching **Photo Art** magazine. The RPS awarded Eric the Gold Medal in their annual exhibition in 1995, and the same year he acted as a consultant to the Duke of Edinburgh Award's Charity Photographic Auction, which took place at Coutts Bank in London. Eric set up cityart.net, a virtual gallery for selling art and photographic art on the Internet in 1997. His own work, and that of a selection of other major photographers, is available for sale either through the site or by contacting Eric by e-mail at eric@cityart.net.

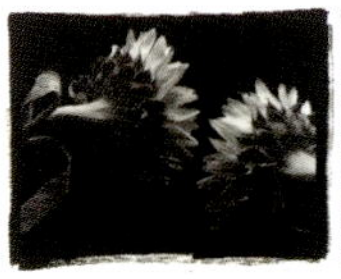
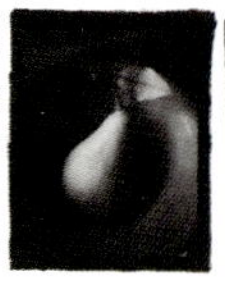
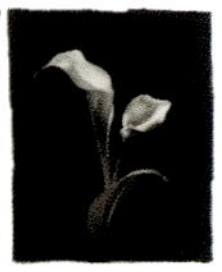

16 89 115

Kenro Izu was born in Osaka, Japan, in 1949, and he moved to New York in 1970, setting up his studio there in 1974. He started to utilise the platinum/palladium printing technique in 1983, and has since made himself a huge reputation as one of the best fine art photographers working in the world today. He has had numerous individual exhibitions throughout America, Japan and Europe, and has also participated in several group exhibitions to great acclaim. After visiting Cambodia in 1993 to photograph Angkor monuments, he founded a non-profit-making organisation called 'Friends Without A Border' to help unfortunate children in Asia. Its first project, the Angkor Hospital for Children, was completed in 1999, and Izu continues to pursue his photography while being involved in the hospital's management. He is represented by the Howard Greenberg Gallery in New York, email: howard.greenberg.gallery@worldnet.att.net.

70 123 130

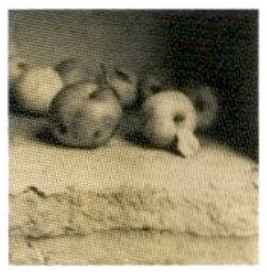
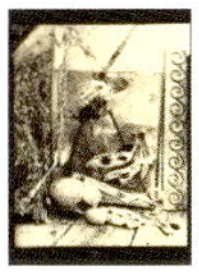
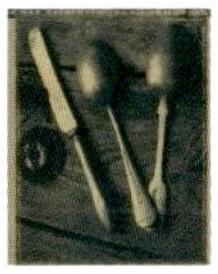

Allan Jenkins is a purist and a traditionalist, working only with natural light and using old-fashioned alternative non-silver processes. These methods were first practised in the 1890s, combining ferric salts and carefully exposed ultraviolet light, which cooks the images slowly into the fibres of the paper through the density of the negative. Allan's work is dark and mysterious; every print a curious mixture of new and old. He describes his pictures as "a fusion between painting and photography, joining forces as an art form influenced by traditional and classical art". Allan is represented by the HackelBury Fine Art Gallery, 4 Launceston Place, London, W8, tel: 020-7937 8688.

20 85

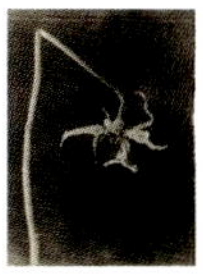
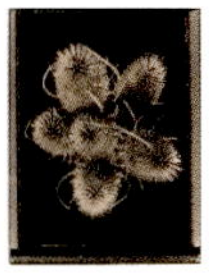

Joseph Ortenzi started out in Toronto, Canada, born two months before JFK was shot, (and is old enough to remember the moon landing) and began photographing at the early age of four with his first blurry, wobbly picture of his Mom. He studied Film and Photography at Ryerson University, but it was his venturing out into the wide world that developed his style, appreciation and experimentation that were to leave a mark. After a few exhibitions in Canada he decided to try for a different environment and sold his possessions, packed his darkroom and cameras and moved to London, England to see who would notice him there. After developing more technical expertise in a large commercial photographic lab he sold out and started shooting anything for money and experience.
From interiors to products to portraits, he balked at nothing, considering anything as an experience of seeing. Finally in 1997, he closed the studio down and returned to his real love, photography just for the pleasure of it, and chose to make his income with something else, so that photography could continue to be a loved experience. Subsequent to this decision, his images continue to attract interest from collectors and publishers alike, while he works on the next project. Examples of his work are held by the Michael Trevillion Picture Library, website: www.trevillion.com, tel: 020-8740 9005.

56

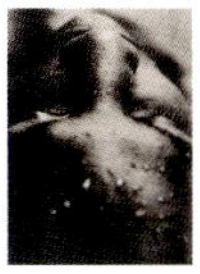

Dean Rogers completed his degree at the Nottingham Trent University in 1996, and since then has been working on a variety of commissions, the more recent of which include a Shane Meadows film, the World Cup event in 1998, a photo feature on British boxing and a project for Channel 4. Dean has most recently exhibited at the British Workhouse Gallery in Dallas, Texas, the Air Gallery in London, the Cable Tel Gallery, Manchester City Art Gallery and at the Paul Smith outlet in London. He is currently working on a solo exhibition for Sheffield Media Centre and on another Shane Meadows project. Examples of his work are held by the Michael Trevillion Picture Library, website: www.trevillion.com, tel: 020-8740 9005.

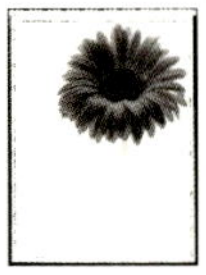
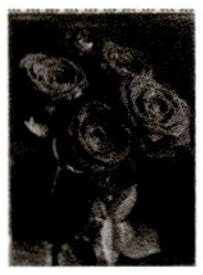
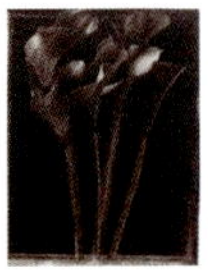

27 86 126

Seamus Ryan is self-taught as a photographer. Having spent the last couple of years taking portraits for book publishers and magazines he became so disillusioned artistically by the disparity between what he was putting into it and what he was getting out of it that he decided to try his hand at flowers and still life. He started by doing flowers very much in the style of Mapplethorpe, but quickly realised that the man had pretty much done it all already. He attended several workshops at Duckspool (Fay Godwin and John Blakemore being two of the more memorable ones) and a printing course with Peter Cattrell at Central St Martin's College. It was his meeting with Melvin Cambettie Davies at Master Mono where he was introduced to both the Polaroid Type 55 and Kodak Ektalure that set him on his current course. Having been made redundant twice in as many years he has now decided to try photography full time. He has designed his own website (www.seamusryan.com) and is doing website design on a freelance basis.

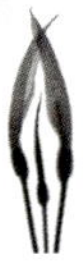
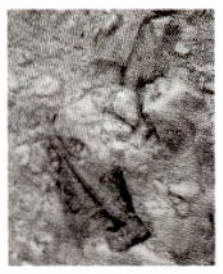

19 74

Ray Spence is a photographer based near Stratford-on-Avon in the UK. Trained as a microbiologist, and a keen organic gardener, much of his influence is drawn from natural forms. Plants, organic structures and the human body are all recurring themes. For many years Ray has specialised in fine art monochrome prints and historical processes such as Cyanotype and platinum/palladium printing. More recent developments have been the use of liquid emulsions and digital manipulation and printing. Ray regularly exhibits, and his work is published and collected widely. He is much in demand as a lecturer and workshop leader. He is the author of the book **Form and Fantasy** and the co-author of **Beyond Monochrome – A Fine Art Printing Workshop**. He is also a Fellow of the Royal Photographic Society and sits on the Distinctions Panels in **Visual Arts** and **Printing** . Ray is represented by The Special Photographers Company in London, tel: 020-7221 3489.

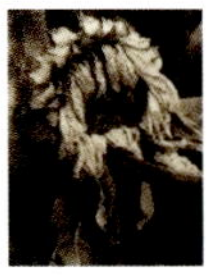

23

Edward Steichen (1879–1973) was born in Luxembourg and he began his photographic career as an impressionistic artist and ended it as Director of Photography at the Museum of Modern Art in New York. In between he embraced every form of photography: abstract, straight, advertising and fashion, bringing his huge enthusiasm and energy to bear to enhance photography as a career, as an art form and as a museum speciality. In 1952 he embarked upon a three-year undertaking to compile a great exhibition of the best photographers in the world, to be called 'The Family of Man', the title of which was taken from a speech by Abraham Lincoln. The exhibition proved to be his greatest achievement: it was viewed by over nine million people in 69 countries and sold millions of copies in book form.

55 82 96

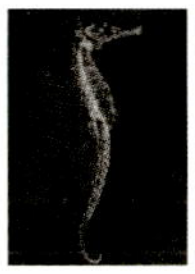 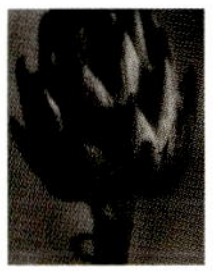 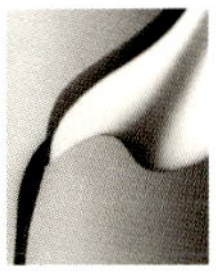

Patrice de Villiers works for advertising giants and editorial clients alike, giving herself plenty of variety in her commercial work, which is predominantly within the field of still life/food. Outside of the studio, she shoots all her pictures on a Yashica point and squirt, considering that the observation is the important element of a picture, not a plethora of kit. Breaking away from a career in journalism into photography was a logical progression for her, and she currently is working on a film treatment alongside her photographic work that allows the indulgence of playing with words and pictures. She can be contacted by email at patrice@delicious-pdev.demon.co.uk.

116 120

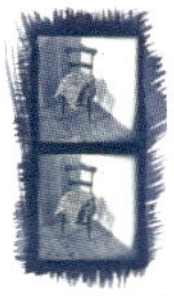 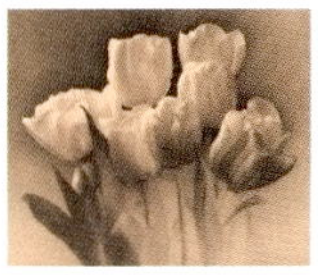

Randall Webb is a freelance photographer and lecturer. He is also a leading authority on the history and practice of photographic printmaking, ranging from the work of Fox Talbot in the 1830s to Andy Warhol in the late 20th century. His interest in early and alternative processing dates from his experiments in 1968 with the now neglected bromoil process. He now runs workshops at museums, art schools and universities on a wide variety of early processes, including salt printing, gum printing, platinum, carbon, photo etching and photo silk screen. Following extensive research, he has recently published a definitive textbook on the subject entitled **Spirit of Salts** , in association with Martin Reed of Silverprint – website at http://www.silverprint.co.uk, email sales@silverprint.co.uk. A few years ago he founded the 120 group of photographers, and he exhibits and sells his work which is printed using examples of alternative printing.

31 52 107 108

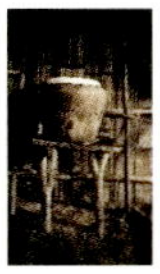 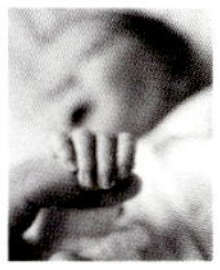 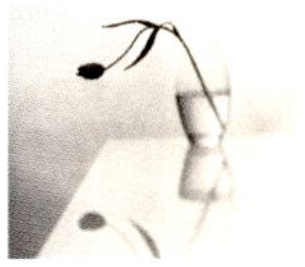 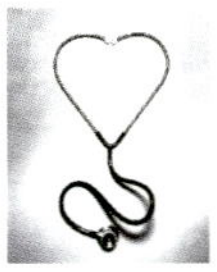

Stephen Widdows started in the photographic industry at the age of 16. For eight years he worked as an assistant until, in 1996, he took on his own studio in Central London. He has now obtained a variety of clients in the fields of advertising, editorial and public relations. Stephen can be contacted and arrangements made to view his portfolio through stephen.widdows@breathemail.net.

Glossary

Backlighting Light that's coming from a position in front of the camera and illuminating the subject from behind.

Bellows Extension The amount of distance between the lens and the film plane in a studio camera is variable, and depends on the amount of extension the bellows is subjected to. For close-up work, the bellows may be extended to two or three times its usual size, and this will mean that a calculation will be required to allow for extra exposure.

Black Reflector Used to soak up light and to ensure that a selected area retains deep shadow.

Bounced Flash Flash that's been reflected from a surface such as a wall or ceiling to diffuse the light.

Cable Release A flexible device that screws into the camera's shutter release button and activates the shutter without the need to touch the camera.

Camera Movements Vertical and swing movements that can be made with the lens and the film plane on a studio camera to perform various functions, such as increased depth of field and correction of converging verticals.

Compressed Perspective Distant perspective that's been brought up close by the use of a telephoto lens.

Dark Slide A sheet film holder that can usually accommodate two pieces of film, and which is then placed in the back of a studio camera prior to an exposure being made.

Depth of Field The distance in front and behind the point at which a lens is focused that will be rendered acceptably sharp. It increases when the aperture is made smaller, and becomes smaller when the lens is focused at close quarters.

Dodging The holding back of certain areas of the negative during printing to reduce print density, allied to the selective increase of exposure to certain areas of the print that require increased density.

Downrating The opposite to uprating, and primarily done to reduce contrast. The film is shot at a lower ISO rating and, to compensate for what is effectively overexposure, the film is developed for a shorter time.

Dual Toning The technique of placing a print in two separate toning baths to pick up elements of both colours.

Extension Tubes A series of rings that can be used with an SLR camera to position the lens further away from the film plane, and to allow close-up pictures to be taken.

Farmer's Reducer A mixture of potassium ferricyanide and sodium thiosulphate that will lighten selective areas of a print.

Field Camera A large format camera that has been especially designed to be used on location.

Fill-in Flash A weakened burst of flash that can be used to subtly fill in the shadows on a subject's face.

Filter Factor An indication of the amount the exposure needs to be increased to allow for the use of a filter. A x2 filter needs one stop extra exposure, x3 one-and-a-half stops more and x4 two stops more.

Fish Fryer A rectangular-shaped tent designed to fit over a flashlight and to spread its illumination evenly in the studio.

Fresnel Lens The front of a fresnel lens consists of concentric rings, each of which forms part of a curved lens surface. These have the same overall convergent effect on illumination as a thicker lens, but the lens loses the heat applied to its inner surface through convection and radiation from its larger external surface area.

Gobo A device like a flag which can be used in the studio to direct light very precisely into a particular area.

Graduated Neutral Density Filter A filter that features a denser area towards its top that helps to even out the contrast levels in a picture if the sky is much brighter than the rest of the scene (see Neutral Density Filter).

Grey Card The Grey Card provides what is assumed to be average density, and a reading taken from its surface will therefore give a good mid-point with a scene of high contrast.

High Key A picture that consists almost entirely of light tones.

Hyperfocal Distance The distance between the lens and the nearest point of acceptably sharp focus when the lens is focused for infinity.

Lith Printing Paper A printing paper that increases the contrast levels in a scene while allowing shadow detail to be retained. Its characteristic feature is a pink tone.

Low Key A picture that consists almost entirely of dark tones.

Macro The term used to describe a close-up picture.

Mirror Lock A lever on an SLR camera that allows the camera's mirror to be locked in the up position before an exposure is made to help reduce vibration.

Monopod A form of support for the camera that utilises one leg, which makes it very easy to set up and move.

Neutral Density Filter Used to cut down the light reaching a film by a stated amount, and absorbs all wavelengths almost equally, ensuring no influence on the tones each colour will record as on black and white film.

Polaroid Type 55 film One of the oldest Polaroid film materials available, which gives the photographer both a print and a negative.

Rangefinder Camera A camera that features two separate images in the viewfinder that come together as the lens is focused.

Reflector Brolly A highly reflective umbrella that attaches to a flashgun to bounce the light back on to a scene.

Selenium Toning A brief immersion in selenium toner diluted at about one part concentrate to 15 parts water should not change print image colour but it will improve the archival permanence of the print. The toner must be used in well ventilated conditions.

Spot Meter A meter that is designed to give an accurate meter reading in difficult lighting conditions by gathering information selectively from three to four areas of a scene.

Thiocarbamide Toning A two-bath process that can, according to relative strengths of the components in the toning stage, give a variety of tones ranging from dark brown to yellow brown.

Uprating Rating a film at a speed higher than its nominal rating, and then compensating for the underexposure that takes place by increasing film development.

Variable Contrast Paper Photographic paper that can produce different levels of contrast depending on the filtration it receives.

White Reflector A board or sheet that is positioned to bounce light into areas of shadow.

Zone System The system perfected by Ansel Adams that divides a scene up into areas of differing tones, to allow metering to be more precisely carried out. Consistent metering, combined with close control of negative development, ensures that a perfect negative can be obtained, allowing a preconceived result to be produced.

Acknowledgements Many thanks to all those who have contributed so very much to this book. To Angie Patchell, who has overseen and edited the whole project, and whose enthusiasm has helped immeasurably to drive it forwards; to Dan Moscrop at Navy Blue Design Consultants, who has worked so hard to turn a collection of pictures into a cohesive and visually stunning volume of work; to Brian Morris at RotoVision, whose belief and support for the project has been invaluable; to Tom Gitterman at the Howard Greenburg Gallery in New York, who gave so much time to help make my visit to that city such a fruitful one; to The Michael Trevillion Picture Library for giving up so much time to put me in touch with photographers whose work they hold on file; and to all the photographers who have contributed their work, and their expertise, so willingly. And, of course, continuing thanks to Sarah and Emilia, who have supported me throughout the entire project, as always.

The Association of Photographers

Based in London, the Association of Photographers has a membership of advertising, editorial and fashion photographers, and photographic assistants, in excess of 1400, and it's also supported by agents, printers, manufacturers and suppliers of photographic equipment, as well as affiliated colleges. The Association, which supports a large and superbly presented gallery, is dedicated to fighting for photographers' rights in addition to promoting the work of contemporary photographers. Contact details: 020-7739 6669, email: aop@dircon.co.uk or visit the website at www.aophoto.co.uk.